SIERRA MAR
COOKBOOK

SIERRA MAR COOKBOOK

POST RANCH INN
BIG SUR CALIFORNIA

by Craig vonFoerster

wine notes
Dominique daCruz

Gibbs Smith, Publisher
Salt Lake City

First Edition
10 09 08 07 06   5 4 3 2 1

Published by
Gibbs Smith, Publisher
P.O. Box 667
Layton, Utah 84041

Orders: 1.800.835.4993
www.gibbs-smith.com

Designed by Fresh Heifers
Printed and bound in Korea

Library of Congress Cataloging-in-Publication Data
von Foerster, Craig.
Sierra Mar cookbook : Post Ranch Inn, Big Sur,
California / Craig von Foerster ; photographs by
Patrick Tregenza.—1st ed.
    p. cm.
Includes index.
ISBN 1-58685-859-9
1. Cookery, American—California style.
2. Sierra Mar Restaurant. I. Title.

TX715.2.C34V66 2006
641.59794—dc22

2006012169

Food brings people together and is the background music to the events of their life.

I remember the food
from the first date
with the woman who
would become my wife,
our dinner the night
I proposed and
our Mendocino
wedding feast.

This book is
dedicated to
my wife, Tamara.

(she remembers too)

INSTINCTIVE
BY WENDY LITTLE

Fourteen years ago, as the first Executive Chef at Sierra Mar, I came up with the impossible concept of a daily-changing menu. A chef's dream that, if not handled properly, could be an execution nightmare. I am thrilled to see it continue under the direction of my friend and culinary associate Craig von Foerster because going there again in my old age now seems doubtful. Big Sur and the Post Ranch Inn setting were indeed inspirational, and opening a small luxury hotel with total creative freedom is something that doesn't happen too often in a lifetime. As I think back on the success of Sierra Mar, I realize that allowing the force that drives us from within to exist is what draws the fine line between a good meal or a mediocre one. I think what really set us off was a real convergence of culinary talent and cooperation. Our menu was rustic, almost comfort-style cuisine, and we had never worked with real "art" like our beautiful plates and glassware that complemented the food so much. We felt like artists ourselves when plating food each day. The unique vista from the exhibition kitchen overlooking the Pacific Ocean gave us all the energy we needed to carry on. We all encouraged each other and inspired each other to do our best and excel each day over the previous day's work. I think back to all the different personalities involved, and I laugh and wonder how it all worked so well! We worked hard, had fun, and laughed a lot. Everyone there relocated for this project, and Craig used to drive his mobile home down to Big Sur, a 50-mile round trip from the peninsula, and park in a friend's driveway just so he could go to work. Today he still does the commute, but his mobile home has long been replaced. My first impression of Craig was a good one. He quickly became known as the "ingredient hog." He would arrive at work before everyone and choose the best ingredients for his creation, something he still stresses today by sourcing local. Craig's cooking, then and now, has become eloquent and fine tuned. His constant curiosity and commitment to the end result and flavor of a dish drive him. Craig imagines the combinations and strives for these tastes without going over the threshold—the process truly instinctive, and the passion is all about food. If you've dined at Sierra Mar, you know what I am talking about, and if you haven't, well, you really should. Craig also cares for his staff with great vigor, making sure they are in complete understanding of what they are cooking, and why or how they could change the outcome of it. I am glad he is ensuring that the next generation will know the difference between great-tasting food and food far from its potential. I am proud of Craig's accomplishments at Sierra Mar and in bringing the daily-changing menu concept forward unto his own. It was a pleasure to write a foreword for Craig's first, but not last, cookbook.

Wendy is currently the chef de cuisine at The Boulders in Carefree, Arizona.

I first met Tod Williamson over 23 years ago on my first day at Flaherty's Seafood Grill in Carmel, California. Tod is currently a sous chef at Sierra Mar and is chiefly responsible for my leaving Maui and coming to Big Sur.

A PASSION FOR FOOD

"a great idea isn't a great dish until it tastes right"

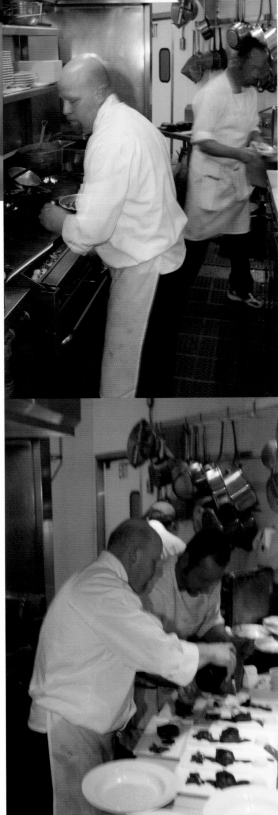

We both went our separate ways after Flaherty's. Then one day I received a phone call: "Craig, you have got to come back to the mainland and work at this new place, The Post Ranch Inn . . . the menu changes every day!" My calm, flavor-driven, classic French and somewhat scientific self and Tod's adventurous, daring, wild, and extremely original culinary style were fated to cook together once again. We were about to realize our dream of taking bold ingredients and classically preparing them. We sure weren't twenty-one any-more, yet we were just as eager and energetic about the possi-bilities. Sierra Mar was and still is the ideal place for both of us—where constant challenge and continuous reward exist. That reunion was thirteen years ago, and, to this day, our sym-biotic relationship pulls us like a magnet toward each other. Whether comparing notes on things we have learned or new ingredients we have experi-mented with, our energy for creating food not competing with food sustains us as we work together with a mutual respect—'70s music and all.

Growing up, dinnertime was sacred at our house. This was emphasized by my mother, who, at the head of the table,

Today hundreds of employees and count-less meals later, Sierra Mar has been recognized by its peers as one of the best restaurants in the country. Through Tony and Tricia's trust, generosity of spirit and care for their employees, a special camaraderie was created and sealed by all those years of working together under pressure to succeed as a great restaurant. Many of our dining room staff commutes one hour to and from work each day including Dining Room General Manager, Wanda Straw. Wanda's focus and attention to detail are what mould the front of the house activities. Being the liaison between a guest and the kitchen isn't for everyone, and we are proud to boast that most of our dining room staff has been here since inception. The Sierra Mar experience wouldn't be complete without their attitude, knowledge and commitment to superior service. Fernando Nunez and most of my cooks have been here ten plus years. In just six years, Alejandro Verdeja went from night janitor with no cooking experience, to being the best line cook I have ever worked with. Today, he is my Sous Chef and has earned the respect of myself and all others in the kitchen. The value of finding the once-in-a-lifetime place of work that becomes a home and your coworkers a family is a rarity. Together we have all grown and created Sierra Mar, the restaurant. The people who work here, and the guests who dine here, have defined Sierra Mar over the years. To many employees it became a second home, while diners have chosen it as the site of marriage proposals, a bonding with nature, anniversary or simple gatherings of friends. Memories were made, stories were told, and it seems like fourteen years ago was only yesterday.

kept the phone close by her side to intercept any would-be caller to inform them that they had violated our dinnertime and to please call back later. This always took place over the screams and protests of my three teenage sisters. My mother was a working single parent of six with little time to spare. Yet, the evening meals were our connecting point with each other every day, and the great taste of mom's food brought us together. Each of my five siblings and I were expected to be at the table for dinner—no excuses. My mother was and still is a great cook, and if I ever complained about my dinner as a child—well mom, please forgive me.

Fourteen years ago, Tony and Tricia Perault traveled from Ann Arbor, Michigan, to Big Sur, California, with their Grand Award wine list in tow to run Sierra Mar Restaurant at the Post Ranch Inn. It was the Post family, Billy and Lucy, along with the vision of Mike Freed, that lured them to take the risk at a small boutique inn that was environmentally conscious and visually unobtrusive to the natural landscape already in place.

As you cook from this book, it is my wish that you learn a few new techniques or find a recipe you'd ask for. Next time you're in Big Sur, come over to the kitchen window, say hello, and enjoy your experience at Sierra Mar.

—Chef Craig von Foerster

The lights came
on this morning
at 5:30 a.m.

It's now 5:30 p.m.
and our day
begins all over
again with the
evening's service.

Sierra Mar voted #1
Hotel Restaurant
in California

Zagat Rating for Top 100
Hotel Restaurants

—*U.S.A. Today*
April 2006

Five seconds is the difference between perfect caramelization and burnt. In the kitchen, everything happens within a matter of seconds. For ten to twelve hours a day, the focus must be absolute, and working nights, weekends or holidays is a given. There seems to be no way to thank a group of people who have given so much to make Sierra Mar a success other than acknowledgement of their loyal contribution. Functioning as a group, the cooks, sous chefs, prep cooks, dishwashers, bussers, hosts and waiters all play a vital role in the reality of a diner's experience. While the chef is the ultimate conduit for the credit or criticism, it is the consistent attention to detail from the staff that completes a restaurant. We are fortunate over the last fourteen years to have been rated excellent in such categories as service, atmosphere, wine selection and food. It wasn't luck, it was and continues to be the intense hard work of those behind and in front of the scenes that keep the accolades positive. My staff at Sierra Mar is diligent, proud, and tenacious. They exude the desire for excellence in everything that they do while maintaining a team spirit. It starts with a love for food as the rest falls rightly into place.

My gratitude and thanks to the Sierra Mar staff for each second of their devoted participation.

—Chef Craig

"Together we have all grown and created Sierra Mar the restaurant."

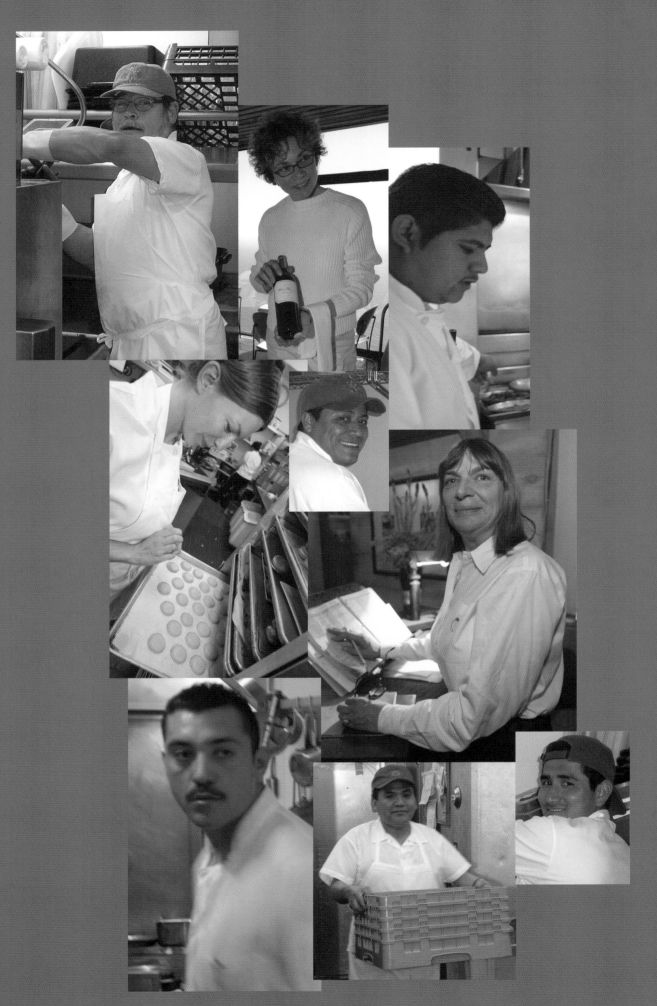

In this world of food and wine, I have been inspired by a very fundamental concept: we need to eat and drink in order to survive, so we might as well do it well.

After spending years working alongside Chef Craig's creations, I have come to understand the components that shape his cooking. Acidity, pH, sugar, spice and richness—these are the characteristics that lead me to select a specific wine versus another.

Wine From The List

My role in the Sierra Mar dining room is more precise than what I am advising you in this cookbook. My selections throughout each menu are the advisable route and a direction to be taken in relation to the structure and flavor component of each dish. I wished to not set limitations to specific producers or vintages in order to offer enough flexibility to close in your selection. The meeting of food and wine is simply natural and ancient and we are all here to carry it on.

With great passion,
Dominique daCruz

"Its wild and reckless dance that plays on my tongue as I am game for any adventure of culinary sport."

julia child

Our daily-changing menu was the approach to finalizing the concept for the *Sierra Mar Cookbook*. If you have dined at the restaurant in the past, it might seem even more familiar.

We created six menus that represent six evenings at Sierra Mar during various times of the year, beginning in January and continuing to year's end. We have included our signature dishes throughout, some helpful techniques and a little bit of our daily food insight, giving each reader a sense of place in our kitchen. Each menu begins with an amuse-bouche, three course selections and is followed by chef's notes that summarize each menu's focus and illustrate what Chef Craig would do with a particular ingredient throughout its season. For example, Menu Three showcases the tomato season. Although not every dish contains a tomato, the menu is very reminiscent of the offering during the tomato season

Wine is a very important part of the dining experience, and Sierra Mar boasts a world-class wine cellar. Dominique daCruz, our wine director, has prepared wine recommendations by varietals for each dish, as well as including some additional remarks on the pairing. Dominique took an obtainable approach by focusing on varietals instead of a specific vintage. By pointing you in the right direction instead of recommending a limited-quantity wine, Dominique narrows the focus, making it convenient for you to choose specifics based on your area offerings. Dominique has been responsible for overall direction and buying for the cellar since 1996.

LOCAL FARMERS MARKETS & PERFECT TIMING | MENU ONE

Amuse-Bouche

FRENCH BREAKFAST RADISH AND
HERBED PLUGRA BUTTER CROSTINI 26

Course One

SPRING ASPARAGUS AND CRAB "OSCAR" WITH
MEYER LEMON SABAYON 28

ROAST BABY BEETS WITH TRIO OF FONDUES 30

NANTES CARROT AND BLACK TRUFFLE RISOTTO 34

SONOMA SAVEURS FOIE GRAS TORCHON WITH
POACHED RHUBARB AND RHUBARB SYRUP 36

Course Two

FARMERS MARKET SALAD WITH
CHAMPAGNE VINAIGRETTE 40

FRENCH FILET BEAN SALAD WITH
SLIVERED ALMONDS, CRISPY SHALLOTS
AND CREAMY TRUFFLE VINAIGRETTE 43

CHILLED SWEET PEA SOUP WITH
MINT AND CRÈME FRAÎCHE 44

Course Three

ROAST RABBIT ROULADES WITH SPRING GARLIC
POTATO PUREE AND MARKET VEGETABLES 47

VEAL LOIN BAKED IN SALT CRUST WITH
MORELS, RAMPS AND ASPARAGUS 53

OPAKAPAKA WITH HERBS de PROVENCE
ROASTED POTATOES, HAM BROTH AND
CHERRY TOMATO–ALMOND RELISH 55

ARTICHOKE RAVIOLI en BARIGOULE, WITH SPRING
VEGETABLES AND SHAVED PARMESAN 56

With our daily-changing menu, we are allowed the distinct contentment of letting our ingredients direct the selections of each evening. It always seemed a little backward to create a dish and *then* source for ingredients. We, by design, are not stuck trying to use under-ripe substandard rhubarb just because it's on a rotation. We get to create something that very afternoon, just hours from serving it—all with what nature provides us.

This first menu marks what happens when spring begins. We capture winter holdovers like crab, Meyer lemons and truffles, and reintroduce them to their new counterparts—asparagus, nantes carrots and French filet beans—all found at most regional farmers markets When the first ten-pound box of bright green sweet peas arrives at the kitchen non-stop from our weekly farmers market, it is just in time for our Chilled Sweet Pea Soup with Mint and Crème Fraîche on page 44.

CHEF'S NOTES

Foie Mousse

White bean Soup

Carrot Soup

Rabbit Terrine

This time of year also renders the phrase "blanch and refresh." This simple technique on page 39 is used for all vegetable preparations and aids in keeping the bounty crisp, yet tender. Delicate meats like the rabbit tenderloin are pancetta-wrapped to protect and flavor, see Roast Rabbit Roulades on page 47, while free-range veal is baked in salt crust on page 53. Both of these techniques keep subtle meats from drying out. Lighter sauces are infused with roasted tomatoes and, although it isn't quite tomato season yet, we'll share how we roast canned tomatoes (see page 256) until the season's first are harvested.

This is the time of year when the kitchen overflows with produce curiously awaiting its new destiny. When nature indicates, we'll put the Sonoma Saveurs Foie Gras Torchon with Poached Rhubarb, page 36, on the menu, not one minute too soon.

FRENCH BREAKFAST RADISH AND HERBED PLUGRA BUTTER CROSTINI

serves 6

HERBED BUTTER
1/4 cup high-quality butter, such as Plugra
1 tablespoon diced chives
2 tablespoons lemon juice
1 teaspoon fleur de sel

Soften butter; whisk vigorously to lighten. Fold in chives, lemon juice and fleur de sel. Transfer to a small piping bag fitted with a star tip.

RADISH
6 French breakfast radishes
1 small watermelon radish

Using the medium teeth of a Japanese mandolin, grate the radishes; place in a container and cover with a damp paper towel.

CROSTINI
1 baguette
Olive oil
Salt and pepper

Preheat oven to 350° F. Slice the baguette into 1/8-inch-thick slices. Lay slices on a baking sheet and brush with olive oil; season with salt and pepper. Bake for 8 minutes, or until lightly browned and crispy; remove and let cool.

FINISH AND PLATE

Pipe a small floret of Herbed Butter in the center of each Crostini. Top with grated radish.

French Breakfast Radish
AND HERBED PLUGRA BUTTER CROSTINI
AMUSE-BOUCHE

SERVE BEFORE

SPRING ASPARAGUS AND CRAB "OSCAR" WITH MEYER LEMON SABAYON

serves 6

When using live crab, you can determine freshness by how active they are. Whole cooked crab is available and can be used in this dish; however, avoid using canned crabmeat. This appetizer is a lighter variation on the traditional steak or veal "oscar." Since my version doesn't contain meat, I don't use the traditional béarnaise sauce. By using only the asparagus and crabmeat components of the "oscar," lemon is the ideal flavor to accent their sweetness without overpowering.

SPRING ASPARAGUS
12 spears green asparagus
12 spears white asparagus

To prepare the asparagus for blanching, hold both ends of one stalk and bend until it breaks. Discard the woody base. Cut the remaining asparagus to the same length. Peel the stalks with a vegetable peeler, then blanch until tender, refreshing in ice water.

BRIOCHE CUPS
2 (4-x-9-inch) Brioche loaves (see page 246)

Brioche is rich buttery bread with a light texture. Although the recipe yields six 4 x 9-inch loaves, brioche can be frozen for up to 1 month. Having it on hand will be convenient as you cook from this book, as we use it in many ways at Sierra Mar.

Preheat oven to 250° F. Cut each loaf into thirds. Cut each piece into a 2 1/2-inch square cube. Press a round cutter down three-fourths of the way through the bread cube and then hollow out the center with a melon baller. Place bread cups on a baking sheet lined with parchment paper and bake for 15 minutes, or until lightly browned. Cool on a wire rack. *Chef's Note:* A low temperature is used when baking brioche cups to prevent the top of the brioche from burning before the base and inside areas are toasted.

MEYER LEMON SABAYON
1/4 cup Meyer lemon juice
2 tablespoons water
1 teaspoon Meyer lemon zest
4 egg yolks
3/4 teaspoon salt
1/8 teaspoon pepper
1/4 cup heavy cream

Bring a medium pot of water to a simmer; place a bowl of ice aside for cooling the sabayon. In a large bowl, mix lemon juice, water, lemon zest, egg yolks, salt and pepper; whisk vigorously until frothy. *Chef's Note:* You can substitute regular lemons, just replace 1 tablespoon of the lemon juice with 1 tablespoon water and 1/2 teaspoon sugar. Place bowl over the pot of simmering water and whisk vigorously until thick and pale yellow in color, about 5 minutes. Place same bowl over ice and whish sabayon base until cool. Whip cream to medium peaks and then gently fold into cooled base. Adjust seasoning with salt and pepper. This can be made up to 3 hours ahead and refrigerated.

DUNGENESS CRAB
10 quarts water
1 cup diced onion
1/2 cup diced celery
1/2 cup diced carrot
1/2 cup diced leek
1 thumb-size piece fresh ginger, smashed
1 lemon, cut in half
6 tablespoons salt
5 bay leaves
15 parsley stems
1 (3-pound) live crab

Place all ingredients except crab in a large pot and bring to a boil; reduce heat and simmer for 15 minutes. Carefully drop crab into pot and simmer for 10 minutes. Remove crab from pot and lay on its back to cool.

When the crab has cooled, pull off the back shell and remove all the crab "butter," or innards, in the center and reserve with the shells for a sauce or soup (see Crab Bisque, page 183). Wash out the center under running water. Pull off and discard the feathery gray gills on the outside of the crab body. Remove all the legs and set aside. Cut the body in half down the center, and then cut each half into thirds following the natural lines between sections. Pick the meat from the body. Crack each of the legs using a mallet or the back of a heavy knife. Extract the crabmeat using a cocktail fork or nut picker. Be careful to avoid small shell fragments. A 3-pound crab yields about 7 ounces body meat and 7 ounces leg meat.

FINISH AND PLATE
2 tablespoons butter
Salt and pepper
Lemon juice
1 teaspoon chopped tarragon
Paper-thin Meyer lemon slices
Chervil sprigs

Preheat oven to 350° F. Place crabmeat on a parchment paper–lined baking sheet with a pat of butter on top and season with salt, pepper and lemon juice. Cover with foil and bake for 4 minutes. Reheat asparagus in boiling water and toss with a little butter, salt, pepper and tarragon. Equally divide the asparagus into the brioche cups (it will extend out over the sides); add the crabmeat and then top with the Meyer Lemon Sabayon. Garnish with paper-thin Meyer lemon slices and chervil.

From The List
NAPA OR SONOMA CHARDONNAY

The citrus and richness of the Sabayon welcomes a rich Chardonnay counterpart from California

ROAST BABY BEETS WITH TRIO OF FONDUES

serves 6

Beets are a direct translation of their soil—earthy and sweet. *Terroir* is a term used by winemakers to describe the relationship of how a wine's characteristics are influenced by the soil that the grapes were grown in. Artisan cheese makers know that animals graze differently at certain times of the year; therefore, the milk they produce will differ slightly in flavor as a direct result of what the animal has eaten. For this, we will notice a change in the flavor of cheese each season. Sweet flavors tend to complement a variety of cheeses and by matching beets' earthy sweetness with the terroir of each cheese, this trio of fondues was born.

ROAST BABY BEETS
1 bunch baby chioggia beets
1 bunch baby golden beets
1 bunch baby red beets
1/4 cup canola oil
1 tablespoon red wine vinegar
2 teaspoons salt
1 teaspoon pepper
1/3 cup large-dice onion
12 sprigs thyme

Preheat oven to 350° F. Cut off the green tops 1/2 inch above the beets and reserve for the Kurobuta Pork on page 206. In a bowl, mix oil, vinegar, salt, pepper, onion and thyme. Separate beets by color in 3 bowls; toss each color with one-third of the oil mixture. Place each color of beet into a separate roasting pan and cover with foil. *Chef's Note: Cooking each color of beet separately keeps colors from running together.* Roast in oven for 35 minutes, or until beets are easily pierced with a paring knife. When the beets are done, they should peel easily. As beets cool, rub peel off with a kitchen towel.

WALNUT PESTO
1/2 cup walnut pieces
1/4 teaspoon chopped garlic
2 tablespoons walnut oil
1/2 teaspoon salt

Preheat oven to 350° F. Lay the walnuts on a sheet pan and bake in the oven for 8 minutes, or until lightly browned and fragrant. Using a mortar and pestle, grind the garlic to a fine paste with the walnut oil. Add walnuts and salt, continuing to grind until mixture resembles a coarse paste.

GRUYÉRE FONDUE
1 1/4 cups grated gruyère cheese
1/2 teaspoon cornstarch
1 clove garlic
1/4 cup dry white wine

Toss the cheese with the cornstarch. With the side of a knife, lightly crush the garlic and rub it on the inside of a small saucepan. Add the wine to the saucepan and heat to a simmer. Do not allow wine to boil. Slowly add the cheese mixture a pinch at a time, whisking constantly to emulsify; add more cheese once the previous addition is completely melted; keep warm. *Chef's Note: My favorite gruyère cheese is Emmi cave-aged gruyère from Switzerland. It has a unique nutty flavor that complements the roasted beets. Most aged gruyère cheeses can be substituted.*

ROAST BABY BEETS | WITH TRIO OF FONDUES

GOAT CHEESE FONDUE
1/2 cup heavy cream
1/2 cup soft-ripened goat cheese

Heat cream; add cheese one piece at a time while whisking constantly to emulsify until all the cheese is incorporated. Transfer to the container of a blender, cover and blend on high for a few seconds. *Chef's Note:* When using soft goat cheese in a classic fondue method, it creates a grainy texture. This method was developed to yield a smoother texture. **Keep warm.**

BLUE CHEESE FONDUE
2/3 cup crumbled blue cheese (such as Fourme d'Ambert or St. Agur)
3/4 teaspoon cornstarch
1 clove garlic
1/4 cup dry white wine

Toss the cheese with the cornstarch. With the side of a knife, lightly crush the garlic clove and rub it on the inside of a small saucepan. Add the wine and heat to a simmer. Do not allow the wine to boil. Slowly add the cheese mixture, one piece at a time. While whisking constantly to emulsify, add more cheese once the previous addition is completely melted; keep warm.

FINISH AND PLATE
Arugula sprouts
Chervil

Dice red beets, slice yellow beets and cut chioggia beets into wedges; keep all the beets warm. Arrange 1 small pool of each fondue on a warm plate. Top Gruyère Fondue with yellow beet slices and garnish with arugula sprouts. Place a small ring mold over the Blue Cheese Fondue and fill with diced red beets; tamp down to hold together. Remove the ring mold and top with a little of the Walnut Pesto. Arrange the chioggia beet wedges over the Goat Cheese Fondue and garnish with chervil.

From The List

SAUVIGNON/SEMILLION BLEND
FROM GRAVES OR PESSAC LEOGNAN

Wine

Semillion takes on the hearty, sweet beets with sauvignon blanc, matching the texture of goat cheese

On keeping fondue warm—
place each fondue
into a ceramic cup
and then place each
ceramic cup into a
shallow bath of warm
water. Make sure the
water goes halfway
up the side and keep
over very low heat
until ready to plate.

NANTES CARROT AND BLACK TRUFFLE RISOTTO

serves 6

If the carrot doesn't taste good raw, it will not make a good risotto. Nantes carrots are a medium-size cylindrically shaped carrot with a sweet, clean flavor. I was first introduced to these delightful orange nibbles by Mark Marino at Earthbound Farms. They are grown locally in Monterey County but are available at most farmers markets. If Nantes are not available, chantenay or any freshly harvested medium-size carrots can be substituted.

RISOTTO
2 tablespoons olive oil
1/4 cup diced onion
1 cup risotto rice
3 3/4 cups carrot juice
2 tablespoons truffle butter
1/2 cup Carrot Nage (recipe facing)
2 tablespoons chopped chives
2 teaspoons lemon juice
Salt and pepper
2 tablespoons diced black truffle, optional

Heat olive oil in a small pot over medium heat and then add onion and sauté until translucent, about 2 minutes. Add risotto rice and stir to coat with oil. Add carrot juice to just cover the rice and bring to a simmer, adding more carrot juice as needed to keep the rice barely covered during cooking, stirring occasionally. Continue adding the juice a little at a time to maintain coverage until all the juice is absorbed. The risotto should have a creamy consistency and the grains of rice are cooked through, yet still firm. Finish off the heat by adding the truffle butter, 3 tablespoons Carrot Nage, chives, lemon juice, salt, pepper and diced black truffle. *Chef's Note:* To make fresh carrot juice, peel carrots and run through a juice extractor. Four medium carrots yield 1 cup of juice.

CRISPY CARROT THREADS
3 quarts rice bran oil
1 large carrot, peeled

In a large pot, heat the oil over medium heat to 325° F. Using the fine teeth of a Japanese mandolin, shred the carrot. Rub the carrot shreds between your fingers to break them apart and separate. Sprinkle the shredded carrot into the oil and fry until bubbling stops. Pull from the oil with a slotted spoon; transfer to a paper towel–lined plate. While the carrot is still hot, fluff with two forks to separate the threads.

CARROT NAGE
4 cups carrot juice
6 tablespoons butter, softened
2 tablespoons truffle butter
1 teaspoon lemon juice
Salt and pepper, to taste

In a small pot over low heat, slowly reduce the carrot juice to 1 cup, whisking occasionally to prevent the juice from separating. Turn up to medium heat, add the butter, 1 tablespoon at a time, whisking constantly to incorporate. Pour the sauce into the container of a blender, cover and run on medium speed until emulsified, about 10 seconds. With the blender running, add truffle butter, lemon juice, salt and pepper. Transfer sauce and keep in a warm place. *Chef's Note: Butter sauces are delicate, therefore keeping the nage warm, not hot, is imperative. A pre-warmed thermos is ideal for keeping this sauce perfect until use.*

FINISH AND PLATE
1 truffle, cut into matchsticks

To shape the Risotto, place a 2 1/2-inch ring mold on the center of each plate and fill with risotto, tamping down gently with the back of a spoon; remove ring. Top with Crispy Carrot Threads. Use the remaining Carrot Nage to sauce the plate and garnish with truffle matchsticks.

From The List
ITALIAN CHARDONNAY OR
BLEND FROM TUSCANY

Wine

Richness and minerals are needed to embrace the sweetness of the carrots and aromatics of the truffles

SONOMA SAVEURS FOIE GRAS TORCHON WITH POACHED RHUBARB AND RHUBARB SYRUP

serves 6

Foie Gras requires a sour or acidic element to balance its richness. In this recipe, we poach the rhubarb in grenadine. Because of its strong pomegranate flavor, it accentuates and pulls forward the sour quality of the rhubarb without dominating the dish's overall flavor balance. Rhubarb signals the first sign of spring vegetables and whets our appetite for the upcoming season.

FOIE GRAS TORCHON
1 1/2-pound grade-A foie gras
3 quarts water
2 tablespoons salt
2 teaspoons salt
1/2 teaspoon white pepper
3 quarts duck fat

DAY ONE
To purge the foie gras, submerge it in the water with 2 tablespoons salt; refrigerate for 12 hours or overnight.

DAY TWO
Remove the foie gras from the water, pat dry with paper towels and set on a cutting board. Cover with plastic wrap and let the foie gras come to room temperature, about 2 1/2 hours. The goal of this next procedure is to remove all the veins and traces of blood while keeping the liver as intact as possible. Separate the two lobes and lay them bottom side up on paper towels to keep in position. Start with the larger lobe by using a pair of needlenose pliers or tweezers and pull on the center vein that was exposed as the two lobes were separated. There are generally two major veins that need to be removed from the larger lobe. Carefully follow the center vein down with the paring knife, gently scraping away to expose the first section of veins while carefully lifting the veins out with the pliers. As you continue to clean, use the tip of a paring knife and a paper towel to clean up smaller veins and spots of residual blood. Repeat this process with the smaller lobe. At room temperature, foie gras is very pliable and forgiving. With care, reform the lobes back to their original shape. Season the foie gras with 2 teaspoons salt and white pepper. Roll the two lobes together in cheesecloth and twist each end to tighten and form a tight cylinder. Tie each end with string and refrigerate for 6 hours or overnight.

DAY THREE
In a pan large enough to allow the duck fat to entirely cover the foie gras, bring the fat to 160° F and submerge the foie gras completely. Remove from heat and let cool to room temperature. Refrigerate overnight or up to 2 weeks; the day before serving, let the duck fat come to room temperature. Gently remove the torchon from the duck fat, clean off excess fat and roll into a towel, twisting and tying at each end; refrigerate 6 hours. *Chef's Note:* To avoid flat spots, hang the torchon from a rack in the refrigerator. To serve, remove towel and cheesecloth, and slice.

SONOMA SAUVERS FOIE GRAS TORCHON | WITH POACHED RHUBARB AND RHUBARB SYRUP

POACHED RHUBARB
3 stalks rhubarb
2 cups grenadine syrup

Peel the outer skin off the rhubarb and reserve. Slice rhubarb on a bias to 1/2-inch thickness. Place the rhubarb slices in a nonreactive saucepan and add the grenadine syrup. Over medium heat, bring to a simmer, and cook gently for 3 minutes, using caution not to overcook rhubarb, as it will disintegrate. The rhubarb should still have a firm texture and a little crunch when done. Remove from heat and allow to cool to room temperature. Reserve the poaching liquid for the Rhubarb Syrup.

RHUBARB SYRUP
1 cup rhubarb poaching liquid

Strain liquid into a saucepan and bring to a simmer over low heat. Reduce to 1/4 cup, about 30 minutes. When the syrup cools, transfer to a squeeze bottle.

DRIED RHUBARB PEEL
Peel from 3 stalks rhubarb

Preheat oven to 200° F. Place the reserved strips of peel on a Silpat-lined or silicon baking sheet and bake for 35 minutes, or until dried.

FINISH AND PLATE
18 brioche toast points or toasted baguette slices
Fleur de sel
Cracked black pepper
Rhubarb Syrup (see page 251)

Cut the torchon in 3/4-inch-thick slices. Place each slice on the center of a plate and season lightly with fleur de sel and cracked black pepper. Place 3 Poached Rhubarb slices next to the Foie Gras Torchon, dot plate with 3 pools of Rhubarb Syrup. Place toast points or baguette slices on each plate and top with Dried Rhubarb Peel.

From The List
VOUVRAY MOELLEUX
FROM THE LOIRE

Wine

Rhubarb is a strong component, the ideal match is an austere sweeter wine

WHEN BLANCHING
GREEN VEGETABLES,
always use a large
amount of well-salted
water, about 1 table-
spoon salt per quart of
rapid boiling water.

BLANCHING VEGETABLES

Have a strainer sitting in a
container of ice water on
hand before blanching.

Blanch the vegetables
in batches so the temper-
ature of the water is not
reduced too much.

Test the vegetables
frequently by pulling one
out and eating.

In each vegetable there
is a perfect intersection
of flavor and texture.
When the vegetable still
has a pop or crispy
crunch but no longer has
a raw green flavor, it is
time to immediately
transfer to the ice water
bath and refresh.

Let the blanching water
return to a rolling boil
before adding the next
batch of vegetables.

Blanch the most delicate
green vegetables first.

FARMERS MARKET SALAD WITH CHAMPAGNE VINAIGRETTE

serves 6

Each week I attend the farmers market in downtown Monterey. The vendors are plentiful with fresh-from-the-farm produce, and a favorite is the Italian sprouting broccoli from Borba Farms. I take a quick side trip to Earthbound Farms as I head down the coast. This leads me to several cases of just-picked baby lettuces, edible flower petals and baby round carrots in perfect time for the evening's Farmers Market Salad.

1 gallon water
4 tablespoons salt
3 cups Italian sprouting broccoli
18 spears asparagus
12 baby round carrots
1 teaspoon salt
1 cup shelled sweet peas
6 small heads baby lettuces
1/4 cup picked herbs (such as chervil, dill or chives)
2 tablespoons edible flower petals
Salt and pepper
Champagne Vinaigrette (see page 247)

Bring water to a boil and add 6 tablespoons salt. Cut off any browned area at the base of the broccoli. To prepare the asparagus, hold both ends of a stalk and bend until it breaks. Discard the woody base and cut the remaining asparagus to the same length. Peel the stalks with a vegetable peeler. Cut off the feathery tops of the baby carrots, leaving 1/2 inch of the green stem. Peel the carrots, cut in half and place in a small pot of cold water with 1 teaspoon salt; bring to a boil. *Chef's Note:* With root vegetables, such as carrots, start them in cold water, they yield a much better texture. When the carrot water begins to boil it usually indicates the carrots are ready. Drain and refresh carrots in ice water. Blanch each of the green vegetables until tender, one at a time beginning with the peas and ending with the asparagus. Refresh each in ice water. To clean lettuces, remove and discard outer leaves. Gently cut the rest of the lettuce leaves individually with kitchen shears. Fill a large bowl three-fourths of the way with cold water, add the lettuce and gently swish. Let lettuce set for a few minutes, allowing dirt to settle in the bottom of the bowl. Gently scoop the lettuces from the top and spin dry. Pick a selection of fresh herbs such as chervil, dill or chives and gently toss with the baby lettuces. Add the edible flower petals and season lightly with salt and pepper. Pour a little of the Champagne Vinaigrette around the outside of the bowl and toss lightly to avoid bruising lettuces. Season and dress the vegetables in a separate bowl, then mix with lettuces and place on chilled plates.

From The List
MORGAN OR KELLER ESTATE
OAKLESS CHARDONNAY

An oakless
chardonnay
from California
or a lower
burgundy
maconnais
white wine

FARMERS MARKET SALAD | WITH CHAMPAGNE VINAIGRETTE

FRENCH FILET
BEAN SALAD | WITH SLIVERED ALMONDS,
CRISPY SHALLOTS AND
CREAMY TRUFFLE VINAIGRETTE

FRENCH FILET BEAN SALAD WITH SLIVERED ALMONDS, CRISPY SHALLOTS AND CREAMY TRUFFLE VINAIGRETTE

serves 6

Sometimes I blame my mother. Yes, I am a chef because my mother was a great cook. As far as green bean casseroles go, my mom's really *is* the best. The flavor of crispy onions atop a creamy sauce was more than just a tempting disguise to get me to eat my green beans. It was my introduction to flavor building, and I had no idea. French filet beans, also known as haricots verts are small, tender and full of sweet flavor. With present-day Creamy Truffle Vinaigrette, crispy shallots and slivered almonds, I'm reminded again just how effective a guise can be.

TOASTED SLIVERED ALMONDS
1/2 cup slivered almonds
2 teaspoons canola oil
1 teaspoon salt

Preheat oven to 350° F. Toss almonds in a mixing bowl with canola oil and salt; transfer almonds to a baking sheet lined with parchment paper. Bake for 8 minutes, or until golden brown and fragrant.

FRENCH FILET BEANS
2 pounds French filet beans

Cut off the stem end of the beans. In a large pot of salted water, blanch the beans in batches until tender but still crisp; refresh in ice water. *Chef's Note: Let the water in the pot return to a boil between batches.* With the tip of a sharp knife or bean frencher, split the beans in half lengthwise.

FINISH AND PLATE
Creamy Truffle Vinaigrette (see page 247)
Salt and pepper
Crispy Shallots (see page 254)

Toss French Filet Beans in a bowl with Toasted Slivered Almonds and Creamy Truffle Vinaigrette. Season with salt and pepper to taste. Divide amongst six chilled plates and top with the Crispy Shallots.

From The List
GRUNER VELTLINER
FROM AUSTRIA

Wine

Versatile white varietal unafraid of any food blends with the acidity of the vinaigrette

CHILLED SWEET PEA SOUP WITH MIND AND CRÈME FRAÎCHE

serves 6

Swank Farms' sweet peas are grown in Hollister, California, which is roughly one hour from our kitchen. From the moment they are harvested, sweet peas start converting sugar to starch. Making this soup the day the sweet peas come in from the farm allows our diners the pleasure of experiencing the true essence of taste that a sweet pea has to offer. Sweet peas are available at most regional farmers markets.

2 cups shelled sweet peas
2 tablespoons butter
1/4 cup diced shallots
2 1/2 cups Vegetable Stock (see page 253)
1 cup cream
6 mint leaves
Salt and white pepper, to taste
Crème fraîche
Mint Oil (see page 249)
Pea tendrils

Blanch sweet peas until tender (they should still pop when eaten) and refresh in ice water; drain and set aside. For the soup base, melt the butter in a nonreactive pot. Add shallots and sauté until translucent but not browned, about 3 minutes. Add the Vegetable Stock and simmer for 20 minutes, then add the cream and simmer for 1 minute more. Remove from heat and let cool for 20 minutes. Place blanched peas, warm soup base and a few mint leaves in the container of a blender, cover and puree on high until smooth. Strain through a chinois, pressing on the solids with the bottom of a ladle to extract all the liquid. Season the soup with salt and white pepper. Chill thoroughly. To serve, add a small swirl of crème fraîche and a few drops of Mint Oil over the top. Garnish with pea tendrils.

From The List
VERMENTINO FROM ITALY OR
ALBARINO FROM SPAIN

One distinctive style is needed... dry, crisp and refreshing just like the soup

CHILLED SWEET PEA SOUP WITH MINT AND CRÈME FRAÎCHE

ROAST RABBIT ROULADES | WITH SPRING GARLIC
POTATO PUREE AND
MARKET VEGETABLES

ROAST RABBIT ROULADES WITH SPRING GARLIC POTATO PUREE AND MARKET VEGETABLES

serves 6

Rabbit meat is very delicate and easily overcooked. By wrapping the tenderloins in pancetta, not only does it add flavor, but it protects them from drying out. To prepare rabbit, ask your butcher to break down the rabbit into foreleg, hind leg or thigh and boneless tenderloin. This dish requires 3 whole rabbits broken down.

STUFFED RABBIT THIGHS
6 rabbit hind legs or thighs
1 large egg
1 egg white
1/2 cup cream
3/4 tablespoon salt
1/4 teaspoon pepper
2 tablespoons chopped chives
Salt and pepper

Place the food processor bowl in the freezer to chill. De-bone rabbit hind legs, making sure to keep the thigh and leg meat intact. Remove as much of the silver skin as possible. Pound out 3 of the de-boned thighs between sheets of plastic wrap until about 1/2 inch thick, and cut the other 3 into cubes. *Chef's Note: De-bone hind legs on cutting board using boning knife. Cut along the center of the leg and thigh exposing the bone. Run the tip of the knife under the bone and remove.* Place the cubed rabbit meat in the bowl of a food processor fitted with a metal blade. Pulse the processor a few times to grind the rabbit meat. Scrape down the sides and run another 20 seconds. Add the egg and egg white and run until incorporated, about 5 seconds. Scrape down the sides again; with the processor running, add the cream in a slow, steady stream. Push mousse through a tamis sieve; season with salt, pepper and chives. To test seasoning, drop an almond-size piece into simmering water, poach about 3 minutes and taste. Adjust seasoning if needed. As an option, you can also add mushroom duxelles or truffle puree to the rabbit mousse. Place a spoonful of mousse in the center of each pounded thigh and roll; carefully tie roll with butcher's twine to secure. This rabbit thigh is finished in the same manner as the Guinea Hen Roulade technique on page 93.

PANCETTA-WRAPPED RABBIT TENDERLOIN
6 pieces rabbit tenderloin
28 thin slices pancetta bacon
See technique on page 50

Lay a 12-x-12-inch sheet of plastic wrap on a flat surface. Unroll the slices of pancetta bacon and lay side by side, slightly overlapping on the plastic wrap, until roughly the length of the tenderloins. Place three tenderloins, side by side, thick end to thin end, 2 inches away from the front edge of the bacon and roll the rabbit in the bacon. Roll entire pancetta-wrapped tenderloin in plastic wrap. Twist ends of wrap in opposite directions to tighten into a cylinder; tie each end of plastic into a knot. Place the roulade into the freezer for about 20 minutes, or until it becomes firm but not frozen. This aids in keeping the circular shape of the roulade for tying. Remove plastic wrap and tie with butcher's twine, tied around the roulade every inch to keep from separating during cooking.

RABBIT JUS

Reserved rabbit forelegs
1/4 cup canola oil
1/4 cup water
1/2 cup large-dice onion
1/4 cup large-dice carrots
1/4 cup large-dice leek
1/4 cup large-dice celery
1 clove garlic, crushed
2 cups Chicken Stock (see page 252)
1 cup Veal Stock (see page 253)
2 cups water
8 whole black peppercorns
1 sprig each thyme, sage, parsley
1/2 teaspoon sherry vinegar
Salt and pepper

With a heavy cleaver, chop the rabbit forelegs into 2-inch pieces. Heat canola oil in a heavy-bottom 4-quart saucepan until almost smoking. Add rabbit legs 1 piece at a time; allow to brown deeply, turning over one by one. When second side is brown, add 1/4 cup water and then scrape pan the bottom of the pan with a wooden spoon to loosen up all the brown bits; keep cooking until dry and bones caramelize again. At this point, add the onion, carrots, leek, celery and garlic. As the vegetables begin to sweat, the liquid will deglaze the pan again. Continue to cook until all the vegetables begin to brown, about 5 minutes. Add Chicken Stock, Veal Stock, water and peppercorns. Bring to a simmer, skimming frequently until reduced by half, around 45 minutes. Add herbs and simmer for another 5 minutes. Strain liquid through a fine sieve and continue to reduce slowly by one-fourth; it is important to skim frequently. Season the jus with sherry vinegar, salt and pepper. Take 1/2 cup of the Rabbit Jus and slowly reduce to 1 tablespoon glacé for the vinaigrette below.

GRAIN MUSTARD–TARRAGON VINAIGRETTE

2 tablespoons sherry vinegar
1 tablespoon warm rabbit demi-glacé
1 tablespoon diced shallots
1/4 teaspoon salt
1 tablespoon grain mustard
1/3 cup canola oil
Pinch black pepper
1 tablespoon chopped chives
1 tablespoon chopped tarragon
1 tablespoon minced red bell pepper

Place the vinegar, reserved warm rabbit glacé, shallots and salt in a mixing bowl and let sit for 15 minutes. *Chef's Note: If the reduced rabbit jus is cold, it will become hard and not mix with the vinegar.* Add the mustard and then slowly add the canola oil in a steady stream while whisking constantly to emulsify; add black pepper. About 10 minutes before serving, add the chives, tarragon, and red bell pepper.

SPRING GARLIC CREAM

1/4 cup spring garlic
1/3 cup cream

Cut off the root end and green top of the spring garlic and peel off the outer layer. Cut the remaining pale green part in half lengthwise and cut into 1/8-inch-thick slices. Place in a small pot and cover with the cream. Simmer for 5 minutes; strain through a fine sieve, reserving cream. Transfer garlic to a blender and run until smooth, adding a bit of the cream if needed. Remove puree from blender and mix with the reserved cream. Keep warm.

SPRING GARLIC POTATO PUREE

2 large russet potatoes (about 1 1/2 pounds)
2 large Yukon gold potatoes (about 3/4 pound)
Cold water to cover
2 tablespoons salt
4 ounces cold butter, cut in cubes
1/8 teaspoon white pepper
Salt

Peel potatoes and then cut the russet potatoes in quarters. Cut the Yukon golds in half and then each half into quarters. *Chef's Note: The Yukon gold potatoes are slightly denser and take longer to cook, therefore they must be cut into slightly smaller pieces so all potatoes are done at the same time.* Put potatoes into a medium pot and cover with cold water; add salt and bring to a boil. Immediately reduce heat to a simmer; cook until potatoes pierce easily with a paring knife, about 10 minutes. Drain potatoes into a colander and let steam for 2 minutes; run the potatoes and butter together through a potato ricer; gently fold in the warm Spring Garlic Cream. As starch content of potatoes vary, the amount of cream needed can vary. If potatoes are a little overcooked, you may not need to add all the cream. Add white pepper and adjust the salt to taste.

MARKET VEGETABLES
1/2 cup shelled sweet peas
18 French filet beans
18 pieces Italian sprouting broccoli
9 baby chantenay carrots
1 teaspoon salt
1 tablespoon butter, melted

FINISH AND PLATE
Salt and pepper
1/2 cup canola oil, divided
6 tablespoons butter, divided
1/4 cup combination of sage, rosemary, and thyme sprigs
1/2 cup Rabbit Jus

Blanch and refresh the peas followed by the beans and then the broccoli. With the tip of a sharp knife or a bean frencher, cut the filet beans in half lengthwise. Cut off the feathery tops of the baby carrots, leaving 1 inch; peel carrots and then place in a saucepan. Cover with cold water and add salt; bring to a boil over medium heat. Simmer until tender. Drain and refresh.

Preheat oven to 350° F.

Stuffed Rabbit Thighs. Season the thighs with salt and pepper. Heat 3 tablespoons canola oil in a large skillet over high heat and add the thighs and brown all over, about 6 minutes. Using a heat-proof spatula, hold the thighs in place, tilt the skillet and drain off the oil. Place 2 tablespoons butter in skillet and as the butter begins to foam, add half the herbs and baste the rabbit thighs with the herb butter. Transfer to a preheated oven and bake for approximately 10 minutes; keep warm.

Tenderloin Roulades. Heat 3 tablespoons canola oil in a skillet; add the roulades and thoroughly brown all around, about 6 minutes. Transfer to a preheated oven and bake for 4 minutes; keep warm.

In a sauté pan, melt 2 tablespoons butter over medium heat. Transfer to and toss vegetables in the pan with the butter. Add 1 tablespoon water and cook for 30 seconds, or until vegetables are warmed through. Season with salt and pepper; keep warm. Slice each thigh into 6 pieces and each roulade into 9 slices. Place 2 quenelles of Spring Garlic Potato Puree on the plate; fan out the tenderloin roulade on the right with the Rabbit Jus, and fan out the stuffed rabbit thigh on the left with the Grain Mustard–Tarragon Vinaigrette. Arrange the Market Vegetables in the center and serve immediately. *Chef's Note:* You can prepare the Tenderloin Roulades, Stuffed Rabbit Thighs, and Rabbit Jus up to a day ahead.

From The List
YARRA VALLEY SHIRAZ
OR RHONE BLEND

Wine

cooler climate
rhone style

1. Lay a 12-x-12-inch sheet of plastic wrap on a flat surface. Unroll the slices of pancetta bacon and lay side by side, slightly overlapping.

2. Place three tenderloins, side by side, thick end to thin end, 2 inches away from the front edge of the bacon.

3. Roll the tenderloins in the bacon with the plastic wrap.

4. When you reach the end, roll entire pancetta-wrapped tenderloin in plastic wrap.

5. Twist ends of wrap in opposite directions to tighten into a cylinder; tie each end of plastic into a knot. Place in freezer for 20 minutes.

6. Remove plastic wrap and tie with butcher's twine; tie around the roulade every inch.

PANCETTA WRAPPING RABBIT TENDERLOINS

VEAL LOIN BAKED IN SALT CRUST | WITH MORELS, RAMPS AND ASPARAGUS

VEAL LOIN BAKED IN SALT CRUST WITH MORELS, RAMPS AND ASPARAGUS

serves 6

Free-range veal is a very delicate meat. We bake it in salt crust to encase it and keep its flavor and texture delicate. With salt crusting, the veal absorbs just the right amount of salt during baking and seals in the moisture. The combination of morels, ramps and asparagus is the pinnacle of spring flavors.

MORELS, RAMPS AND ASPARAGUS
24 ramps
2 large bunches asparagus
3 cups morel mushrooms
1/3 cup Chicken Stock (see page 252)
4 thyme sprigs
2 tablespoons white wine
3 cloves garlic, lightly crushed
1 shallot, cut into quarters
1 tablespoon olive oil
3 tablespoons butter

Preheat oven to 350° F. Cut off the root ends of the ramps and discard. Cut off and reserve the green leafy part 1 inch above the white base of the ramp. Blanch the green tops for 5 seconds, refresh and pat dry with paper towels. Blanch the white part of the ramp for 1 to 2 minutes, or until tender. Peel, blanch and refresh the asparagus. Wash the morels (see page 238) and toss in baking dish with Chicken Stock, thyme, white wine, garlic, shallot and olive oil. Cover with foil and place in preheated oven. Bake for 25 minutes, or until mushrooms are soft. Strain mushroom cooking liquid through a fine sieve into a small saucepan and reduce by half over medium heat. Whisk in butter, one piece at a time, until incorporated; keep warm.

SALT CRUSTED VEAL LOIN
8 egg whites
3 cups salt
1/2 cup flour
1 (1 1/2-pound) whole veal loin
See technique on page 54

Preheat oven to 375° F. With a stand mixer, whip egg whites to medium peaks; add salt and flour. Continue mixing to stiff peaks. Lay out the reserved ramp leaves, side by side and overlapping, to the approximate length of the veal loin. Wrap the loin tightly in the ramp leaves. On a parchment-lined baking sheet, spread out a 1/2-inch-thick layer of salt crust mixture slightly wider and longer than the loin. Lay the veal loin in the center of the crust and completely encase the veal with the remaining salt crust. Place in oven and bake for 9 minutes. Turn entire loin over by removing from oven, laying another parchment-lined sheet pan on top, and flipping the pans over quickly. Return to the oven and bake for 9 minutes more, or until the internal temperature is 135° F. Remove from the oven and let rest for 5 minutes. Remove the Veal Loin from the salt crust and slice.

FINISH AND PLATE
Salt and pepper
Lemon juice

Add the Morels, Ramps and Asparagus to the butter sauce and gently warm over low heat. Season with salt, pepper and a few drops of lemon juice. Place some of the morel, ramp and asparagus mixture in the center of the plate. Top with sliced Salt Crusted Veal Loin and spoon remaining sauce around.

From The List

CLASSIC MERLOT FROM POMEROL OR
BORDEAUX STYLE FROM NAPA

Earthy aromatics blend into the saveurs of salt and morels while taking on the edgy ramps

1. Lay out blanched ramp leaves, side by side and overlapping, to the approximate length of the veal loin.

2. Wrap the loin tightly in the ramp leaves.

3. On a parchment-lined baking sheet, spread out a 1/2-inch layer of salt crust slightly wider and longer than the tenderloin.

4. Lay the tenderloin in the center of the crust.

5. Completely encase the veal with remaining salt crust and bake.

6 & 7. After resting in salt crust, remove loin and slice.

SALT
CRUST
FOR VEAL
TENDERLOIN

OPAKAPAKA WITH HERBES de PROVENCE ROASTED POTATOES, HAM BROTH AND CHERRY TOMATO–ALMOND RELISH

serves 6

Opakapaka is Hawaiian pink snapper and is considered the most sought after snapper swimming in Hawaiian waters. It has a delicate sweet flavor that complements spring's first harvest of cherry tomatoes. If opakapaka is not available, American red snapper is the perfect substitute for this dish.

HERBES de PROVENCE POTATOES
1 pound fingerling potatoes
2 tablespoons olive oil
1 tablespoon dried herbes de Provence
Salt and pepper

Preheat oven to 375° F. Wash and cut potatoes in half; toss with the oil, herbes de Provence, salt and pepper. Arrange on a parchment-lined sheet pan; bake for 30 to 35 minutes, or until lightly browned and cooked through.

HAM BROTH
1/2 cup olive oil, divided
1/2 cup julienned shallots
4 cloves garlic, chopped
4 cups Chicken Stock (see page 252)
1/4 cup diced ham
1/3 cup cubed baguette (crust removed)

Heat 3 tablespoons oil in a pot over medium heat and then add the shallots and garlic; cook until translucent, about 2 minutes. Add Chicken Stock and ham; simmer for 20 minutes. While broth is simmering, heat remaining oil in a skillet over medium heat and pan-fry the bread cubes until golden brown, about 3 minutes; drain on paper towels. Transfer broth to the container of a blender with the fried bread, cover, and puree until smooth. Keep warm.

CHERRY TOMATO–ALMOND RELISH
1/4 cup toasted slivered almonds
2 teaspoons canola oil
1/4 teaspoon salt
1 pint cherry tomatoes
1/4 cup chopped Italian parsley
1 tablespoon sherry vinegar
3 tablespoons extra virgin olive oil
1 teaspoon fleur de sel
1/2 teaspoon freshly ground black pepper

Preheat oven to 350° F. Toss almonds with oil and salt. Place on a lined baking sheet; bake for 8 minutes, or until golden brown. Wash the tomatoes under cold running water; remove stems and cut in half. Toss in a bowl with almonds and remaining ingredients just before serving.

FINISH AND PLATE
3 tablespoons canola oil
6 (4-ounce) opakapaka fillets, skin on
Salt and pepper
2 tablespoons butter
1 teaspoon lemon juice

Heat the oil in a large skillet over high heat. Season the opakapaka with salt and pepper; add the fillets skin side down into the skillet. Reduce heat a little and press down on the fillets with a spatula for 10 seconds to prevent skin from curling. Cook until the skin is browned and crisp, about 4 minutes, turn over fillets, brown the other side about 3 minutes and hold the fillets in place with a spatula and drain off the oil. Add the butter to the skillet and when it begins to foam, add lemon juice and baste the fish. Ladle 2 ounces of broth into each bowl; place a small mound of potatoes in the center. Top with an opakapaka fillet and Cherry Tomato–Almond Relish.

From The List
ROSE de PROVENCE
OR BANDOL

Wine

A rose cuts through the fish and the herbs, leaving beautiful aromatics and a sturdy finish

ARTICHOKE RAVIOLI en BARIGOULE WITH SPRING VEGETABLES AND SHAVED PARMESAN

serves 6

Wendy Little, Sierra Mar's first executive chef, taught me this method of cooking artichokes roughly thirteen years ago. The en Barigoule technique is a stewing process that infuses aromatic vegetables, herbs and wine. Castroville, the artichoke capital of the world, is in close proximity, and during their peak season, we always anticipate the artichokes' defined flavor with other spring vegetables. The pasta dough needs to rest 2 hours in the refrigerator before use.

BARIGOULE BROTH

8 medium artichokes
2 to 3 lemon slices
2 cups white wine
1/4 cup olive oil
3/4 cup julienned yellow onion
1/2 cup julienned leeks
1/2 cup julienned carrots
3/4 cup julienned fennel
1/2 cup julienned celery
2 cloves garlic , sliced
1 tablespoon salt
2 tablespoons lemon juice
12 parsley stems
3 bay leaves
4 tarragon sprigs
1 strip orange peel
6 cups water

Lay the artichoke on a cutting board, firmly grasp the stem and with a serrated knife, cut off the top two-thirds of the leaves just above the heart. Turn the artichoke around and cut off the stem. Pull off and discard the outer green leaves. Trim off any remaining green areas with a sharp paring knife and scrape out the choke "hairs" with a spoon. Place artichokes into water with a few lemon slices to prevent oxidation. To remove the raw alcohol taste, bring white wine to a boil and continue cooking for 2 minutes; set aside. In a large nonreactive pot, heat the olive oil; add the onion, leeks, carrots, fennel, celery and garlic, and stir to coat with oil. Add the artichokes, cover pot, turn heat to low and steam the artichokes for 5 minutes. Add the salt, lemon juice, parsley stems, bay leaves, tarragon and orange peel. Cover with water and reserved wine. Place a kitchen towel over the artichokes, keeping them submerged, and simmer until tender, about 15 to 20 minutes. Let the artichokes cool in their liquid and then strain through a chinois; reserve this broth for finishing the dish. *Chef's Note:* Barigoule, in the south of France, is the method for stewing artichokes.

ARTICHOKE RAVIOLI FILLING

6 medium artichoke hearts, cooked in Barigoule Broth
1/4 cup mascarpone
1 teaspoon salt
1/2 teaspoon lemon juice

Roughly chop the artichoke hearts and puree until smooth in a food processor fitted with a metal blade. Press through a tamis sieve into a mixing bowl; whisk in the mascarpone, salt and lemon juice.

FINISH AND PLATE

Pasta Dough (see page 247)
1 egg, lightly beaten
1 bunch asparagus, cut into 2-inch pieces
1/2 cup shelled peas
1/2 cup shelled fava beans
5 cups Barigoule Broth
1/3 cup Roasted Tomatoes (see page 256)
12 basil leaves
2 tablespoons olive oil
1/4 cup shaved Parmesan cheese

Using a pasta machine, roll out the pasta into thin sheets. With a round cutter, cut pasta sheets into eighteen 3 1/2-inch circles. Brush the outer edges of the pasta with lightly beaten egg. Place 2 teaspoons of the Artichoke Ravioli Filling in the center of each pasta circle. Fold one side of the pasta over the filling and press down on top of the opposite edge, forming a half-circle, being careful to remove any air pockets. Crimp the edge with the tines of a fork to seal. Bring a large pot of salted water to a boil; blanch and refresh the green vegetables, starting with the peas first, then the asparagus and fava beans last. Remove the outer skin from the blanched fava beans and set aside. Bring the Barigoule Broth to a simmer and add the Roasted Tomatoes; simmer for about 5 minutes to infuse the tomato flavor. Bring a large pot of salted water to a rapid boil, drop in ravioli and cook for 2 minutes, or until the pasta is al dente. Drain ravioli and add to the Barigoule Broth with the basil, olive oil and vegetables; simmer 1 minute more. Serve immediately topped with shaved Parmesan cheese.

From The List
MORE ROSE

Appellations of Tavel, Bandol or Corbieves a good place to start

MONTEREY BAY SALMON, TASTE MEMORY & TOTAL UTILIZATION | MENU TWO

Amuse-Bouche

AVOCADO PANNA COTTA WITH CURED SALMON,
JALAPEÑO SYRUP AND CILANTRO PESTO 62

Course One

SMOKED SALMON–WRAPPED DAY BOAT SCALLOPS WITH
QUAIL EGG, FENNEL EMULSION AND SALMON ROE 67

HOISIN-GRILLED QUAIL WITH SHIITAKE MUSHROOM
POTSTICKER, PEANUTS AND PLUM SAUCE 68

CARPACCIO OF AHI TUNA WITH QUAIL EGG
ONE-EYED SUSANS AND GRIBICHE 71

CEYLON TEA–GLAZED SALMON WITH HOISIN-BRAISED
BACON AND PEA TENDRIL SALAD 72

Course Two

CURED MONTEREY BAY SALMON WITH YUKON GOLD
POTATO SALAD AND RED ONION–FENNEL RELISH 74

ROAST BEET SALAD WITH HORSERADISH CRÈME FRAÎCHE,
WALNUT PESTO AND BITTER GREENS 77

SAFFRON SEAFOOD SOUP 80

Course Three

WILD MONTEREY BAY SALMON WITH
LEMON-MINT COUSCOUS, CUCUMBER THREADS
AND DILL-SHALLOT VINAIGRETTE 83

CORIANDER-CRUSTED LAMB LOIN AND PANCETTA-
WRAPPED TENDERLOIN WITH PANISSE, MILLEFEUILLE OF
EGGPLANT PÂTÉ AND CURRIED CARROT NAGE 84

TRIO OF GUINEA HEN PREPARATIONS 88

SWEET CORN FLAN WITH MOREL MUSHROOMS
AND CRISPY LEEKS 95

When the local Monterey Bay salmon season begins in late spring, we are able to purchase salmon the day it is caught. Straight from the boat to my awaiting cooler, it journeys back to Big Sur with me as the smell of the ocean directs my thoughts to the curing and tea-glazing that await. We are lucky to have access to wild salmon and its natural intense flavor. When comparing wild versus farm-raised salmon, the difference is in the flavor. Wild salmon tastes rich, complex and natural; however, as our season comes to an end and access to wild salmon is limited, farm-raised Loch Duar from Scotland is a valid source for a couple of reasons. Loch Duar maintains better farming conditions by rotating lots each season and by allowing sufficient living space per fish. The results are a "natural" atmosphere for farmed salmon that transitions down through to the taste.

The range of flavors you can create with salmon give this second menu its momentum, as versatility is one of its trademarks. During salmon season we create around flavors of avocados, fennel, bacon, lemon and mint. Techniques like curing, smoking or pan roasting build upon salmon's flexibility. Tasting the difference, be it corn, quail or lamb, is a simple thing everyone can do to broaden skills in the kitchen. My staff and I do a lot of tasting in the kitchen. Our motto: A great idea isn't a great dish until it tastes right.

Taste memories are the lifelong database your palate keeps in storage just waiting for culinary situations to present themselves. The sweet, intense flavor of freshly harvested corn from a small farm stand outside of Noblesville, Indiana, is one of my best childhood taste memories and direct inspiration for Sweet Corn Flan with Morel Mushrooms and Crispy Leeks on page 95. During my professional sojourn to Hawaii, my exposure to several grades of line-caught ahi tuna gave me an ideal flavor standard to hold myself to for the Carpaccio of Ahi Tuna with Quail Egg One-Eyed Susans and Gribiche on page 71.

Along with the featured flavors of salmon, this menu will lead you in breaking down a guinea hen and completing a trio using all of its components. This practice of total utilization focuses on how to achieve a range of different flavors with ingredients from one source. These taste progressions on one plate begin and end on harmonious and pronounced flavor.

My cooler and I just arrived at the kitchen and Sean brings to my attention that they have filleted the last salmon for tonight's course one. I pop open the cooler, he laughs, we both reach for our filet knives—problem solved.

AVOCADO PANNA COTTA WITH CURED SALMON, JALAPEÑO SYRUP AND CILANTRO PESTO

serves 6

AVOCADO PANNA COTTA
2 sheets gelatin
2 tablespoons + 1 teaspoon lime juice
1 1/2 cups avocado puree (about 2 avocados)
1 1/4 teaspoons salt
1/2 teaspoon Tabasco

Bloom the gelatin by submerging in cold water for 5 minutes. Remove and squeeze out excess liquid. Place lime juice and gelatin in a small pot and warm over low heat until gelatin has dissolved. Peel and pit avocados; transfer to the container of a blender, cover and run on medium until a smooth puree. Add the gelatin mixture, salt and Tabasco and blend until incorporated. Coat the inside of six 1-ounce plastic soufflé cups with nonstick spray, fill 3/4 with avocado puree and tap lightly on hard surface to remove air bubbles. Refrigerate for 2 hours or until set.

CILANTRO CRUST
1 bunch cilantro
1 tablespoon lime zest

Wash and roughly chop cilantro. Place in the container of a food processor fitted with a metal blade. Add lime zest and run machine until a coarse paste is formed.

CURED SALMON
1/4 cup kosher salt
1/4 cup brown sugar
1 tablespoon whole coriander seed
1 teaspoon whole cumin seed
4-ounce salmon fillet (about 1 inch thick), skin on
See technique on page 64

Mix the salt, sugar, coriander and cumin in a bowl. Distribute one-third of the salt mixture in a nonreactive dish. Place salmon fillet on top skin side down. Cover the salmon with remaining salt mixture. Refrigerate for 48 hours, draining off the liquid that collects in the dish each day. Remove the salmon from the salt mixture and rinse under cold running water; pat dry with a towel. Coat the top of the salmon with the Cilantro Crust, wrap in plastic, lay on a sheet pan, cover with another sheet pan and place a 5-pound weight on top; refrigerate for 24 hours. Unwrap salmon, scrape off Cilantro Crust, remove the skin and dice. *Chef's Note:* Since curing is a 3-day procedure, this is ideal to make ahead and have on hand for the panna cotta, or serve sliced in other preparations.

FINISH AND PLATE
Cilantro sprigs
Jalapeño Syrup (see page 250)
Cilantro Pesto (see page 254)

Turn each cup of chilled Avocado Panna Cotta upside down in the center of a plate and carefully punch a hole in the bottom of each cup with a pairing knife. Using the tip of the knife, pull the plastic cup bottom away from the panna cotta to release, allowing panna cotta to come out. Top with diced Cured Salmon and a small sprig of cilantro; dot with Jalapeño Syrup and Cilantro Pesto.

Avocado Panna Cotta
WITH CURED SALMON, JALAPEÑO
SYRUP AND CILANTRO PESTO

AMUSE-BOUCHE

SERVE BEFORE

1. Mix the salt, sugar, coriander and cumin in a bowl. Distribute a third of the salt mixture in a nonreactive dish.

2. Place the salmon fillet on top of the salt mixture skin side down.

3. Cover salmon with remaining salt mixture. Refrigerate for 48 hours.

4. Drain off the liquid that collects in the dish each day. Remove salmon from the salt mixture and rinse under cold running water; pat dry with a paper towel.

5. Coat the top of the salmon with the Cilantro Crust, wrap in plastic and refrigerate for 24 hours between two sheet pans, weighted down.

6. Unwrap salmon and then scrape off Cilantro Crust. Slice salmon as is or remove skin and dice.

CURING
SALMON

3 CRUSTING OPTIONS
FOR CURING SALMON

The crusting on cured salmon can be a fusion of several flavors. We also blend the following combinations and they can be applied in place of the Cilantro Crust from the previous page.

DILL-GREEN PEPPERCORN
1 bunch dill
2 tablespoons green peppercorns

FENNEL FROND
2 tablespoons crushed fennel seed
1/2 cup chopped fennel fronds

TARRAGON-ORANGE PEEL
2 tablespoons orange peel
1/2 cup chopped tarragon

These are variations of the cured salmon recipe from page 62. They all follow the same procedure by running ingredients through a food processor fitted with a metal blade until the mixture becomes a coarse paste.

SMOKED SALMON–WRAPPED
DAY BOAT SCALLOPS | WITH QUAIL EGG,
FENNEL EMULSION
AND SALMON ROE

SMOKED SALMON–WRAPPED DAY BOAT SCALLOPS WITH QUAIL EGG, FENNEL EMULSION AND SALMON ROE

serves 6

To preserve the season's bounty of wild Monterey Bay salmon, Dimas, my local fish purveyor from Sea Harvest Fish Market, has his smoker running 24 hours a day. The salmon is taken off the boat, immediately cured and then smoked. The neutral quality of scallops make them a perfect seafood vehicle. They blend with and accentuate the salmon's intense flavor while fennel infuses a sharp nutty quality.

SALMON-WRAPPED DAY BOAT SCALLOPS
12 slices smoked salmon
12 day boat scallops
1/4 cup canola oil
Salt and pepper

Cut smoked salmon slices into strips the same width as the scallops. Wrap each scallop in smoked salmon, overlapping by 1 inch. *Chef's Note: Tying is not necessary because when cooked, the salmon and scallop will seal together.* Heat 2 tablespoons canola oil over high heat in each of two large skillets. Season the scallops lightly with salt and pepper, keeping in mind the smoked salmon is already salty. When oil is hot, add 6 salmon-wrapped scallops to each pan and cook approximately 45 seconds per side, or until a golden brown crust forms; transfer to a warm platter and keep warm.

FENNEL EMULSION
4 medium bulbs fennel
1 teaspoon chopped fennel fronds
1/4 cup Beurre Blanc (see page 246)

Cut off tops of fennel and reserve fronds. Cut each bulb into quarters and remove the core. Run through a juice extractor to yield 1 cup fennel juice. Place juice in a small saucepan. Bring to a simmer over medium heat. The pale green solids will begin to separate; strain juice through a fine sieve over another small pot. The remaining juice should be clear. Slowly reduce the liquid to 2 tablespoons. Add the fennel juice reduction to the Beurre Blanc and pulse with an immersion blender. Add fennel fronds and adjust seasoning.

FINISH AND PLATE
12 quail eggs
2 tablespoons butter
1 ounce salmon roe
Chervil sprigs

Crack the quail eggs into individual cups. Heat butter in a nonstick skillet and pour in the quail eggs, one at a time, to keep the whites from running together. When the white has just set and the yolk is still runny, transfer to a cutting board. Using a round cutter the same size as a scallop, cut each egg into a round, keeping the yolk in the center. Place 2 scallops on each plate and then top each with a quail egg. Sauce with Fennel Emulsion, scatter salmon roe around scallops and garnish with chervil sprigs.

From The List
COOLER CLIMATE
CALIFORNIA CHARDONNAY

Not too oaky, let the extreme flavors and strong herb note show

HOISIN-GRILLED QUAIL WITH SHIITAKE MUSHROOM POTSTICKER, PEANUTS AND PLUM SAUCE

serves 6

This dish is a variation of a Tod Williamson creation. All the elements are influenced with Asian classics—hoisin, shiitake and plum. Hoisin is a sweet thick sauce made from fermented soybeans, sugar, garlic, five spice and a little chili. The idea of plating these flavors together is pure Tod, who started this dish. I finished it by infusing plum sauce and a mushroom potsticker. We both think you'll enjoy it!

SHIITAKE MUSHROOM POTSTICKERS
6 potsticker wrappers
Shiitake Duxelles (see page 256)
1 large egg white
2 tablespoons cornstarch
3 tablespoons canola oil
2 tablespoons Sweet Soy (see page 253)
1/4 cup water

Lay potsticker wrappers on a cutting board. Place 2 teaspoons of Shiitake Duxelles in the center of each wrapper. In a small bowl, whisk together egg white and cornstarch, forming a thick paste. Brush the egg white mixture around the outer edge of the wrapper; fold over and seal by pressing down with the tines of a fork. Heat oil in a 12-inch nonstick skillet over medium heat and then add the potstickers; cook about 20 seconds per side or until browned. Drain off the excess oil; add the Sweet Soy and water. Cover the skillet and cook the potstickers for 2 minutes, adding more water if needed. Uncover and reduce the liquid until the Sweet Soy has glazed the potstickers; keep warm.

HOISIN SAUCE
1/4 cup hoisin
2 teaspoons sesame oil
1 teaspoon chopped garlic
1 teaspoon siracha*

Mix all ingredients together in a bowl.

*Siracha is an Asian chili paste found at most Asian markets and in some regional grocers.

TOASTED PEANUTS
1 cup blanched, shelled peanuts
1 tablespoon canola oil
2 teaspoons salt

Preheat oven to 350° F. Toss peanuts with oil and salt; lay out on a parchment-lined baking sheet. Bake for 8 to 10 minutes, or until golden brown. Remove and cool. Fold parchment in half over peanuts and roll with a rolling pin to crush. Set aside.

FINISH AND PLATE
6 quail
Salt and pepper
2 tablespoons canola oil
Plum Sauce (see page 253)
3 Santa Rosa plums
Green onions, julienned

Rinse and dry quail; cut off the last joint of the wing. Season the quail inside and out with salt and pepper and then brush with a little oil. Grill the quail on a hot char broiler for 2 minutes on each side. Brush the quail all over with Hoisin Sauce and grill another 3 to 4 minutes, basting and turning frequently to avoid burning. Cook until medium. *Chef's Note: The quail should still be a little pink on the inside.* Remove quail from grill and roll in Toasted Peanuts. Drizzle Plum Sauce across the plate in a zigzag pattern. Place a Shiitake Potsticker in the center and top with grilled quail. Slice plums and fan out on each plate. Garnish with julienned green onions.

From The List

RHEINGAU REISLING OR ALSACE VARIETALS

Wine

A sweet white
wine meets
its match
in spice
and acidity

CARPACCIO OF AHI TUNA | WITH QUAIL EGG
ONE-EYED SUSANS
AND GRIBICHE

CARPACCIO OF AHI TUNA WITH QUAIL EGG ONE-EYED SUSANS AND GRIBICHE

serves 6

The best tuna is graded 1+ and is largely reserved for the Japanese export market. However, through Honolulu Seafood Company I am able to purchase 1+ tuna that is line caught and shipped overnight from Hawaiian waters to the restaurant. For Ahi Tuna Carpaccio, a firm texture is of utmost importance. Grading of tuna can be subjective, therefore a level of trust with your fishmonger is very important.

AHI TUNA CARPACCIO
12 ounces 1+ or 1 ahi tuna, center cut

Place tuna loin skin side down on a cutting board. Cut horizontally across the loin, removing the top third all in one piece (this piece has the least amount of sinew—ideal for carpaccio). Reserve the rest of the loin for other applications. Slice the top piece across the grain into six 1/4-inch-thick portions; place each portion on a sheet of plastic wrap. Cover with another sheet of plastic wrap and gently pound with a mallet until 1/8 inch thick. With a sharp 4-inch-round cutter, cut each slice into a circle. Store tuna rounds between sheets of plastic wrap. Keep refrigerated until serving.

QUAIL EGG ONE-EYED SUSANS
12 slices brioche, 1/4 inch thick
12 quail eggs
3 tablespoons butter, divided

With a cookie cutter, cut a 1 1/2-inch circle out of the center of each brioche slice. The outer part of the bread can be used for Walnut Crust (see page 206). With a 3/4-inch cutter, cut a smaller circle in the center of the bread round like a doughnut. Crack each of the quail eggs into individual cups. Melt 2 tablespoons butter in a nonstick skillet over medium heat; add the brioche rings and fry until golden brown; turn the brioche over and add the remaining butter. Pour a quail egg into the center of each brioche; fry until the whites are set and the yolks are still soft, about 2 minutes. Transfer to a warm plate.

GRIBICHE
1 egg
1/2 teaspoon red wine vinegar
1/2 teaspoon sherry vinegar
1/2 teaspoon Dijon mustard
1 teaspoon minced shallots
1 cornichon, minced
1 teaspoon capers, rinsed and chopped
1/4 teaspoon salt
1 teaspoon Fennel Ala Greque (see page 255)
3 tablespoons high-quality extra virgin olive oil
Salt and black pepper
1 tablespoon Fines Herbs (see page 255)

Drop egg into boiling water and cook for 3 minutes and 30 seconds; transfer egg to an ice-water bath. When cool, peel the egg and place in a mixing bowl. Mash with a fork; add the vinegars, mustard, shallots, cornichon, capers, salt and fennel. Add the oil in a steady stream while mixing with a fork to incorporate. *Chef's Note:* You do not want to completely emulsify the oil into the egg, which will create a mayonnaise-like consistency. Season with salt and black pepper to taste. Add the Fines Herbs just before serving.

FINISH AND PLATE
6 pounded tuna rounds
Extra virgin olive oil
Fleur de sel
2 tablespoons chopped chives
Herb Salad (see page 255)

Place 1 piece of Ahi Tuna Carpaccio on the center of each plate; drizzle with olive oil, season with fleur de sel, chives and the Gribiche. Place 2 One-Eyed Susans on the tuna and garnish with Herb Salad.

From The List
A CLEAN, CLEAN
SAUVIGNON BLANC

Lipid enough to respect the tuna and herbal enough for the gribiche

CEYLON TEA–GLAZED SALMON WITH HOISIN-BRAISED BACON AND PEA TENDRIL SALAD

serves 6

Ceylon tea is a black pekoe tea leaf that has been fermented before drying. The subtle nuance of Ceylon's exotic flavor paired with the spicy Hoisin-Braised Bacon give versatile salmon a simple Asian influence with an elegant taste.

CEYLON TEA GLAZE
1/2 cup mirin
1/2 cup sake
1 tablespoon sugar
2 teaspoons loose Ceylon tea
1 tablespoon soy sauce

In a saucepan over medium-low heat, slowly reduce mirin, sake and sugar by two-thirds to a syrup consistency. Remove from heat and add the loose tea. Let steep for 5 minutes. Add soy sauce and set aside.

HOISIN-BRAISED BACON
1 (12-ounce) piece slab bacon
3 tablespoons canola oil
1 thumb-size piece ginger, sliced
Chicken Stock, as needed (see page 252)
1/4 cup hoisin

Preheat oven to 275° F. Score the bacon in a crisscross pattern 1/8 inch deep on the fat or skin side; heat oil in a skillet over high heat and add the bacon scored side down. Reduce heat to low and cook for 10 minutes, or until the bacon is a rich brown color. Turn bacon over and slowly cook for 10 minutes more. Drain off most of the fat and then add the ginger and enough Chicken Stock to come two-thirds of the way up the sides of the bacon. Transfer to preheated oven and cook for 45 minutes. Remove and brush bacon with hoisin and then return to oven and bake 30 minutes more. *Chef's Note: As bacon is braising, add more stock as needed to keep the liquid at the same level.* Remove and let cool in the pan. Once cool, remove bacon from pan and cut into 1/4-inch-thick slices. Strain the braising liquid and return to the pan. Reduce over medium heat to a thick glaze, about 30 minutes, and add the bacon pieces. Cook until bacon begins to crisp and is completely glazed with the hoisin reduction. Remove from heat and let cool.

SALMON
Salt and pepper
12 slices fresh salmon, 1 1/2 inches thick

Lay salmon slices on a baking sheet, season with salt and pepper and then brush with Ceylon Tea Glaze. Cook under preheated broiler for 3 minutes, basting with the tea glaze.

RICE WINE VINAIGRETTE
1 teaspoon soy sauce
3 tablespoons rice vinegar
2 teaspoons diced shallots
1/2 teaspoon Coleman's dry mustard
1/2 teaspoon salt
6 tablespoons canola oil

Place soy sauce, vinegar, shallots, dry mustard, and salt in a bowl and let sit for 15 minutes. Add the canola oil in a slow, steady stream, whisking constantly to incorporate.

FINISH AND PLATE
2 cara cara oranges
1 pound pea tendrils
1/2 cup toasted cashews
Salt

Peel oranges and cut into segments. Place pea tendrils, cashews, and orange segments in a mixing bowl, season lightly with salt and toss with Rice Wine Vinaigrette to taste. Place 2 slices of Hoisin-Braised Bacon on the plate; top each with a slice of Salmon. Place salad behind and drizzle with Ceylon Tea Glaze.

From The List
TOKAY PINOT GRIS FROM ALSACE
Sexy Alsatian
noble grape
spicy sweet
and inviting

Wine

CEYLON TEA–GLAZED SALMON WITH HOISIN-BRAISED BACON AND PEA TENDRIL SALAD

CURED MONTEREY BAY SALMON WITH YUKON GOLD POTATO SALAD AND RED ONION–FENNEL RELISH

serves 6

This dish is an example of how we use a classic flavor combination of mustard and fennel with salmon. Combining a casual chunky potato salad with the paper thin slices of cured salmon adds contrast. By simply playing with different textures, you can create very different flavors using the same ingredients.

YUKON GOLD POTATO SALAD
1 1/2 cups cubed (1/8-inch) Yukon Gold potatoes, peeled
2 quarts water
3 tablespoons salt
1/3 cup Creamy Mustard Vinaigrette (see page 247)
1 tablespoon chopped chives

Place potatoes, water and salt in a pot and bring to a boil over medium heat. Reduce heat to a simmer. *Chef's Note: To test the potatoes for doneness, taste them. The potato should not be mealy or overcooked. The potatoes only take a few minutes to cook after reaching a boil.* Drain potatoes into a strainer and dip strainer into ice water for 20 seconds—just long enough to stop the cooking but not long enough to waterlog the potatoes. Drain and toss in a bowl with Creamy Mustard Vinaigrette and chives.

RED ONION–FENNEL RELISH
2 tablespoons seasoned rice vinegar
2 tablespoons finely diced red onion
2 tablespoons finely diced fennel bulb
1/2 teaspoon dry mustard
1/4 teaspoon salt
1/4 cup canola oil
1/4 teaspoon black pepper
2 tablespoons chopped fennel fronds

Place vinegar, red onion, fennel bulb, dry mustard and salt in a mixing bowl and let sit for 15 minutes. Add oil in a slow, steady stream while whisking constantly; add black pepper. A few minutes before serving, add fennel fronds.

FINISH AND PLATE
18 thin slices Fennel Cured Salmon (see page 65)
Herb Salad (see page 255)

Place a 4-inch-round mold in the center of the plate and lay the salmon slices inside, creating a circle. Place a 2-inch mold in the center of the salmon and fill with the Yukon Gold Potato Salad; top with Herb Salad and spoon Red Onion–Fennel Relish over the salmon.

From The List
VERDELHO FROM PORTUGAL

clean acidic
but persistent
Palate cleasner

CURED MONTEREY BAY SALMON | WITH YUKON GOLD
POTATO SALAD AND RED
ONION–FENNEL RELISH

ROAST BEET SALAD | WITH HORSERADISH
CRÈME FRAÎCHE, WALNUT
PESTO AND BITTER GREENS

ROAST BEET SALAD WITH HORSERADISH CRÈME FRAÎCHE, WALNUT PESTO AND BITTER GREENS

serves 6

Horseradish in combination with beets is the ultimate union of spicy heat and sweet coolness. Although white beets are not common, they can be grown easily. Ask a vendor at your local summer market to grow some for you, or better yet, try it for yourself at home.

ROAST BABY BEETS

1 bunch baby chioggia beets
1 bunch baby golden beets
1 bunch baby red beets
6 tablespoons canola oil
3 tablespoons red wine vinegar
2 teaspoons salt
1 teaspoon pepper
1/2 cup diced (1-inch) onion
12 sprigs thyme

Preheat oven to 350° F. Cut off the green tops 1/2-inch above the beets and reserve for the Kurobuta Pork on page 206. In a bowl, mix oil, vinegar, salt, pepper, onion and thyme. Separate beets by color in 3 bowls; toss each color with one-third of the oil mixture. Place each color of beet into a separate roasting pan and cover with foil. *Chef's Note:* Cooking each color of beet separately keeps colors from running together. Roast for 35 minutes, or until beets are easily pierced with a paring knife. When the beets are done, they should peel easily. As beets cool, rub peel off with a kitchen towel starting with the lightest color first.

ROAST LARGE BEETS

3 large red beets
3 large chioggia beets
3 large golden beets
3 large white beets
1/4 cup canola oil, divided
Salt and pepper

Preheat oven to 350° F. Cut off the green tops from beets. Cut 12 6-x-6-inch pieces heavy-duty aluminum foil. Set one beet in the center of each foil square and drizzle with 1 teaspoon canola oil. Season with salt and pepper. Seal each beet in foil and place directly on the oven rack. Cook for about 50 minutes, or until beets are easily pierced with a paring knife. Cool beets; remove foil and rub off peel with kitchen towel.

HORSERADISH CRÈME FRAÎCHE
1/3 cup crème fraîche
1 1/2 teaspoons prepared horseradish
1/2 teaspoon lemon juice
1/2 teaspoon salt

Place all ingredients into the bowl of a stand mixer; using a whisk attachment, beat on high until medium peaks form.

FINISH AND PLATE
2 heads green Belgium endive
1 head red Belgium endive
1 head frisee
1/4 pound baby arugula
2 heads baby lettuces
Walnut Pesto (see page 32)
1/3 cup Champagne Vinaigrette (see page 247)
Beet Oil (see page 249)
Parsley Oil (see page 249)

Chef's Notes: For every step in this recipe, work with each color of beet separately. Slice the Roast Large Beets into 1/8-inch-thick slices, starting with the white beets, followed by the golden, chioggia and red beets. Use a Japanese mandolin for perfect slices. Then cut out 2-inch circles from each slice with a round cutter. Cut each color of baby beets into quarters. Wash and spin dry all the greens, leaving the red endive leaves whole and cutting the green endive leaves on a bias. To plate, overlap the large beet rounds in the center of each plate, alternating colors. Place a dollop of the Horseradish Crème Fraîche in the center of the ring. Toss each color of baby beets separately in the Champagne Vinaigrette (reserving some vinaigrette for the greens) and mound them atop the Horseradish Crème Fraîche. Sprinkle with Walnut Pesto. Season the greens with salt and pepper, toss with remaining Champagne Vinaigrette and arrange on top of the baby beets. Drizzle Beet Oil and Parsley Oil around the plate.

From The List
ROUSSANNE FROM THE RHONE OR
CALIFORNIA'S CENTRAL COAST

Wine

To keep
structure
between earth
and nuttiness
a moderate
alcohol
content

SAFFRON SEAFOOD SOUP

serves 6

A chef's natural desire is to make his or her food taste better. We are constantly refining and making small adjustments so each diner receives the pleasure of our uncontrollable curiosity, and, in the end, we have tasted the difference. For fifteen years I have been making this soup—slight adjustments were made along the way. The kitchen wisdom: don't be afraid to work towards that flavor in your mind and taste all along the way.

SAFFRON SOUP BROTH

1/4 cup olive oil
1 1/2 cups diced (1-inch) yellow onions
1 cup diced (1-inch) carrots
1 cup diced (1-inch) celery
2 cups diced (1-inch) leeks
1/4 cup roughly chopped garlic
2 tablespoons fennel seed
1/2 teaspoon red chili flakes
4 cups Roma tomatoes
4 cups Fish Fumet (see page 252)
4 cups clam juice
2 cups water
2 tablespoons olive oil
2 cups diced (1/4-inch) leeks, brunoise
4 teaspoons chopped garlic
3/4 cup Oven-Roasted Tomatoes (see page 256)
1 teaspoon saffron
1/4 cup pernod
Salt

Heat 1/4 cup olive oil in a 6-quart pot; add onions, carrots, celery and leeks. Sauté until the onions are translucent, about 5 minutes. Add garlic, fennel seed and red chili flakes. Cook for 3 minutes more, add the Roma tomatoes and cook until they start to break down, roughly 5 minutes more. Stir and scrape the bottom of the pan frequently. Add fumet, clam juice and water; bring to a simmer for 45 minutes. Pour hot stock through a fine sieve, pushing down with a ladle to extract all of the liquid; discard vegetables and reserve stock. Set aside 1/2 cup broth for Rouille. In a 6-quart pot, heat 2 tablespoons olive oil; add the brunoise leeks, garlic, Oven-Roasted Tomatoes and saffron. Cook until the leeks are translucent, about 3 minutes; add pernod and simmer until almost dry. Add reserved stock and bring back to a simmer for 10 minutes, season with salt.

ROUILLE

1/2 pound Yukon gold potatoes (about 2 medium)
2 teaspoons chopped garlic
1/4 teaspoon saffron
1/2 teaspoon red chiles
1 teaspoon salt
2 teaspoons lemon juice
1/2 cup Saffron Soup Broth
6 tablespoons extra virgin olive oil

Cook the potatoes in salted boiling water until easily pierced with a paring knife, about 25 minutes. When cool enough to handle, peel the potatoes and place in the container of a blender; add garlic, saffron, red chiles, salt, lemon juice and reserved Saffron Soup Broth. Cover and puree on medium speed until smooth. With the blender running, add the olive oil in a slow steady stream to incorporate.

FINISH AND PLATE
12 mussels
12 clams, such as manila or pacific steamer
6 calamari
6 prawns
6 (2-ounce) pieces fish, such as California
rock cod, sea bass or halibut
French bread

Chef's Note: It is important to use fresh fish or shellfish that your fishmonger recommends. Scrub mussels under cold running water with a stiff brush; submerge under cold water for a few seconds, drain and discard any that are not tightly closed or have broken shells. Pull out and discard the fibrous beard that is between the two halves of the shell. Scrub clams under cold running water and discard any that do not close tightly. Rinse calamari under cold running water. Hold the body firmly in one hand, grasping the tentacles in the other; gently but firmly pull the head away from the body. Cut tentacles away from the head; discard head and remove the hard beak from the center of the tentacles. Peel the purple-grey membrane away from the body; pull out the quill from the inside of the body and discard. Rinse the body under cold running water and cut into rings. Peel and devein the prawns.

In a pot, bring the Saffron Soup Broth to a simmer; add the clams and cook until beginning to open, about 2 minutes. Add the mussels and cook 1 minute more. Add the fish pieces and prawns; simmer until the fish is almost cooked through and the clams and mussels are all open, discarding any that remain closed. Add the calamari rings and tentacles and cook 1 minute more. Serve with a side of Rouille and french bread.

From The List
SOUTH OF FRANCE WHITE

crisp floral
and aromatic,
these are
ideal qualities
for saffron

WILD MONTEREY BAY SALMON WITH LEMON-MINT COUSCOUS, CUCUMBER THREADS AND DILL-SHALLOT VINAIGRETTE

WILD MONTEREY BAY SALMON WITH LEMON-MINT COUSCOUS, CUCUMBER THREADS AND DILL-SHALLOT VINAIGRETTE

serves 6

Salmon's rich flavor need not compete with several taste elements on the same plate. Accenting salmon with a little acidity from the Dill-Shallot Vinaigrette and swaying this acidity by introducing a tangy Lemon-Mint Couscous provides a refreshing summer meal, balanced with flavor that tastes natural, not difficult.

LEMON-MINT COUSCOUS

2 cups couscous
2 cups water
2 tablespoons salt
7 tablespoons olive oil, divided
1/2 cup toasted pine nuts
6 tablespoons lemon juice
1/4 cup packed julienned mint leaves
1/4 cup packed julienned parsley leaves

Preheat oven to 350° F. Place the couscous in a heat-proof bowl. Bring the water, salt and 1 tablespoon olive oil to a boil and pour over couscous. Mix well, then cover the bowl with plastic wrap. Let sit in a warm place for 10 minutes. Spread out pine nuts on a baking sheet and bake for 6 minutes or until lightly toasted. Uncover and fluff up the couscous with a fork. Add the remaining ingredients and adjust seasoning to taste.

CUCUMBER THREADS

1 English cucumber
1/4 cup crème fraîche
2 teaspoons lemon juice
Salt

With the medium shredding attachment on a Japanese mandolin, julienne the cucumber by running it through the mandolin approximately 5 times on each side until you reach the seeds. Repeat until all the sides have been shredded. When ready to serve, toss the cucumber in a bowl with the crème fraiche, lemon juice and salt.

PICKLED RED ONION

2 cups sliced red onion
1 1/2 cups red-label rice wine vinegar
1/4 cup sugar
1 1/2 teaspoons salt

Peel the red onion and slice across into thin rings using a Japanese mandolin. Place first 3 ingredients in a pot and bring to a boil; place the red onions in a stainless steel or ceramic bowl and pour vinegar mixture over the top. Let cool in liquid.

FINISH AND PLATE

6 (5-ounce) portions salmon
Salt and pepper
3 tablespoons canola oil
1 English cucumber, sliced into rounds
Dill-Shallot Vinaigrette (see page 248)

Preheat oven to 350° F. Remove the skin and the pin bones from the salmon. Cut slices 1 1/2 inches thick across the widest part of the salmon. Roll slices into pinwheels. Tie around the outside with butcher's twine. See halibut technique on page 167. Season salmon with salt and pepper. Heat the oil over high heat in ovenproof skillet large enough to hold all the salmon without crowding. Add salmon and cook until you can see a brown crust form on the bottom; do not turn over. Transfer to preheated oven and bake for 6 minutes. Make a circle of sliced cucumbers in the center of each plate. Place a ring mold over the cucumber circle and fill with Lemon-Mint Couscous, pressing down so the couscous will hold its shape when the mold is removed. Cut and remove string from the salmon and then place on top of the couscous. Twist the dressed cucumber into a nest with a fork. Drizzle the Dill-Shallot Vinaigrette around the fish and then top with Cucumber Threads and Pickled Red Onion.

From The List
CENTRAL COAST WHITE

Bright and spicy wine from Santa Barbara or Arroyo Grande

CORIANDER-CRUSTED LAMB LOIN AND PANCETTA-WRAPPED TENDERLOIN WITH PANISSE, MILLEFEUILLE OF EGGPLANT PÂTÉ AND CURRIED CARROT NAGE

serves 6

Chef's love other chefs' cookbooks, and we all have our coveted chef. My first familiarity with Panisse came from one of my favorites, John George Vongerichten's *Simple Cuisine*. Panisse is a cake made from garbanzo flour, and when paired with lamb and the aggressive spices of coriander and curry, its nutty flavor holds true. Eggplant, at its peak in late summer, rallies alongside the forward flavors in this dish.

CORIANDER CRUST
1/4 cup whole coriander seeds
2 tablespoons whole fennel seeds
1 teaspoon yellow mustard seeds

Mix all the spices together. Transfer to a spice grinder. Process seeds to a coarse grind and store in an air-tight container.

PANISSE
1 1/2 cups milk
1 1/2 cups Chicken Stock (see page 252)
1 cup garbanzo flour
2 tablespoons olive oil
Salt

Place the milk and Chicken Stock in a heavy-bottom pot over medium heat; when warm, add the garbanzo flour in a steady stream while whisking vigorously. When the mixture is smooth, continue cooking, whisking constantly, until it reaches a boil. The mixture will thicken; cook for 1 minute more. Add half the oil and salt. Transfer to a 9-inch-square cake pan, smoothing with a rubber spatula. Cover with plastic wrap and refrigerate. When cool, turn out of the pan and then cut into triangle-shaped pieces. Pan-fry in olive oil until brown and crispy on the outside. Keep warm.

EGGPLANT PÂTÉ
2 medium eggplants
2 tablespoons canola oil
1 clove garlic, minced
2 teaspoons sea salt
1/2 teaspoon curry powder
1/4 cup extra virgin olive oil

Preheat oven to 350° F. Cut eggplants in half lengthwise. Brush the cut side with canola oil. Place the cut side down on a parchment-lined sheet pan. Bake for 40 minutes, or until the eggplant is soft to the touch; remove and allow to cool. Scoop out the flesh and discard the skin, place the eggplant pulp in a strainer over a bowl; allow to drain for 2 hours. Chop the drained eggplant and garlic together until the eggplant resembles a paste. Sprinkle the salt and curry over top. Continue chopping, incorporating the spices into the pulp. Transfer eggplant to a mixing bowl and add olive oil in a steady stream, whisking to incorporate completely. Set aside.

CORIANDER-CRUSTED LAMB LOIN
AND PANCETTA-WRAPPED TENDERLOIN

WITH PANISSE, MILLEFEUILLE OF EGGPLANT
PÂTÉ AND CURRIED CARROT NAGE

MILLEFEUILLE

3 quarts rice bran or peanut oil
1/2 cup flour
Salt and pepper
1 medium globe eggplant

Heat the oil to 325°F in a pot large enough to allow for the oil to boil up during frying. Place the flour in a bowl and season with salt and pepper. Cut the eggplant in half lengthwise. Slice into paper-thin half-circles with a Japanese mandolin. Dredge eggplant slices in the seasoned flour and fry in small batches until browned and crispy, about 3 minutes. Transfer to a paper towel-lined plate to drain.

PANCETTA-WRAPPED LAMB TENDERLOIN

2 pieces lamb tenderloin
14 thin slices pancetta bacon

The lamb loin and tenderloin come from the saddle. When the saddle is cut across, you have the lamb T-bone or double-cut lamb chop. Have your butcher extract the loin and tenderloin whole. Clean the loins and tenderloins of sinew and fat. Lay a 12-x-12-inch sheet of plastic wrap on a flat surface. Unroll the slices of pancetta bacon and lay side by side, slightly overlapping on the plastic wrap, until roughly the length of the tenderloins. Place the tenderloins, side by side thick end to thin end, 2 inches away from the edge of the bacon closest to you and roll the tenderloins in the bacon. When you reach the end, turn plastic and roll entire pancetta-wrapped lamb loin in plastic wrap. Twist ends of wrap in opposite directions to tighten in a cylinder; tie each end of plastic into a knot. Place the roulade into the freezer for about 20 minutes, or until it becomes firm but not frozen. This aids in keeping the circular shape of the roulade for tying. Remove plastic wrap and tie butcher's twine around the roulade every inch to keep from unrolling during cooking.

CURRIED CARROT NAGE
1 tablespoon canola oil
2 teaspoons curry powder
1 slice ginger
1 clove garlic , diced
1/8 teaspoon red chili flakes
3 cups carrot juice
6 tablespoons butter
1/2 teaspoon salt

FINISH AND PLATE
6 tablespoons canola oil, divided
Salt and pepper
6 (3-ounce) portions lamb loin
Mint Oil (see page 249)

Mix the oil and curry powder in a small pot and place over medium heat; when the mixture begins to sizzle, add the ginger, garlic, red chili flakes and carrot juice. Bring to a simmer. Slowly reduce by three-fourths, whisking occasionally. Add the butter, one piece at a time, while whisking constantly to incorporate. Strain through a chinois, firmly pressing down on the solids with the bottom of a ladle to extract all the liquid. Transfer the sauce to the container of a blender, cover and pulse to completely emulsify. Season with salt and keep warm.

Preheat oven to 350° F. Finishing this dish requires two skillets. In a skillet large enough to hold the Pancetta-Wrapped Lamb Tenderloin, heat 3 tablespoons canola oil over high heat, add lamb roulade and then reduce heat to medium and brown on all sides until the pancetta is crispy and the lamb is medium-rare, about 8 minutes. Keep warm. Season the loins with salt and pepper and coat with the Coriander Crust. Heat the remaining canola oil over high heat in a skillet large enough to hold all 6 lamb loins. Cook 3 minutes on each side, or until crust is browned. Transfer loins to preheated oven for 3 minutes, or until medium rare; remove and let rest for 5 minutes. While the lamb loins rest, heat the Eggplant Pâté in a small saucepan. Stack 2 Panisse triangles on the plate, followed by the Millefeuille; alternating layers of Pâté then eggplant chips, ending with the pâté. Slice roulade into six pieces, placing one on each plate. Slice the lamb loin and position next to the tenderloin roulade. Sauce the plate with Curried Carrot Nage and dot with Mint Oil.

From The List
GRENACHE FROM THE
PRIORAT OF SPAIN

Balanced with good fruit intensity and enough structure

TRIO OF GUINEA HEN PREPARATIONS

serves 8

The dark meat of guinea hen thighs and legs has a well-defined flavor, and with different preparations and cooking techniques, you can focus on these flavors. Plated as a trio, the guinea hen lends texture, taste and adventure with each succession, accentuating the variety of tastes between dark and light meat. The trio can also be divided into 3 individual entrees all standing on their own flavor merits.

GUINEA HEN

3 (2 1/2-pound) Guinea Hens
See technique on page 90

Place guinea hen breast side up, wings closest to you on a cutting board. Cut off and reserve the wings. With your finger, find the cartilage running down the center of the breast. With a boning knife, make a cut just to the right of the cartilage and cut all the way from the front to the back, getting as close to the cartilage as possible. When you reach the end closest to you, which is the wishbone, follow it down and to the right until you come to the wing joint. Pull the wing down to expose the joint so it is easier to cut through the gap. Cut through the skin above the thigh, exposing the thigh joint, and pull the thigh down and away from the bird to expose or dislocate the joint. Cut through the joint and cut down the breastplate all the way to the wing to remove the meat from the carcass, lay half of bird on cutting board and then cut through the skin connecting the breast with the thigh. Remove the tender from the inside of the breast and reserve for Guinea Hen Mousse. Separate the leg and thigh by cutting between the bones at the joint; reserve the legs for the Guinea Hen Potpie. Place the thigh skin side down and make an incision on either side of the thigh bone, slip your knife point under the bone and remove it, set aside the thigh meat for roulade and the bone for stock. After breaking down the other side, chop the carcass into 2-inch pieces with a heavy cleaver for the Guinea Hen Jus (see page 251).

GUINEA HEN MOUSSE

6 guinea hen tenders
1 egg
1/2 cup cream
3/4 teaspoon salt
1/4 teaspoon pepper
1 tablespoon black truffle puree
2 tablespoons chives

Place the bowl of a food processor in the freezer for 30 minutes. Place guinea hen tenders in processor bowl fitted with a metal blade and run until the meat is minced, about 30 seconds. Add the egg and continue running until the egg is just incorporated. Stop processor. Chef's Note: It is important to only run the processor while ingredients are being added. If the mousse is over processed, it will be tough and chewy. With processor running again, add half the cream in a steady stream. Stop the processor and scrape down the sides with a rubber spatula. With the machine running again, add the remaining cream in a steady stream. Push mousse through a tamis sieve. Season with salt and pepper, followed by the truffle puree and chives. Chef's Note: To test seasoning, drop an almond-size piece into simmering water and poach about 3 minutes. Taste and adjust seasoning if necessary.

GUINEA HEN ROULADE

6 guinea hen thighs, deboned and pounded
Salt and pepper
See technique on page 93

GUINEA HEN POTPIE

6 guinea hen legs
Salt and pepper
5 tablespoons canola oil, divided
1 cup large-dice yellow onion
1/2 cup large-dice carrots
1/2 cup large-dice celery
3 1/2 cups Chicken Stock (see page 252)
6 sprigs fresh thyme
5 tablespoons Roux (see page 252)
1/2 cup small-dice yellow onion
1/4 cup small-dice celery
1/4 cup small-dice carrots
1 teaspoon salt
1/2 teaspoon pepper
1/2 teaspoon chopped thyme
Pâte Brisee (see page 247)

Season thighs with salt and pepper; equally divide Guinea Hen Mousse between thighs and roll up to enclose. Tie each with three pieces of butcher's twine; refrigerate.

Preheat oven to 350° F. *Chef's Note:* Potpies can be prepared up to one day ahead. Season guinea hen legs with salt and pepper. Heat 2 tablespoons oil over medium heat in a large skillet and add the guinea hen legs and brown on all sides, about 6 minutes in all. Transfer to a roasting pan. Drain the oil and wipe out skillet; add 1 tablespoon oil. Add large-dice onion, carrot and celery and cook until lightly browned, about 4 minutes. Add the cooked vegetables to the legs; add the Chicken Stock and thyme sprigs. Cover roasting pan with foil and bake for 45 minutes, or until the meat pulls away easily from the bone; let cool to room temperature. Remove legs from roasting pan and strain the braising liquid through a fine strainer. Discard the vegetables and skim the fat from the top of the liquid (yields about 2 cups liquid). When the legs are cool enough to handle, pick the meat from the bones and set aside. Discard the bones and skin. Transfer 2 cups braising liquid into a 2-quart sauce pan and keep warm. Place the Roux in a mixing bowl; add half the liquid, whisking rapidly until smooth and thickened. Add the roux-stock mixture back into the saucepan and bring to a boil, whisking vigorously until smooth; reduce heat to low. In a sauté pan, heat 1 tablespoon oil; add small-dice onion and cook until translucent. Add onion to the thickened stock; repeat with celery and carrots. Add salt, pepper and thyme. Adjust seasoning, if needed. Add reserved guinea hen leg meat and divide between eight 3-ounce ramekins. Roll Pâté Brisee to 1/8-inch thickness and then cut into rounds 1 inch larger than the ramekin diameter. Place round on top of ramekin and pinch to seal on the rim of the ramekin. Bake in oven until browned on top, about 12 minutes.

(recipe continued on page 92)

TECHNIQUES

1. Place breast side up, wings closest to you on cutting board and cut off the last two joints of the wing.

2. Find the cartilage running down the center of breast.

3. With a boning knife, make a cut just to the right of the cartilage.

4. Cut down the length of the bird following along the outside of the wishbone and through the joint connecting the wing.

5. Cut through the skin above the thigh; pull the thigh down and away from the bird to expose or dislocate the joint. Cut through the gap.

6. Pull down on the thigh to dislocate the joint.

7. Cut all the way down the breastplate to separate the meat from the carcass.

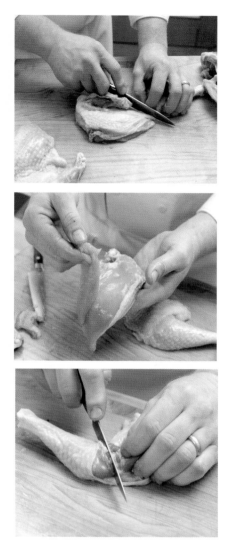

8. Cut through the skin that connects the breast with the thigh.

9. Remove tender from the inside of the breast and reserve for mousse.

10. Separate the leg and thigh by cutting between the bones at the joint; reserve legs for potpie.

11. Place the thigh skin side down and make an incision on either side of thigh bone.

12. Slip your knife point under the bone and remove, reserving for galantine.

13. Chop carcass with heavy cleaver for the jus.

BREAKING DOWN A GUINEA HEN

(recipe continued from page 89)

FINISH AND PLATE
6 guinea hen breasts
6 guinea hen thigh roulades
Salt and pepper
1/2 cup canola oil, divided
10 tablespoons butter
12 sprigs thyme, divided
1/2 cup Guinea Hen Jus (see page 251)
Potato Puree (see page 256)
Wild Mushroom Vinaigrette (see page 248)
1/2 cup cooked peas

Preheat oven to 350° F. Season the guinea hen breasts and thigh roulades with salt and pepper. Have ovenproof dishes ready for breasts and thighs after pan roasting. Heat 2 tablespoons oil in a 12-inch skillet over high heat; add 3 breasts skin side down and reduce heat to medium-high. When the skin sides are brown, approximately 6 minutes, turn over and brown other side for 3 minutes. Holding the breasts in place with a spatula, tilt the skillet and drain off all the oil; add 2 tablespoons butter and let foam. Add 3 sprigs thyme on top of the butter and baste the breasts. Transfer breasts to an ovenproof dish and top with the thyme butter. Repeat for remaining breasts. Finish in the oven for 7 minutes, or until the juices run clear when pierced with a skewer at the thickest point. Follow with same procedure for the thigh roulades, cooking on all sides approximately 8 minutes and finishing in oven for 9 minutes. Remove breasts and thigh roulades from oven and let rest 5 minutes. While breasts and roulades are resting, heat the Guinea Hen Jus, and reheat the peas in 2 tablespoons butter until tender. Using four separate small plates, place the potpie on one plate and place a mound of Potato Puree on the second plate, top with 2 slices of breast. Sauce with the Guinea Hen Jus. For the third plate, spoon some Wild Mushroom Vinaigrette on the plate and top with 3 slices of Guinea Hen Galantine. Finally, place a small spoonful of fresh peas on the fourth plate.

From The List
LIGHTER CORBIERES, MOSTLY CARIGNANE

Wine

Delicate,
sturdy
offering
flexibility
over the trio

TECHNIQUES

1. Lay deboned thigh out between two sheets of plastic wrap and pound flat.

2. Season with salt and pepper.

3. Place a spoonful of mousse in the center of the thigh.

4. Roll thigh around the mousse.

5. Tie each thigh with butcher's twine every inch.

6. Cut the excess twine.

GUINEA HEN
ROULADE

CORN FLAN | WITH MOREL MUSHROOMS, AND CRISPY LEEKS

SWEET CORN FLAN WITH MOREL MUSHROOMS AND CRISPY LEEKS

serves 6

To this day, new corn still tastes like summer in Indiana. Back then I didn't know that the natural sugars in corn begin their conversion to starch shortly after harvest. I sure acted like I knew, the way each roasting ear was quickly and enthusiastically devoured. For our corn flan, we use Swank Farms sweet corn, the intense corn flavor prevails, sans the corn cob holders.

CORN FLAN

2 cups corn kernels (about 5 ears)
1/2 cup half-and-half
3/4 cup heavy cream
4 eggs
2 egg yolks
Salt
Cayenne pepper

Preheat oven to 325° F. Place corn kernels in a small saucepan over medium heat with the half-and-half and cream. Simmer for 5 minutes. Strain corn, reserving the liquid. Puree the cooked corn kernels in a blender until smooth. Push the puree through a fine sieve or chinois and add cream mixture. Whisk the eggs and egg yolks together in a bowl; temper in the cream mixture and season with salt and cayenne pepper. *Chef's Note:* Tempering is bringing a mixture to a desired temperature or texture. The hot corn liquid, if added directly to the eggs without whisking, will cook the eggs, hence tempering or slowly adding it is necessary. Spray six 4-ounce ramekins with a nonstick and fill to just below the top with flan batter. Place ramekins in a water bath, cover with foil and bake for 30 to 35 minutes, or until set. Keep warm.

OVEN-ROASTED MOREL MUSHROOMS

24 morel mushrooms
2 tablespoons water
1 tablespoon butter
4 sprigs thyme
2 cloves garlic, chopped
1 shallot, sliced
Salt and pepper

Preheat oven to 350° F. Remove the bottom stem of the morels and reserve for Mushroom Nage. Cut each mushroom in half lengthwise. Wash the morels by soaking in cold water for a few minutes, swishing to loosen any dirt (see page 238). Gently remove mushrooms from water and transfer to a colander to drain. Place cleaned mushrooms, water, butter, thyme, garlic, shallot, salt and pepper in an ovenproof dish. Cover with foil and bake for 25 minutes, or until the mushrooms are soft. Strain mushroom liquid and reserve for Mushroom Nage; keep warm.

MUSHROOM NAGE

1 cup Mushroom Jus (see page 251)
Reserved morel stems
Reserved morel liquid
6 tablespoons butter
1 teaspoon truffle butter
1/4 teaspoon salt
1/4 teaspoon lemon juice
1/8 teaspoon pepper

Place the Mushroom Jus in a small pot with the reserved morel stems and mushroom roasting liquid; over low heat, reduce to 1/4 cup. Keep reduction over low flame and add butter, 1 tablespoon at a time, whisking constantly to incorporate. Pour hot liquid into the container of a blender, cover and run on high, adding the truffle butter, salt, lemon juice and pepper. Keep warm.

FINISH AND PLATE

Chives, cut in 2-inch pieces
Chervil leaves
Crispy Leeks (see page 254)

Run a knife around the ramekin of each Corn Flan; turn out onto a plate. Sauce the flan with Mushroom Nage. Place Oven-Roasted Morel Mushrooms around each flan and top with chives, chervil and Crispy Leeks.

From The List
BEAUJOLAIS GRAN CRU

A red full of strength and lighter floral fruit with earthy goodness

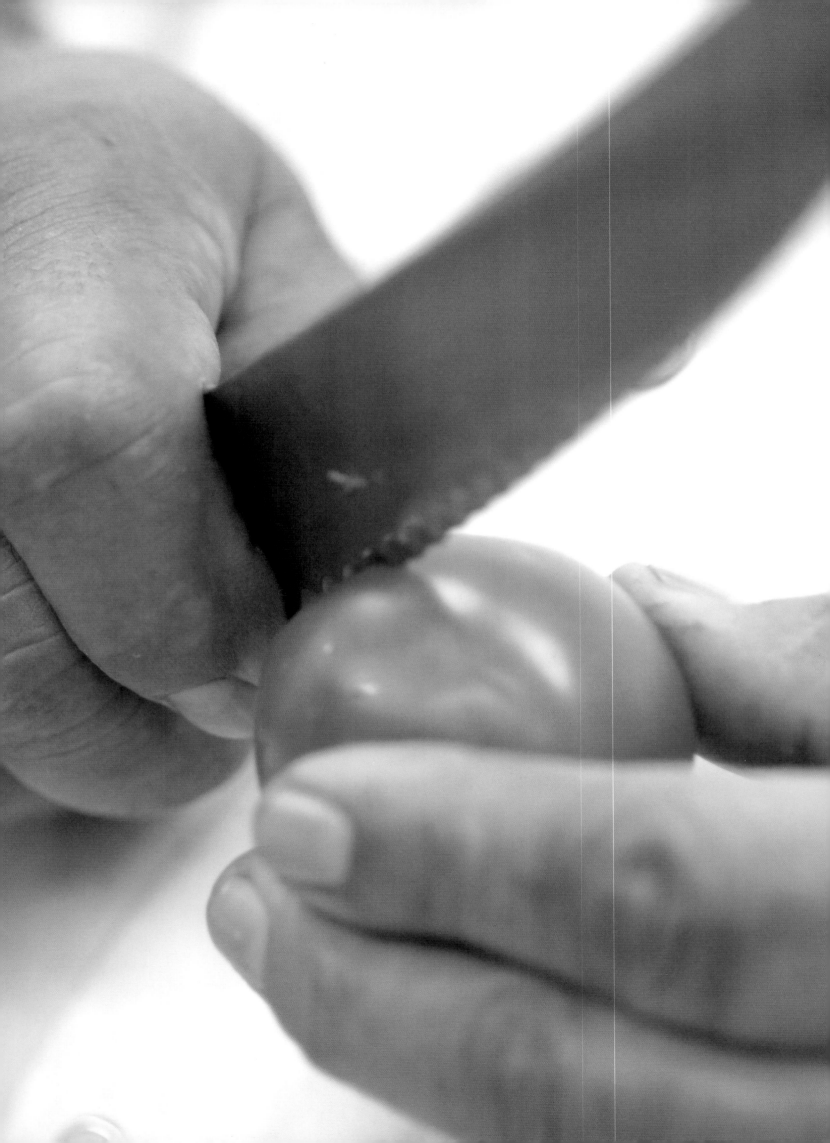

TOMATOES, TERROIR & THE ARTISTRY THEY INSPIRE

MENU THREE

HEIRLOOM TOMATO AND
BREAD SALAD SEE PAGE 113

Food doesn't have to look like modern art to be considered gallery worthy. It does, however, need to keep the palate engaged with a savory journey in anticipation of forthcoming flavors. Every year during tomato season, simple Layers of Heirloom Tomatoes and Buffalo Mozzarella, page 102, falls unassumingly into the art of eating. Our appreciation for the multitalented fruit of the tomato inspires us in menu three, where you'll find our beloved stretching beyond traditional partners such as basil oil and garlic confit to dance with a lively grain-mustard balsamic vinaigrette or a handsome ponzu.

Our focus is also directed by the harmonious terroir of Big Sur. The wild lavender perfumes the Post Ranch just about the same time Steve Beck's dry-farmed tomatoes ripen. Lavender-Tomato Tart Tatin, page 124, shows as the perfect accompaniment for roast rack of lamb. From the property's herb garden, we pick basil, cilantro and mint's new growth for many oils and purees, keeping each dish in circular community with the land.

This time of year we start previewing figs and soon Fig-Shiitake Sauce and Guinea Hen Breast with Blue Cheese Polenta, page 123, is on the menu. Today, I am teaching interns how to roll sweetbreads, page 108, explaining that when they are wrapped in pancetta and seared over high heat, the caramelization or browning will seal in the juices, therefore allowing their flavor no escape.

I just noticed Fernando has stopped scoring the tomatoes and is cleaning some Big Sur nopales, indicating he's seen the fresh prawns I picked up this morning at Sea Harvest. Instinctively, Tod's already prepping his Pasilla Chili Butter. Dominique shows me the local Sauvignon Blanc he'll be recommending for tonight's Escolar with Sweet Corn Pudding, Prawns, Nopales Salad and Pasilla Chili Butter, page 129. We never tire of the spirit in Big Sur that continually inspires the artist within us all.

HEIRLOOM TOMATO CONSOMMÉ

serves 6

CONSOMMÉ
2 pounds ripe heirloom tomatoes
1/2 teaspoon salt
6 leaves basil

Cut the tomatoes into quarters and then place in the bowl of a stand mixer fitted with paddle attachment. Add salt and basil. Run on low speed for 5 minutes to crush tomatoes. Transfer crushed tomatoes and liquid to a cheesecloth-lined chinois; set over a non-reactive container tall enough to have 3 inches clearance between the bottom of the container and the chinois. Refrigerate and let consommé drip overnight. Adjust seasoning with salt if needed. Serve chilled in shot glasses.

Heirloom
TOMATO CONSOMMÉ
AMUSE-BOUCHE

SERVE BEFORE

LAYERS OF HEIRLOOM TOMATO
AND BUFFALO MOZZARELLA

serves 6

Buffalo mozzarella is a fresh cheese made from the milk of a water buffalo. It has a much more complex flavor than cow's milk mozzarella. Finding a cheese shop in your area that can provide you with buffalo mozzarella is well worth the endeavor for this dish. When layered with simple, juicy heirloom tomatoes and fresh basil, you can taste the difference.

4 pounds heirloom tomatoes
1 pound buffalo mozzarella
Fleur de sel
Chianti Wine Vinaigrette (see page 247)
Basil leaves
18 blanched and peeled cherry tomatoes
Basil Oil (see page 248)

Select a variety of heirloom tomatoes and then slice the tomatoes and buffalo mozzarella about 1/4 inch thick. Lay a slice of tomato down on a plate, sprinkle with fleur de sel, and drizzle with a small amount of Chianti Wine Vinaigrette. Top with a slice of buffalo mozzarella and then lay a few basil leaves with tips protruding on each layer. Continue layering in this order to create three layers. Top with a few blanched and peeled cherry tomatoes; drizzle with Basil Oil.

From The List
ITALIAN WHITE WINE
OR SAUVIGNON BLANC

Wine

Of course
Italian
white...Alto
Adage area
would do well

LAYERS OF HEIRLOOM TOMATO AND BUFFALO MOZZARELLA

ABALONE DORÉ WITH CHERRY TOMATO–BASIL BROWN BUTTER

serves 6

Due to overharvesting and pollution, wild abalone is not available commercially. Our abalone comes from The Abalone Farm, located in Harmony, California, just 2 hours south of Big Sur. To appreciate the subtle sweet flavor of abalone, a light preparation is recommended. Abalone will lose its sweet flavor and light texture when overcooked; therefore pay heed to the shorter cooking time. Doré creates the perfect coating for abalone to seal in its juices as well as preventing overcooking.

ABALONE DORÉ
6 live abalone
1/4 cup flour
Salt and pepper
2 large eggs
3 tablespoons Clarified Butter (see page 246)

Remove abalone from its shell by running a sharp knife between the meat and the shell. Remove the intestinal sac. The black skirt surrounding the white muscle is edible; however, you can remove it for esthetic reasons by scrubbing the meat with a stiff brush under cold running water. Slice into thin slices and pound each slice vigorously with a mallet until abalone is tender. I prepare the live abalone at the restaurant, however, the Abalone Farms also offers prepared portions for sale. Season the flour with salt and pepper. Lightly beat the eggs in a small bowl. Dredge the abalone in the flour and then the egg. In a large skillet, heat the Clarified Butter over high heat; add the coated abalone one piece at a time. By the time the last one is added, begin turning the first few over. The abalone takes only about 5 seconds per side to cook in a hot pan.

CHERRY TOMATO–BASIL BROWN BUTTER

6 tablespoons butter
3 tablespoons milk solids (see page 246)
1 tablespoon finely chopped garlic
24 basil leaves
1 pint assorted cherry tomatoes, cut in half
1 1/2 teaspoons capers
2 1/4 teaspoons lemon juice
3/4 teaspoon salt
Pepper

Chef's Note: When melted, butter separates into 2 components; the fat, or clarified butter, and the milk solids, or whey. The milk solids are the part of butter that actually browns. I add extra milk solids to my brown butter sauces. This results in a creamier, less oily finished sauce due to a lower proportion of butter fat (see Clarified Butter and Milk Solids, page 246). This sauce moves very quickly, so have all the components ready to go before starting. Over medium heat, place butter in a 10-inch skillet and heat until melted; add the milk solids and heat until foamy. The bottom of the pan will begin to brown, and the foam will have some brown flecks followed by a nutty aroma. Remove pan from heat and quickly add garlic and let cook for a few seconds. Carefully add basil leaves, as they will splatter a little, tomatoes, capers, lemon juice, salt and pepper. Mix well and serve immediately.

FINISH AND PLATE

Balsamic Syrup (see page 250)

Place Abalone Doré in the center of warmed plates. Circle with Balsamic Syrup and spoon Cherry Tomato–Basil Brown Butter over the top.

From The List
BLANC de BLANC FROM CASSIS FRANCE

Wine

Lively and
slightly nutty
flavor for the
challenge of
brown butter

PANCETTA-WRAPPED
VEAL SWEETBREADS | WITH FAVA BEANS AND WILD
MUSHROOM VINAIGRETTE

PANCETTA-WRAPPED VEAL SWEETBREADS WITH FAVA BEANS AND WILD MUSHROOM VINAIGRETTE

serves 6

I first tried sweetbreads about ten years ago in San Francisco at Nancy Oaks' Boulevard restaurant and have been a devoted fan ever since. Throughout my career at Sierra Mar, and many variations, this version is not only my favorite but its recipe is frequently requested by our guest diners. The contrast of textures, the earthy mushroom flavor and the vinaigrette's acidity complement the richness of the sweetbreads.

VEAL SWEETBREADS
1 pound veal sweetbreads
2 quarts cold water
2 tablespoons salt
2 1/2 cups heavy cream
2 large cloves garlic, crushed
3 tablespoons roughly chopped shallots
4 sprigs thyme
2 bay leaves
1 teaspoon salt
1/4 teaspoon black pepper
See technique page 108

To purge, place the sweetbreads in the cold water with 2 tablespoons salt and soak for 6 hours or overnight. Place the cream, garlic, shallots, thyme, bay leaves, salt and pepper in a 2-quart saucepan and bring to a simmer for 5 minutes to infuse the cream; add the veal sweetbreads and simmer for 15 minutes, or until sweetbreads are firm to the touch. Lay out a 12-x-18-inch piece of aluminum foil and cover it with a same-size piece of parchment paper. Remove sweetbreads from the poaching liquid and rub each piece with a dry towel to remove the outer membrane. Lay the sweetbreads on the parchment paper and then roll the veal in foil and paper to form a cylinder. *Chef's Note: Cut the larger lobes of sweetbreads in half, if needed, to form a uniform cylinder. Twist each end of the foil in opposite directions to tighten and compress the veal into a tight cylinder.* Transfer to a bowl of ice water until cold, about 5 minutes. Refrigerate until ready to use.

FINISH AND PLATE
6 slices pancetta bacon
1/4 cup flour
2 teaspoons salt
1 teaspoon pepper
4 tablespoons canola oil
1/3 cup blanched and shelled fava beans
2 teaspoons water
1 teaspoon olive oil
Salt and pepper
Wild Mushroom Vinaigrette (see page 248)
1/3 cup Herb Salad (see page 255)
See technique on page 108

Remove the foil and parchment paper. Cut the sweetbread roll into six even discs. Wrap one slice of pancetta bacon around the outside of each piece. Secure by tying with butcher's twine. Season the flour with salt and pepper. Roll the Pancetta-Wrapped Veal Sweetbreads in the seasoned flour, shaking off excess. Heat oil in a 12-inch skillet over medium heat; add the sweetbreads one at time. Cook for about 3 minutes per side until nicely browned. After second side is golden brown, turn the sweetbreads on their side and slowly roll in the pan to crisp the bacon, cooking 2 to 3 minutes more. Transfer to a paper towel–lined plate to drain; keep warm. In a small sauté pan, heat fava beans in water and olive oil, season to taste with salt and pepper. Place a Pancetta-Wrapped Veal Sweetbread in the center of each plate; sauce with Wild Mushroom Vinaigrette, scatter the fava beans around the plate and top with a petite portion of Herb Salad.

From The List

COTE DU RHONE

Light yet terroir-filled rasteau or cairanne villages for a supple palate feel

1. Layout a 12-x-18-inch piece of foil with the same size parchment paper on top.

2. Remove the sweetbreads from the poaching liquid and rub each piece with a dry towel, removing outer membrane.

3. Place sweetbreads on foil lined with parchment paper.

4. Roll into a cylinder.

5. Twist each end of the foil in opposite directions to tighten and compress the sweetbreads into a tight cylinder.

6. Transfer the rolled sweetbreads into an ice water bath to chill.

7. Cut the larger lobes in half if needed to form a uniform cylinder.

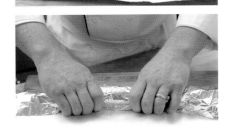

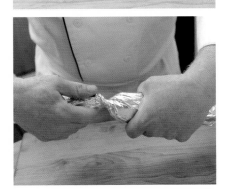

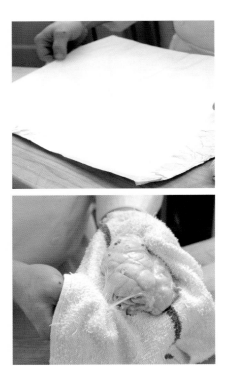

ROLLING SWEETBREADS

HEIRLOOM TOMATO NIGIRI WITH MATSUTAKE ROLL AND PONZU

serves 6

This hand-molded tomato nigiri gives the palate a break from the tomato's usual accompaniments of basil and garlic. In keeping with Japanese influence, the matsutake's piney flavor holds up and completes the balance of this dish. In the United States, matsutake mushrooms are foraged late summer through the fall. Mikuni Wild Harvest ships us matsutake mushrooms directly from the field each day. They are located in the Pacific Northwest, one of the prime regions for foraging matsutakes.

SUSHI RICE

2 cups short-grain white rice
2 cups water
1/3 cup seasoned rice vinegar
2 teaspoons salt
3 1/2 tablespoons sugar
1 tablespoon mirin

Place the rice in a fine strainer; thoroughly rinse under cold running water until water runs clear. Transfer to a rice cooker; add water and cook according to manufacturer's instructions. Place the vinegar, salt, sugar and mirin in a small pot and heat until the sugar and salt dissolve; do not boil. When the rice is cooked, turn it out into a mixing bowl. *Chef's Note:* Red-labeled vinegar is already seasoned; green–labeled vinegar is unseasoned. Pour the vinegar mixture over the cooked rice. Mix the rice with a spatula or wooden spoon in a left to right slicing motion to separate the grains until all the vinegar is absorbed while simultaneously fanning the rice with a piece of cardboard or a hand-held fan. Continue fanning the rice while mixing until it reaches room temperature; this aides in the separation of grains and will ensure the rice will not be gummy.

TOMATO NIGIRI

4 large heirloom tomatoes, such as Cherokee purple, marvel stripe, green zebra or any firm, ripe heirloom variety
1/2 recipe Sushi Rice
1 tablespoon wasabi
1 sheet nori paper, cut into 3-x-1/4-inch strips

Blanch and peel the tomatoes, see page 119. Cut tomatoes into quarters, or sixths if using large tomatoes, and then cut away the seeds and pulp. Each tomato should yield 4 petals. Form a small ball of Sushi Rice in the palm of your hand and press into an oval shape, rub a little wasabi on the rice and top with a tomato petal. Wet one end of a nori strip and wrap around the rice and tomato, pressing the moist strip ends together underneath.

MIRIN SOY-GLAZED MATSUTAKE MUSHROOMS

1/2 cup sake
1/2 cup mirin
1 (1-inch) piece ginger, lightly crushed
2 tablespoons sugar
3 tablespoons + 1 teaspoon soy sauce
3 tablespoons canola oil
3 cups sliced matsutake mushrooms (shiitake mushrooms may be substituted)

In a small saucepan over medium heat, bring sake, mirin, ginger and sugar to a simmer and reduce by two-thirds. Add the soy sauce and strain through chinois. In a large skillet, heat the oil over high heat and add the matsutakes; cook over medium heat until lightly browned, about 5 minutes. Add the mirin-soy reduction, toss to coat, and cook for 1 minute more to caramelize.

HEIRLOOM TOMATO NIGIRI | WITH MATSUTAKE ROLL AND PONZU

PONZU

2 tablespoons mirin
1/2 cup soy sauce
2 tablespoons tamari
2 tablespoons yuzu juice
2 tablespoons seasoned rice vinegar
1 (2-inch) square kombu seaweed

Heat mirin in a small pot over medium heat for 1 minute to remove alcohol. Mix all ingredients together and let set for 24 hours; strain out kombu. Chef's Note: Yuzu is a Japanese citrus. The bottled juice is available in Asian markets or through Fresh and Wild (see Purveyor's List on page 258). If not available, substitute 1 tablespoon lime juice and 1 tablespoon lemon juice combined.

FINISH AND PLATE

5 sheets nori paper
Sushi rolling mat
1 recipe Sushi Rice
Wasabi, to taste
1 avocado, peeled and cut into 12 wedges
Pickled ginger

Lay one sheet of nori paper on sushi rolling mat and cover with Sushi Rice approximately 1/4 inch thick, leaving the last 1/2 inch of nori paper uncovered at the end furthest from you. With one finger, make an indentation across the center of the rice and spread with a desired amount of wasabi. Place 2 avocado wedges end to end across; layer with Mirin Soy-Glazed Matsutake Mushrooms. With the rolling mat, lift the end of the nori nearest you and roll it over the filling. To seal, moisten the exposed nori at the far end with a paste made by mashing together a few grains of Sushi Rice and a few drops of water. Cut roll into 6 even pieces. Repeat with remaining nori paper and ingredients. This dish can be served family style on large platters. Arrange sliced matsutake rolls and Tomato Nigiri on the platter. Serve with pickled ginger, wasabi, and Ponzu.

From The List
SAKE

Wine

You can take a break from wine and if the situation like this presents itself do so

HEIRLOOM TOMATO AND BREAD SALAD

serves 6

This classic rustic Italian tomato and bread salad has been on Sierra Mar's menu since opening. We bring together 2-year-old Reggiano Parmigiano, sharp local Rucola arugula and 8-year-old aged balsamic vinegar with crunchy bread for a flavorful salad. By bringing together artisan-produced ingredients, this salad lets everyone know its tomato season!

GRAIN-MUSTARD BALSAMIC VINAIGRETTE

1/4 cup good-quality aged balsamic vinegar
1 tablespoon whole-grain mustard
2 teaspoons honey
1 tablespoon diced shallots
1 teaspoon salt
1/2 cup canola oil
2 tablespoons extra virgin olive oil
1/2 teaspoon freshly ground pepper

Place the vinegar, mustard, honey, shallots and salt in a mixing bowl and let stand for 15 minutes. Add the oils in a slow, steady stream while whisking constantly to emulsify; add freshly ground pepper.

FINISH AND PLATE

4 cups whole-grain bread (crust removed), cut into 1/2-inch cubes
1/4 cup olive oil
Salt and pepper
1/2 English cucumber
2 pounds assorted heirloom tomatoes
Fleur de sel
1 pound Rocolla arugula
1/2 red onion, julienned
Shaved Reggiano Parmigiano

Preheat oven to 350° F. Toss the bread cubes in a bowl with the olive oil and season with salt and pepper; lay out on a parchment-lined baking sheet. Bake for 10 minutes, or until browned and crunchy. Cut the cucumber in half lengthwise and remove the seeds with a spoon; thinly slice. Place bread cubes in a large mixing bowl and generously dress with the Grain-Mustard Balsamic Vinaigrette; let sit for 2 minutes, allowing the cubes to soak up the dressing and soften slightly. Cut the tomatoes into wedges and toss with bread cubes; season lightly with fleur de sel. Add the arugula, onion and cucumber; toss very gently, adding a little more vinaigrette. Divide between 6 plates and top with shaved Reggiano Parmigiano.

From The List
PINOT GRIGIO

Well made
and complex

TEMPURA
SOFT-SHELL CRAB   WITH MISO VINAIGRETTE
                   AND CUCUMBER SALAD

TEMPURA SOFT-SHELL CRAB WITH MISO VINAIGRETTE AND CUCUMBER SALAD

serves 6

We receive live Maryland soft-shell crabs in season starting around Mother's day. (See Chef's Note below for substitutions.) Seabeans are a salt-loving plant that grows wild in the coastal regions of the Pacific Northwest and is foraged during the summer months. It's pleasant crunch and fresh salty ocean flavor add depth to this dish. Less is more as the straightforward Japanese Miso Vinaigrette lets the crab flavor reign.

SOFT-SHELL CRABS
6 prime dressed soft-shell crabs

Chef's Note: Using live crabs is the best way to ensure quality and freshness. If you prefer, your fishmonger can dress the crabs for you, or if live crabs are not available, prepared fresh or frozen soft-shell crabs can be substituted.

TEMPURA BATTER
2 cups flour
2 cups cornstarch
2 teaspoons baking soda
2 tablespoons wasabi powder
1 tablespoon salt
1 whole egg
1 egg white
2 1/2 cups cold soda water
2 tablespoons white sesame seeds
2 tablespoons black sesame seeds

In a large bowl, mix the flour, cornstarch, baking soda, wasabi powder and salt. In another bowl, whisk together the egg and egg white. Add the cold soda water and the egg to the dry ingredients and mix well; add more soda water or cornstarch to adjust consistency if needed. Fold in the sesame seeds and set batter aside. *Chef's Note:* Test the batter by coating and frying a piece of vegetable. It should coat evenly but not too thick.

CUCUMBER SALAD
2 English cucumbers
1/2 cup Crispy Shiitakes (see page 254)
1 package daikon sprouts
1/4 cup julienned pickled ginger
1/2 pound seabeans, optional
Salt to taste
Lemon juice
Garlic Confit Oil (see page 254)

Bring pot of water to a boil; blanch the seabeans for 5 seconds and then refresh in ice water. Using the medium teeth on a Japanese mandolin, julienne the cucumber into a bowl, stopping when you reach the seeds. Add the Crispy Shiitakes, daikon sprouts, pickled ginger and seabeans. Season the salad with salt and drizzle with lemon juice and Garlic Confit Oil to taste.

FINISH AND PLATE
3 quarts rice bran oil for frying
Miso Vinaigrette (see page 248)
1/4 cup pickled ginger

Heat oil to 350° F in a pot large enough to allow oil to rise up while frying. Dip the Soft-Shell Crabs into the Tempura Batter one at a time; remove and let the excess batter drip off. To prevent crabs from sticking to the bottom of the pot, hold onto one side of the crab, dip halfway into the hot oil and count 5 seconds. The batter will expand and allow the crab to float. Fry until golden brown and crispy, about 3 minutes, turning the crab over in the oil to cook both sides. Transfer the cooked crabs to a paper towel–lined plate and keep warm. Tempura fried foods need to be served immediately, so while the crabs are cooking, twist a portion of the Cucumber Salad into a haystack with a fork. Make a pool of Miso Vinaigrette and top with pickled ginger. When all the crabs are done, place in front of salad and serve.

From The List
AUSTRIAN RIESLING

Wine

With dry
notes, yet
floral, mineral
and well
structured

GOLDEN TOMATO THAI GAZPACHO

serves 6

Being fascinated with Thai flavor combinations—sour, sweet and spicy—I knew instinctively the sensation of taste I wanted to achieve when creating this recipe. Infusing vinegar, lemongrass and kaffir lime leaf with exotic galangal and siracha chili paste made this vision a reality. Each year at Tomato Fest, we feature Thai Gazpacho using Lemon Boy Heirloom Tomatoes, which contribute a light color and provide the ideal base for an intense Thai flavor.

5 pounds ripe tomatoes, Lemon Boy or other yellow heirloom variety such as marvel stripe
1 1/4 cups rice vinegar
10 kaffir lime leaves
4 lemongrass stalks, chopped
1/2 cup lime juice
3 tablespoons fish sauce
1 medium red onion, finely diced
1 cucumber, seeded and finely diced
2 cups green papaya, peeled and finely diced
20 mint leaves, julienned
20 Thai basil leaves, julienned
1/4 cup julienned cilantro leaves
2 tablespoons siracha
1 (1-inch) piece galangal, peeled
Mint Oil (see page 249)

Cut tomatoes into quarters. Place in the bowl of a stand mixer fitted with the paddle attachment. Run on low speed for 5 minutes to crush the tomatoes and release the juices. Transfer to a cone-shaped strainer over a bowl and press with the back of a ladle to extract all the juice; discard the seeds and peels. The liquid after straining should resemble slightly thick tomato juice. Simmer vinegar, lime leaves and lemongrass for 3 minutes, then remove from heat and let cool. Strain vinegar mixture into the tomato puree, add lime juice, fish sauce, diced vegetables, papaya, herbs and siracha. Place in bowl over ice to chill. Just before serving, grate the galangal into the gazpacho with a ginger grater or microplaner. *Chef's Note:* If fresh galangal is not available, use dried of the same amount and steep in the rice vinegar with the lemongrass and lime leaves. Drizzle Mint Oil over the top and serve in chilled bowls.

From The List
ALVARINHO FROM DE VINHO
VERDE REGION OF PORTUGAL

Wine

Tight and zesty with plenty of acidity to meet the challenge of this dish

GOLDEN TOMATO THAI GAZPACHO

MARVEL STRIPE TOMATO | FILLED WITH BASIL
PESTO AND SQUASH
BLOSSOM RISOTTO

MARVEL STRIPE TOMATO FILLED WITH BASIL PESTO AND SQUASH BLOSSOM RISOTTO

serves 6

The combination of creamy risotto and the bright acidity of a marvel stripe tomato offers the palate a pleasant contrast. This dish showcases the heirloom tomato at its best, surrounded by companions that keep the tomato front and forward. Cherokee Purple, Aunt Ruby's German Green or Hillbilly tomato may be substituted. For sourcing varieties, visit www.tomatofest.com.

TOMATOES
6 heirloom tomatoes, such as marvel stripe
Boiling water
Ice water

With the tip of a sharp knife, remove the core of each tomato and cut a shallow X through the skin on the bottom. Bring a large pot of water to a rapid boil; drop tomatoes in a few at a time. Ripe heirloom tomatoes take about 10 to 12 seconds before they are ready to peel, gently transfer to an ice water bath. *Chef's Note: A good rule is to test one tomato from your assortment to get an approximate time. If tomatoes are in the boiling water too long, they become grainy and mealy. If the tomato slips right out of the peel it is overcooked, therefore the peel should come away with gentle pulling. Slightly firm Roma tomatoes during the winter months could take as long as 30 seconds and cherry tomatoes as little as 6 seconds.* Using your fingers and the tip of a paring knife, peel the tomatoes by grasping the edge of the peel at the X and gently pulling away. Gently work the melon baller down into the core end of each tomato, removing pulp and seeds and being careful not to break through the sides or out the bottom. Leave about 1/3-inch thickness on the inside of the tomato to prevent it from collapsing.

VEGETABLE NAGE
2 1/2 cups Vegetable Stock (see page 253)
6 tablespoons butter
1/4 teaspoon lemon juice
Salt and pepper

Place Vegetable Stock in a saucepan and slowly reduce to 1/4 cup; over medium heat, whisk in butter, 1 tablespoon at a time. Transfer to the container of a blender, cover, and blend on high speed about 10 seconds or until completely emulsified. Season with lemon juice, salt and pepper. Keep warm until ready to use.

PARMESAN TUILLE
1/2 cup grated Parmesan cheese

Preheat oven to 350° F. Make a tuille template by cutting a 1/2-x-4-inch rectangle out of a piece of heavy paper, cardboard or thin plastic. Line a sheet pan with Silpat. Lay the template on the Silpat and sprinkle Parmesan cheese to just cover the exposed area. The tuilles will spread during cooking, so leave a 1-inch space around each. Bake until lightly browned and bubbling, about 8 minutes. Remove from oven and, working quickly while still hot, remove tuilles by running a small metal spatula underneath to loosen. Wrap each tuille three-fourths of the way around a small cylinder such as the thin end of a rolling pin or handle of a whisk, forming a horseshoe shape. The tuille is very pliable while hot. If needed, return the tuilles to the oven to reheat and shape. When cool, tuilles should be crunchy.

BASIL PESTO AND SQUASH BLOSSOM RISOTTO
1 3/4 cups Vegetable Stock (see page 253)
1 batch parcooked Risotto Base (see page 253)
1/3 cup pinenuts
1/2 cup julienned squash blossoms
1/4 cup basil pesto
2 tablespoons butter
3 tablespoons Parmesan cheese
1 1/4 teaspoons salt
1 1/4 teaspoons lemon juice
1 1/4 teaspoons pepper

Bring Vegetable Stock to a simmer. Place Risotto Base in a small pot over medium heat and add enough stock to just cover. Maintain at a simmer, stirring with a wooden spoon and adding more stock as needed to keep risotto barely covered. When all the stock has been absorbed, but a creamy liquid is surrounding the rice, remove from heat and add the remaining ingredients, adjust seasoning to taste and serve immediately.

FINISH AND PLATE
Salt and pepper
Olive oil
6 cherry tomatoes, sliced
Basil Oil (see page 248)
Basil for garnish (optional)

Preheat oven to 350° F. Season the Tomatoes inside and out with salt and pepper; drizzle with olive oil and warm on a sheet pan in the oven for 2 minutes. Transfer to serving bowls and fill with Basil Pesto and Squash Blossom Risotto. Spoon warm Vegetable Nage around the tomato. Top with a Parmesan Tuille, place sliced cherry tomatoes in the Vegetable Nage and then drizzle with Basil Oil. Garnish with fresh basil.

From The List
PIEDMONTE CHARDONNAY FROM
CONTERNO OR ROCCA

Gaja,
a nice
splurge

ROAST GUINEA HEN BREAST | WITH BLUE CHEESE, POLENTA
AND FIG-SHIITAKE SAUCE

ROAST GUINEA HEN BREAST WITH BLUE CHEESE POLENTA AND FIG-SHIITAKE SAUCE

serves 6

We purchase figs from Preston of Hamada Farms on our weekly trip to the farmers market. Usually, he takes me to the back of the van and we eat fresh figs as I make my selection. Pairing figs with ingredients that allow their unique sweetness to prevail remains the best complement to the fig. Blue cheese and shiitake mushrooms play well with a fig's interesting characteristic.

ROAST GUINEA HEN BREAST
6 guinea hen breasts
Salt and pepper
4 tablespoons canola oil
1/4 cup butter
8 sprigs thyme

Preheat oven to 350° F. Season the guinea hen breasts with salt and pepper. Heat the canola oil over high heat divided between two 12-inch cast-iron or nonstick skillets. Add three breasts skin side down to each skillet. Reduce heat to medium. Continue to cook until the skin is golden brown and crispy, about 6 minutes. Turn breasts over; cook until second side is browned. Holding the breasts in place with a spatula, drain off the excess oil, return to the heat, and add 2 tablespoons butter to each skillet. When foamy, add the thyme sprigs and baste the breasts. Transfer to oven for about 7 minutes or until the juices run clear when pierced with a skewer. Keep warm.

BLUE CHEESE POLENTA
1 1/2 cups Chicken Stock (see page 252), Vegetable Stock (see page 253), or water
1 1/2 cups half-and-half
1/2 cup coarse polenta meal
3 tablespoons butter
Salt
4 ounces blue cheese, such as St. Agur, Roquefort or Stilton

In a heavy-bottom pot, bring the stock and half-and-half to a boil. Add polenta meal in a steady stream, whisking constantly, until the mixture returns to a boil and thickens slightly. Reduce heat to a low simmer, stirring frequently with a wooden spoon, scraping the bottom to prevent scorching. Simmer for 45 minutes; add butter and salt. When butter is incorporated, transfer to a container, cover with plastic wrap and keep warm. When ready to plate, fold in the blue cheese.

FINISH AND PLATE
Fig-Shiitake Sauce (see page 253)
Swiss Chard (see page 256)

Place a small mound of Swiss Chard in the center of each plate with 2 quenelles of Blue Cheese Polenta behind it. Place Roast Guinea Hen Breast on the chard and finish with the Fig-Shiitake Sauce.

From The List
LIGHTER STYLE ZINFANDEL

With moderate alcohol, prevalent spice, sweet fruit and good tannins

ROAST RACK OF LAMB WITH LAVENDER-TOMATO TART TATIN AND BALSAMIC REDUCTION

serves 6

During the summer, local farmers bring eggplant and squash blossoms just picked from their gardens. Lavender also grows freely all over the property at Post Ranch Inn. Down the road at Esalen, Steve Beck brings some of his intensely flavored dry-farmed tomatoes to complete this Provençal dish that features the terroir of Big Sur.

LAVENDER-TOMATO TART TATIN
2 tablespoons Sherry-Lavender Gastrique (see page 250)
18 cloves Garlic Confit (see page 254)
18 black olive halves
Lavender flowers
18 Roasted Tomatoes (see page 256)
6 (3-inch round) circle puff pastry
See technique on page 126

Preheat oven to 375° F. I use a 3-inch Teflon tart mold for this tart; however, a 4-ounce ramekin will work if you adjust the size of the puff pastry as needed. Drizzle 1 teaspoon of the gastrique in the bottom of each tart mold. Arrange the Garlic Confit cloves and olives around the bottom of the pan, sprinkle a few lavender flowers and cover with 3 Roasted Tomato halves placed smooth side down. Top with the puff pastry. Place the tarts on a sheet pan and cover with Silpat. Bake for approximately 20 minutes. *Chef's Note: Laying Silpat over the top prevents the puff pastry from rising too much and separating the tomatoes. Anything heavier compacts the pastry too much, making it too hard.* **Keep warm.**

RATATOUILLE
1/2 cup + 1 tablespoon olive oil, divided
1/4 cup diced red bell pepper
4 teaspoons chopped garlic, divided
Salt and crushed red pepper
1/4 cup diced eggplant
1/4 cup diced zucchini
1/4 cup diced yellow onion
1/4 cup Oven-Roasted Tomatoes (see page 256)
2 tablespoons julienned basil
Salt

Chef's Note: The key to this ratatouille is to cook each vegetable separately before combining together. In a nonstick skillet, heat 2 tablespoons oil over high heat and then add red bell pepper. Cook for 2 minutes, tossing frequently; add 1 teaspoon garlic, salt and crushed red pepper and cook another 30 seconds. Transfer cooked peppers to a parchment-lined sheet pan. Repeat procedure for eggplant, zucchini and yellow onion, using 1 extra tablespoon olive oil for the eggplant because it absorbs much of the oil. When all of the vegetables have cooled, mix together with Oven-Roasted Tomatoes and basil; adjust seasoning with salt. Set aside until ready to use.

SQUASH BLOSSOMS
12 squash blossoms
3 quarts rice bran oil for frying
Fromage Blanc Batter (see page 246)

Open each squash blossom and remove the center pistil. Fill with 2 tablespoons Ratatouille and then twist the ends to seal. Heat oil to 350° F in a pot large enough to allow the oil to rise up during frying; dip each squash blossom into the Fromage Blanc Batter and fry until crispy and golden brown, about 3 minutes. Remove and drain on paper towels; serve immediately.

ROAST RACK OF LAMB
2 Jamison Farms lamb racks
Salt and pepper
3 tablespoons canola oil
2 tablespoons butter
1 sprig rosemary
5 sprigs lavender

Preheat oven to 350° F. Generously season the lamb rack with salt and pepper 6 hours prior to cooking; cover with plastic wrap and refrigerate. Before cooking, remove from the refrigerator and let sit at room temperature for 1 hour. Heat oil in a 14-inch skillet; add the lamb rack, bone side up. When a brown crust begins to form, about 5 minutes, turn and cook until evenly browned on all sides, ending bone side down. Hold the lamb in place with a metal spatula, tilt the skillet and drain off the oil. Add the butter. When foaming, add rosemary and lavender, baste the lamb rack and transfer to preheated oven for 8 to 12 minutes, or until an internal temperature of 140°F for medium rare. Remove from oven, transfer to a platter and let rest for 5 minutes before slicing; keep warm.

FINISH AND PLATE
Balsamic Reduction (see page 250)

Turn out the Lavender-Tomato Tart Tatin in the center of the plate by placing the plate on top of the tart and turning over; remove mold. Place 2 Squash Blossoms in front, slice one chop off either end of the Roast Rack of Lamb and place in front of the tart; sauce with Balsamic Reduction. Chef's Note: One end of the lamb rack has a smaller eye and a section of fat, so by taking one chop from either end, it makes the portions even.

From The List
NEW WORLD GRENACHE

Wine

Accepts lamb well and takes on the challenge of lavender and balsamic reduction

TECHNIQUE

1. Drizzle 1 teaspoon of the Sherry-Lavender Gastrique into each mold.

2. Arrange 3 Garlic Confit cloves and olives on the bottom of each mold and a few lavender flowers.

3. Add 3 Roasted Tomato halves on top of the garlic and olives smooth side down.

4. Cut the puff pastry into circles and press over the tomatoes.

5. Lay Silpat over the top during baking to provide pressure that prevents the pastry from rising and separating the tomatoes.

6. Turn tart onto plate by placing plate over mold and flipping; remove mold.

TOMATO TART TATIN

ESCOLAR WITH SWEET CORN PUDDING, PRAWNS,
NOPALES SALAD AND PASILLA CHILI BUTTER

ESCOLAR WITH SWEET CORN PUDDING, PRAWNS, NOPALES SALAD AND PASILLA CHILI BUTTER

serves 6

Fernando Nunez has been a cook at Sierra Mar since the very first day. Fernando's wife harvests nopales in Big Sur, and Fernando created this accompaniment salad influenced by his Mexican heritage. Fernando's pride and care for products and preparation go into each dish he is involved with in the kitchen. We are lucky to have him on staff.

ESCOLAR
1/2 teaspoon whole cumin seeds
6 (3-ounce) pieces escolar
Salt and pepper
3 tablespoons canola oil
2 tablespoons butter
1 teaspoon lime juice

Toast the cumin seeds in a small skillet over high heat, stirring frequently to keep from burning. When the cumin becomes aromatic and a light smoke rises from the pan, transfer to a spice grinder and process to a coarse grind. Set aside 1/2 teaspoon for Prawns. Season the escolar with salt and pepper. Heat oil in a large skillet over high heat; add escolar, reduce heat to medium, and cook for 3 to 4 minutes, or until a brown crust begins to form. Turn and cook 3 minutes more; holding the fish in place with a spatula, drain oil from skillet. Add butter. When it begins to foam, add the lime juice and half the ground cumin seeds. Tilt the pan and baste the escolar with the seasoned butter; set aside and keep warm.

NOPALES SALAD
2 pounds nopales
1 1/2 onions
1 head garlic
1 gallon water
1/2 bunch cilantro
Salt
1/2 cup diced onion
1/2 cup diced fresh tomato
1/4 cup chopped cilantro
See technique on page 131

To clean the nopales you will need a rubber glove and a sharp knife. Hold the nopales with your gloved hand using a sharp knife, cut off all the thorns, not the green skin. Dice the thorn-free nopales into 1/2-inch pieces. Cut whole onion and garlic in half; bring water to a boil and then add onions, garlic, cilantro, salt and nopales. Boil for 30 minutes and then drain into a colander. Remove garlic, cilantro, onions and discard. Rinse nopales thoroughly under cold water to remove all the viscous juices. Reserve a few pieces of nopales for garnish. Measure 3 cups cooked nopales and toss with 1/2 cup diced fresh onion, fresh tomato, cilantro and more salt. Set aside until ready to use.

CORN PUDDING
6 to 8 ears corn
2 1/2 cups corn water
3 tablespoons butter
3/4 teaspoon salt

Remove the husks and silk from corn; shave the kernels off each cob and reserve. Place the cobs in a pot and add enough water just to cover; bring to a simmer for 45 minutes, adding more water if needed to keep the cobs covered. Strain the corn water into a container; place reserved kernels in a small pot and barely cover with corn water. Bring to a simmer for 10 minutes, or until corn is tender. Strain the kernels, once again reserving the liquid. Transfer the corn kernels to the container of a blender, cover, and puree, adding a little of the reserved corn liquid if needed. Press the puree through a fine sieve with the bottom of a ladle. Whisk butter and salt into the strained puree and cover with plastic wrap to prevent a skin from forming. Keep warm until ready to serve.

PRAWNS

2 tablespoons canola oil
12 fresh prawn tails, peeled and deveined
Salt and pepper
2 tablespoons butter
1 teaspoon lime juice
1/4 teaspoon ground toasted cumin seeds

Heat the canola oil in a large skillet over medium heat; add the prawns, season with salt and pepper. Cook for a minute, turning frequently until turning pink but still opaque in the center. Hold the prawns in place with a spatula and tilt the skillet to drain off the oil. Return to heat and then add the butter. When foamy, add the lime juice and cumin, basting the prawns with the butter. Serve immediately.

PASILLA CHILI BUTTER SAUCE

3 tablespoons pasilla chili juice (about 1 chili)
1/2 cup Beurre Blanc (see page 246)
2 teaspoons Cilantro Pesto (see page 254)
1 teaspoon lime juice
Salt

Remove seeds and core from the chile and then cut into quarters. Run through a juice extractor; 1 chile should yield 3 tablespoons juice. Just before serving, warm the Beurre Blanc; add the pasilla juice, Cilantro Pesto, lime juice and salt to taste. *Chef's Notes: Serve this sauce immediately. If it sits, the green color will diminish. If you do not own a juice extractor, roast the chili, peel and remove the seeds, and then puree it in a blender with a little Beurre Blanc. The bright green color will disappear but the flavor is still excellent.*

FINISH AND PLATE

Thin slices nopales
Cilantro sprouts

Place a pool of Corn Pudding in the center of a shallow bowl. Place Escolar on top. Mound Nopales Salad toward the back of the Escolar and cover with 2 Prawns. Top with cilantro sprouts, thin slices of tomato and nopales. Spoon Pasilla Chili Butter Sauce around the plate.

From The List
GRUNET VELTLINER OR
VIURA AND SAUVIGNON BLANC

Greener well-structured white wine shall travel well with the entire dish

TECHNIQUE

1. To clean the nopales, you will need a rubber glove and a sharp knife.

2. Hold nopales with a gloved hand and with a sharp knife, shave off all the little bumps that contain thorns but not the remaining green skin.

3. Dice the nopales into 1/2-inch pieces.

4. Add onions, garlic, cilantro, salt and diced nopales to boiling water. Boil 30 minutes.

5. Remove onion, garlic, cilantro and rinse nopales to remove all the viscous juices.

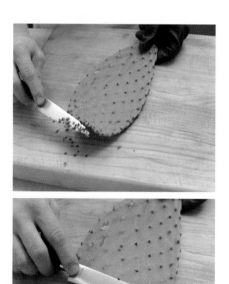

CLEANING NOPALES

PRESERVES, MARMALADES & CAPTURING FLAVORS THAT SUSTAIN US

MENU FOUR

Amuse-Bouche

"BLT" TOMATO JAM WITH BRAISED BACON
AND BABY ARUGULA 136

Course One

TERNION OF FOIE GRAS WITH AUTUMN PRESERVES 139

CELERIAC CANNOLI WITH PUMPKIN SEED
VINAIGRETTE AND APPLE SALAD 142

GRILLED SQUAB BREAST WITH SQUAB LIVER MOUSSE
CROSTINI, ENDIVE AND CASSIS SAUCE 145

GRILLED MONTEREY BAY SARDINES WITH CARAMELIZED
FENNEL TART TATIN, SALSA VERDE AND TAPENADE 148

Course Two

RED WINE–POACHED SEKEL PEAR WITH PIERRE ROBERT,
HEARTY GREENS AND CANDIED WALNUTS 153

SALAD OF GRILLED BLACK MISSION FIGS,
BITTER GREENS AND BLEU DE HAUT JURA
CHEESE WITH A PORT REDUCTION 156

SEAFOOD BOURIDE WITH RED PEPPER PICADA 158

Course Three

PANCETTA-WRAPPED SIKA VENISON LOIN WITH PISTACHIO
PUREE, HUCKLEBERRY SAUCE AND PUMPKIN DUMPLINGS 161

ALASKAN HALIBUT WITH POTATO RÖSTI, SAVOY SPINACH,
PERNOD-POACHED OYSTERS AND SEVRUGA CAVIAR 164

ROAST DUCK BREAST WITH STAR ANISE CONSOMMÉ,
PEKING DUCK WONTONS, SOY-BRAISED MUSHROOMS
AND PLUM SAUCE 169

BUTTERNUT SQUASH RAVIOLI WITH
SAGE-PECAN BROWN BUTTER 172

For Menu Four, Dominique felt an hommage to the Loire Valley Varietals was in order.

"The Loire Valley is a large wine-growing area offering great diversity of sub-regions each supporting contrasting styles. It extends from Sauvignon Blanc in the upper Loire to the Muscadet in the east of Nantes, passing by the Anjou-Saumur and the Touraine where the Chenin Blanc is king. The whites range from very light, crisp, mineral focused to dense, spicy or nutty.

The reds of the region are also very distinctive and although a little on the lighter side, they stay respectful to more delicate preparations. Cabernet Franc in Chinon for example, and Pinot Noir in the Sancerre and even some Gamay in there.

These wines have structure, character and, regardless of their finesse, are not afraid to take on a wide array of foods. Despite their greatness and amazing quality to value ratio, they are very understated and rightfully deserving of a better exposure."

—Dominique daCruz, Sommelier

Chef's tasting menus that include wine pairings are a very important part of the Sierra Mar experience.

Our grandmothers knew the philosophy behind preserving and canning. Perhaps it was just their way of life or maybe they already knew what we have come to realize—wintertime produce, albeit good, lacks variety. It therefore becomes essential to preserve autumn and its flavors of currants, plums, quince, persimmons and huckleberries in order to sustain the rustic meat, game and fowl throughout the impending winter months.

In this menu, we quietly welcome the change in landscape as fall has left us to the comfortable task of flavoring vinaigrettes with autumn fruit emulsions, and pureeing hearty vegetables like celeriac or butternut squash for our vegetarian cannoli and ravioli.

Jams, gastriques and syrups all play a vital role in our daytime prep. Grinders blend savory spices of nutmeg, clove and ginger as the term brûlée, tapenade and picada debut on the menu. Nuts are spiced or candied, and signature dishes like Alaskan Halibut with Potato Rösti, Savoy Spinach, Pernod-Poached Oysters and Sevruga Caviar, page 164, receives the welcome of a long lost relative.

Stocks simmering on the stove remind me of how important it is to make your own rich broth from scratch and the positive effects it has on a dish's outcome, see stock recipes on pages 252–253. I continue to break down the peking duck for this evening's Roast Duck Breast with Star Anise Consommé, Peking Duck Wontons and Soy Braised Mushrooms with Plum Sauce, page 169. I just preserved the plums this morning to use over the next several months as an important way of life continues in the kitchen.

CHEF'S NOTES

"BLT" TOMATO JAM WITH BRAISED BACON AND BABY ARUGULA

serves 6

TOMATO JAM

2 pounds heirloom tomatoes, paste variety
1/4 cup sugar
1/4 cup balsamic vinegar
2 cloves garlic, chopped

Blanch and peel the tomatoes (see page 119). Cut in half to remove the seeds and then roughly chop tomatoes. Place the sugar, vinegar and garlic in a nonreactive pot and bring to a boil. Add the tomatoes; reduce heat to a low simmer, stirring frequently, until thickened to a jam consistency, about 1 hour.

BRAISED BACON

1 (8-ounce) piece slab bacon
3 tablespoons canola oil
1/2 cup chopped (1-inch) onion
1/4 cup chopped (1-inch) carrot
1/4 cup chopped (1-inch) leek
2 cloves garlic
2 sprigs thyme
2 cups Chicken Stock (see page 252)

Preheat oven to 275° F. Score the fat or skin side of the bacon. Heat the oil in an ovenproof skillet over high heat and then add bacon, scored side down. Reduce heat to low and cook for 10 minutes, until it is deep brown in color. Turn bacon over and cook for 10 minutes more; drain off most of the fat and then add vegetables. Cook until they begin to caramelize, about 5 minutes; add garlic, thyme and enough Chicken Stock to come three-fourths of the way up the sides of the bacon. Transfer skillet to the oven for 1 hour, basting the bacon and occasionally adding more Chicken Stock to maintain the same amount of liquid. Remove from oven and let bacon cool in braising liquid. When cool, remove from liquid and cut into 1/4-inch-thick slices.

CROSTINI

Sourdough baguette
3 tablespoons olive oil, divided
Salt and pepper

Slice a crusty sourdough baguette into 1/4-inch slices. Cut a rectangle out of the center of each slice. In a nonstick skillet, heat 1 1/2 tablespoons olive oil over medium heat; add the bread slices and a light sprinkling of salt and pepper. Cook until golden brown, about 2 minutes. Turn over slices and add remaining oil to the pan and brown the second side. Set aside.

FINISH AND PLATE

Micro arugula or Herb Salad (see page 255)

Heat slices of Braised Bacon under a broiler for 3 minutes, or until lightly browned. Place a piece of bacon on each Crostini, spoon 1 tablespoon Tomato Jam over bacon and then top with micro arugula or Herb Salad.

"BLT"
TOMATO JAM WITH
BRAISED BACON AND BABY ARUGULA
AMUSE-BOUCHE

SERVE BEFORE

TERNION OF FOIE GRAS | WITH AUTUMN PRESERVES

TERNION OF FOIE GRAS WITH AUTUMN PRESERVES

serves 6

The connection between foie gras and preserved autumn fruit is nature's way of communicating her serendipitous plan. Symmetry between the tartness of quince, persimmon and apple lets you taste the alignment of texture and flavor in these three preparations of foie gras. The Foie Gras Torchon needs to be started 4 days prior to serving.

QUATRE ÉPICES CARAMEL POWDER
1/4 cup water
1/2 cup sugar
1 teaspoon Quatre Épices (see page 256)

Line a sheet pan with Silpat and set aside. In a small pot, mix together the water and sugar and then bring to a boil over medium heat. When the sugar turns a golden brown, about 5 minutes, add the Quatre Épices powder and pour out on the Silpat and let cool. When cool, the sugar caramel will harden and look like glass. Pull caramel sheet off the Silpat and then break it into smaller pieces. Grind pieces to a powder in a clean spice grinder. You may need to sift to remove larger pieces. Over grinding can heat the powder and cause clogging. Store in an airtight container until ready to use. *Chef's Note: If you are not using the same day, add 1 tablespoon of rice to the powder in the airtight container. This absorbs the excess moisture and prevents caking. Sift through a dry fine strainer to remove rice before using.*

FOIE GRAS MOUSSE
1 (1 1/2-pound) grade A foie gras
3 quarts cold water
2 tablespoons salt
2 teaspoons salt
1/2 teaspoon freshly ground white pepper
1 tablespoon cognac
2 teaspoons black truffle oil

Purge and devein the foie gras according to instructions on page 36. Season the foie gras with 2 teaspoons salt and white pepper. Transfer to a zipper-lock bag and add the cognac and black truffle oil; remove excess air, seal and place in another zipper-lock bag. Remove the air and seal again; refrigerate for 4 hours. Bring a large pot of water to a boil and drop the zipper-lock bag of foie gras into the water and simmer for 8 minutes. Open one corner of the bag and drain off the fat; reserve. Reseal and transfer the bag of foie gras to the refrigerator; when completely firm, about 2 hours, remove from the bags and scrape off the congealed yellow fat and add to the reserved fat. Warm the fats and strain through a chinois. Press the foie gras through a tamis sieve and whisk in the reserved fat. The fat should be just melted and not hot. Transfer to a container and cover with plastic wrap. Make the crème brûlée right away while the mousse is still soft.

FOIE GRAS "CRÈME BRÛLÉE"
2 tablespoons Pear Gastrique (see page 250)

Place 1 teaspoon Pear Gastrique in each of six 1-ounce ramekins; refrigerate to allow gastrique to harden. Fill ramekin with Foie Gras Mousse, smoothing the top with a spatula. Refrigerate until set, about 2 hours.

QUINCE MARMALADE
4 cups water
3/4 cup sugar
2 teaspoons lemon juice
1 cup grated quince

Place water, sugar and lemon juice in a nonreactive saucepan; bring to a boil. Peel the quince and grate using the largest side of a box grater. Transfer quince to liquid immediately after grating to prevent oxidation. Reduce the heat to low and cook until thick, about 30 minutes.

PERSIMMON MARMALADE
3 cups water
3/4 cup sugar
1 teaspoon lemon juice
1 1/4-inch slice ginger
4 medium Fuyu persimmons, peeled and grated

Chef's Note: The two most common types of persimmons are Fuyu and Haichiya. Haichiya is a pointed persimmon and is best when cooked. Fuyu is a flat variety and can be eaten raw or cooked. When grating the persimmons, be careful not to grate the seeds in the center. Place the water, sugar, lemon juice and ginger in a small nonreactive saucepan; bring to a boil. Add the persimmon and simmer until thick, about 30 minutes. Remove and discard the ginger. Refrigerate until ready to serve.

APPLE-ROSEMARY JELLY
1 pound apples, such as Gala or Pippin
1 3/4 cups water
1 tablespoon lemon juice
3 sprigs rosemary
Sugar

Roughly chop apples, including skin and core; place in a nonreactive saucepan with water, lemon juice and rosemary. Simmer gently until the apples are mushy, about 45 minutes. Pour mixture into a jelly bag or cheesecloth-lined chinois and let strain for 4 hours. Measure the liquid and for every 1 1/4 cups of apple liquid add 3/4 cup sugar. Place sugar and liquid in a nonreactive saucepan over low heat. Stir until the sugar has dissolved; increase heat and bring mixture to a boil. Boil vigorously for 6 minutes, or until jelly is at the soft-set state (221° F). *Chef's Note:* To test the jelly, place a plate in the freezer; when plate is chilled, drop a ball of jelly on the plate's surface and wait 3 seconds. Push it with your finger; if the surface wrinkles when you push it, then it is set. Skim and discard any foam; pour jelly into a 4-x-8-inch Pyrex or nonstick baking dish and let cool for 5 minutes. Cover with plastic wrap on the surface of the jelly and refrigerate for 1 hour, or until set. The plastic wrap on the actual surface of the jelly prevents a skin from forming. Remove plastic wrap when jelly is cool and cut into small cubes.

POMEGRANATE SYRUP
1/4 cup grenadine syrup
1/4 cup water
1/2 cup pomegranate seeds

Chef's Note: I have found the easiest way to extract the pomegranate seeds is to cut the pomegranate in half and hold over a large bowl, placing the cut side away from your body. Tap the back of the pomegranate with a wooden spoon until all the seeds pop out. This can be a bit messy but very effective. Reserve 30 pomegranate seeds for garnish. Place grenadine syrup, water and pomegranate seeds in a small nonreactive pot and bring to a simmer. Simmer until the liquid is reduced by one-fourth and is a syruplike consistency, about 10 minutes. Strain through a fine sieve, pressing down on the seeds with the bottom of a ladle to extract all the juices. When cool, pour into a squeeze bottle.

SEARED FOIE GRAS

6 (1-ounce) portions grade-A foie gras
Salt and pepper
Fleur de sel
Cracked pepper

Portion the foie gras by separating the 2 lobes. Place the larger lobe on a cutting board. Put a thin blade knife in hot water; cut the foie gras into 1/2-inch-thick slices, taking care not to use too much force, as the foie gras will crumble or break. Dip the knife back into the hot water between cuts, as this aids in rendering a smooth cut. Lay each slice flat; using the tip of a paring knife, cut a shallow 1/8-inch crisscross pattern, or scoring, into the foie gras. *Chef's Note: Scoring is commonly used to help render fat under skin. Here we are using the technique for aesthetic reasons.* Season each slice on both sides with salt and pepper; let slices sit at room temperature for 15 minutes. Heat a skillet over medium heat; add the foie gras, scored side down. Sear until a brown crust forms, about 15 seconds; turn over and cook until done, about 15 seconds more. When foie gras is done, it will have a firm texture that yields to gentle pressure, but it should not appear dried out. Transfer foie gras to a paper towel–lined plate to drain and then sprinkle with fleur de sel and fresh cracked pepper; serve immediately. I like to have this dish plated completely before searing foie gras.

FINISH AND PLATE

Brioche (see page 246)
Butter
Foie Gras Torchon (see page 36)
Fleur de Sel
Reserved pomegranate seeds
Apple Cider Gastrique (see page 249)
1 pear
1 apple, cut into batonettes
1 head frisee
Lemon juice
Salt and pepper

Slice brioche into 1/4-inch-thick slices and brush with butter; cut in half and toast. Serve 3 halves per plate. Place 1 slice Foie Gras Torchon on each plate and season with fleur de sel; arrange small dots of Pomegranate Syrup around and scatter pomegranate seeds. Place one quenelle each of Quince Marmalade and Persimmon Marmalade. Scatter the cubes of Apple-Rosemary Jelly. Dust the top of the Foie Gras Crème Brûlée with Quatre Épices Caramel Powder. Using a propane torch, brûlée the powder. *Chef's Note: The caramel powder recaramelizes immediately so that the heat of the torch will not have time to melt the Foie Gras Mousse.* Place Foie Gras Crème Brûlée in the center of each plate; at the far end of the plates, zigzag Apple Cider Gastrique and place the Seared Foie Gras on top. Cut the pear all the way down either side of the core; lay cut side down and slice. Fan pear slices out over the Persimmon Marmalade. Dress apple batonettes and frisee with a drizzle of lemon juice and gastrique and season to taste with salt and pepper. Place on top of the pear and persimmon marmalade.

From The List
COTEAUX du LAYON

Wine

Moelleux or really sweet, both will suit the foie gras and preserves

CELERIAC CANNOLI WITH PUMPKIN SEED VINAIGRETTE AND APPLE SALAD

serves 6

Celeriac is a root variety of celery and is categorized as an autumnal root vegetable. It is often called celery root, although its shape is nothing like traditional stalk celery. Celeriac is round and dense with a thick peel. The meat inside can be cooked or served raw, or a combination of both as in this dish. White in color, with a creamy texture, its flavor is entirely celery.

CANNOLI SHELL
3 quarts rice bran or peanut oil
12 spring roll wrappers, cut into 3-x-3 1/2-inch squares
Metal cannoli cylinder or cannoli mold
1 egg, lightly beaten

Heat the oil to 325° F in a pot large enough to allow the oil to rise up during cooking. The cannoli mold is a 4-inch-long metal tube. Wrap a piece of spring roll wrapper around the mold and seal together by brushing the overlapping edges with the egg. Hold the cannoli mold by one end with a pair of tongs and submerge into the hot oil. Fry the wrapper for 20 seconds to seal before releasing the mold. This prevents the mold and wrapper from sinking to the bottom and sticking. Cook until crispy and golden brown, about 90 seconds. Remove the mold from the oil and transfer to a paper towel–lined plate to drain. When cool enough to handle, slide the shell off the mold. Repeat for remaining shells.

CELERIAC PUREE
3 cups celeriac (about 2 small heads)
3 quarts water
2 tablespoons salt
1 cup heavy cream
Salt
White pepper

Peel and coarsley chop the celeriac. Place in a medium pot and cover with cold water. Add 2 tablespoons salt and bring to a boil over high heat. Reduce heat to a simmer for about 15 minutes, or until the celeriac pieces are easily pierced with a paring knife. Drain into a colander allowing the celeriac to steam dry for a few minutes. While the celeriac is sitting, reduce the cream in a heavy-bottom pot over medium heat until thick enough to coat the back of a spoon. Add the cooked celeriac and continue cooking over medium heat while mashing the celeriac with a heavy whisk or potato masher to release more moisture. When celeriac and cream mixture is noticeably thicker, transfer to the container of a blender, cover, and puree until smooth. Season to taste with salt and white pepper.

FINISH AND PLATE
1/4 cup pumpkin seeds, toasted and chopped
2 teaspoons canola oil
1/2 teaspoon salt
1/2 cup julienned celeriac
1/2 cup julienned apple
Creamy Cider Vinaigrette (see page 247)
Pumpkin Seed Vinaigrette (see page 248)

Preheat oven to 350° F. Toss the pumpkin seeds with canola oil and salt and lay out on a sheet pan. Bake for 8 minutes, or until browned and fragrant. Transfer the hot Celeriac Puree to a piping bag fitted with a fine tip; place the tip as far in the Cannoli Shell as possible and fill. Place 2 filled cannoli on each plate. Toss celeriac, apple and pumpkin seeds with Creamy Cider Vinaigrette. Place salad on top of cannoli and then spoon Pumpkin Seed Vinaigrette around it.

From The List
POUILLY FUME

Wine

Powerful, aromatic sauvignon blanc with bracing qualities, will take on vinaigrettes and more

CELERIAC CANNOLI | WITH PUMPKIN SEED
VINAIGRETTE AND
APPLE SALAD

GRILLED SQUAB BREAST | WITH SQUAB LIVER MOUSSE
CROSTINI, ENDIVE AND
CASSIS SAUCE

GRILLED SQUAB BREAST WITH SQUAB LIVER MOUSSE CROSTINI, ENDIVE AND CASSIS SAUCE

serves 6

Underappreciated squab tastes best when prepared rare to medium-rare, and because it is a dark-meat bird, the taste is rich and savory. Squab adapts successfully to a wide range of preparations and I prefer combining squab's unique flavor with the tart accent of currant. The Currant Jam Vinaigrette and Cassis Sauce can be made the day before.

SQUAB SEASONING
1/2 tablespoon allspice
2 tablespoons coriander
1/2 teaspoon cumin
3 juniper berries
1 tablespoon black pepper
1 whole clove

Chef's Note: Coffee grinders work perfectly for grinding spices. Use all whole spices. Mix all the spices together; grind and store in a sealed jar for up to 1 month.

CURRANT JAM
1 cup granulated sugar
1/2 tablespoon pure apple pectin powder
1 1/2 cups black currants, fresh or frozen
1 teaspoon butter

Preheat oven to 225° F. The butter helps prevent foaming. If not using it, it will be necessary to skim the foam that rises to the surface of the jam during cooking. In a metal bowl, mix together the sugar and apple pectin; set in a warm place for 1 hour or in the preheated oven for 15 minutes. *Chef's Note:* If the sugar is warm, it will dissolve quickly when added to the fruit. In a heavy nonreactive pot, warm the currants over low heat, turning frequently with a heatproof spatula. When the currants are warm, about 5 minutes, turn heat to high and add the sugar-pectin mixture; mix well. The sugar will dissolve quickly. Bring the mixture to a hard boil, stirring and scraping the bottom of the pot frequently. When the jam reaches a boil, quickly add the butter, if using, and cook for 4 minutes, stirring occasionally. Use caution when stirring, the boiling jam will splatter. Remove from heat and transfer to resealable canning jars, cover and cool.

CURRANT VINAIGRETTE
2 tablespoons red wine vinegar
1 tablespoon diced shallots
1 tablespoon Currant Jam
1 teaspoon salt
1/4 teaspoon Coleman's dry mustard
6 tablespoons canola oil
1/2 teaspoon black pepper

Place the vinegar, shallots, Currant Jam, salt and dry mustard in a bowl and let steep for 15 minutes. Add the canola oil in a slow, steady stream while whisking constantly to emulsify. Season with pepper.

CASSIS SAUCE

3 tablespoons canola oil
2 cups squab bones, cut into 2-inch pieces
1/4 cup water
1/2 cup diced (1-inch) yellow onion
1/4 cup peeled diced (1-inch) carrot
1/4 cup diced (1-inch) celery
1 cup white wine
1/4 cup brandy
1 cup orange juice
1/4 cup lemon juice
2 cups Chicken Stock (see page 252)
1 cup Veal Stock (see page 253)
1 cup water
2 tablespoons Red Wine Gastrique (see page 250)
1/4 cup crème de cassis

Heat the canola oil in a heavy-bottom pot until almost smoking. Add the squab bones one piece at a time and let cook undisturbed until deeply browned. Turn bones over one piece at a time and brown the second side; carefully add 1/4 cup water to deglaze the pot. When the steam subsides, scrape the browned bits from the bottom of the pot with a wooden spoon. When the pot is dry and the bones begin to caramelize again, add the onion, carrot and celery. The liquid from the vegetables will deglaze the pot again. Continue cooking until vegetables begin to brown, about 5 minutes. Off the flame, add the white wine and brandy, scraping the bottom of the pot with a wooden spoon. Return to the burner over low heat and slowly reduce, about 20 minutes, or until almost dry. Add the orange juice and lemon juice and slowly reduce until a syrupy consistency, about 20 minutes more. Add the Chicken Stock, Veal Stock and water. Simmer for 30 minutes, skimming frequently. Strain through a chinois into another pot, pressing on the solids with the back of a ladle to extract all the liquid; return to a simmer. Add the Red Wine Gastrique and cassis; slowly reduce by one-fourth, skimming frequently. Keep warm.

SQUAB LIVER MOUSSE

3 squab livers, about 2 ounces each
1 cup milk
1 tablespoon butter
1/4 teaspoon salt
1/4 teaspoon Quatre Épices (see page 256)
2 tablespoons brandy
2 tablespoons butter

Soak the squab livers in milk overnight to purge. Drain the livers in a colander and rinse under cold water; pat dry with a paper towel. In a small skillet, melt 1 tablespoon butter. Add the livers and season with salt and Quatre Épices; cook for about 30 seconds or until the livers are firm but still pink in the center. Carefully add the brandy off the flame, return to heat and flame off the alcohol. Let cool to room temperature and transfer to the container of a food processor fitted with a metal blade. Add the remaining butter while the processor is running and puree until smooth. Push through a tamis sieve and refrigerate.

PISTACHIOS
1/4 cup pistachios
1/2 teaspoon oil
1/2 teaspoon salt

Preheat oven to 350° F. In a bowl, toss the pistachios with the oil and salt. Transfer to a baking sheet and then place in oven for 8 minutes, or until lightly browned and fragrant; let cool. Crush with a rolling pin.

FINISH AND PLATE
6 squab breasts
Salt
6 slices baguette
3 tablespoons canola oil
1 head each Belgian endive, red and green

Season the squab breasts with salt and Squab Seasoning. Grill squab breasts on a hot broiler, about 4 minutes per side for rare to medium-rare; keep warm and let rest for 5 minutes. Brush the baguette slices with oil on each side; grill until browned. Spread a little Squab Liver Mousse on baguette slice, and set in the middle of a plate. Cut off the base of the endive to separate the leaves; reserve 12 leaves and julienne the rest. Toss the endive in a bowl with Pistachios, salt and Currant Vinaigrette. Slice squab breast; fan out on top of the crostini. Garnish with endive salad; sauce with Cassis Sauce and a few drops of the Currant Vinaigrette.

From The List
MOULIN TOUCHAIS

Chenin blanc
on the sweet
side, good
austerity when
young enough,
astringence
for the
endive and
the squab

GRILLED MONTEREY BAY SARDINES WITH CARAMELIZED FENNEL TART TATIN, SALSA VERDE AND TAPENADE

serves 6

From the 1920s to the 1940s, sardines were the most important commercial fish in California, according to the Monterey Bay Aquarium. Commercial extinction due to high demand ended the abundance in the 1950s. In 1980, Pacific sardine populations slowly began to recover. The licorice characteristic of fennel facilitates the strong flavor of sardines.

MONTEREY BAY SARDINES
12 sardines, Monterey Bay or any available
1 tablespoon kosher salt
Freshly ground black pepper
16 thin slices lemon
5 sprigs thyme
6 bay leaves
10 cloves garlic, crushed

Lay the sardines down flat on a cutting board. With a sharp knife, make a shallow incision the length of the belly. With the knife tip, scrape out and discard the innards. Rinse inside and out under cold running water. Remove the scales by rubbing the skin with your thumb under cold running water, moving from the tail to the head, being careful not to tear the skin. Pat dry with paper towels inside and out. Cut off the head and then, holding the sardine firmly in one hand, grasp the bone where the head used to be and gently tug to loosen. Pull out the bones in one piece. Trim any ragged edges with a paring knife. Season the cleaned sardines with salt and pepper. In a shallow, nonreactive dish, place 12 slices of lemon over the bottom; place a sardine on top of each one. Sprinkle with thyme sprigs and then lightly crumbled bay leaves and crushed garlic; top with the remaining lemon slices. Cover and refrigerate for 4 hours. Remove sardines from the herbs and lemon slices; set aside until ready to grill.

CARAMELIZED FENNEL TART TATIN
2 fennel bulbs
3 tablespoons olive oil
Salt and pepper
2 tablespoons Fennel Gastrique (see page 249)
6 (2 1/2-inch) rounds puff pastry

Preheat oven to 350° F. Cut off and discard the stalk-like fennel tops. Remove and discard the tough outer layer of the fennel bulb. Hold on a cutting board, core end up. Using a paring knife, cut around the core, angling the knife to the inside to remove. Cut the bulb into 1/4-inch-thick slices. Heat the olive oil in a cast-iron or nonstick skillet over medium heat. Arrange a single layer of the fennel slices in the skillet, season with salt and pepper and cook until lightly browned, about 4 minutes per side. Transfer to a paper-towel–lined plate to drain; repeat until all fennel is done. In the bottom of a 4-ounce ramekin, drizzle 1 teaspoon fennel gastrique. Top with a few slices of fennel and finish with a puff pastry round. *Chef's Note:* The puff pastry should be cut to the same size as the opening of whatever mold used to make the tart tatin. Set the ramekins on a sheet pan, lay a Silpat on top and bake until done, about 20 minutes. Keep warm. The Silpat keeps the pastry from rising too much.

TAPENADE
1 cup good-quality green olives, pitted
1 tablespoon golden raisins
2 tablespoons capers in salt, rinsed
2 cloves garlic
2 anchovy fillets
1 tablespoon olive oil

Use good-quality green olives like Pichioline or Nyon. Soak the golden raisins in hot water for 5 minutes; drain. Place the olives, raisins, capers, garlic and anchovies in food processor fitted with a metal blade. Run the processor until the ingredients form a coarse paste, about 30 seconds, stopping to scrape down the sides. With the motor running, slowly add the oil. Set aside until ready to use.

SALSA VERDE
2 tablespoons capers, rinsed and chopped
2 tablespoons diced shallot
1 teaspoon chopped garlic
1 tablespoon lemon juice
2 tablespoons extra virgin olive oil
2 tablespoons chopped parsley

Place capers, shallot and garlic in a bowl; add the lemon juice and oil, mixing well. Just before serving, add chopped parsley; if it is added too early the acid from the lemon juice will turn it brown. Set aside until ready to use.

FINISH AND PLATE
Olive oil
Herb Salad (see page 255)
Fennel Ala Grecque (see page 255)

Heat a char broiler. Brush the Monterey Bay Sardines with olive oil and grill 2 minutes per side. Turn out a Caramelized Fennel Tart Tatin in the center of the plate. Place 2 grilled sardines on top followed by a small quenelle of Tapenade and a small Herb Salad with a few slivers of Fennel Ala Grecque. Mix the parsley in the Salsa Verde and scatter around the sardines.

From The List
MUSCADET

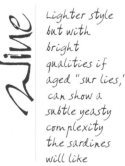

Wine

Lighter style but with bright qualities if aged "sur lies," can show a subtle yeasty complexity the sardines will like

Contributing photographers

Peter Monteforte
pages 22, 60, 61 (bottom), 132,
176, 177 (bottom)

Gabriel Skvor
pages 10, 11, 12, 16, 59, 61 (top), 105,
135 (bottom), 174, 177 (top), 213, 225

Larry Dale Gordon
page 24

Holger Leue
pages 2, 58

Galen Rowell
page 79, 210

RED WINE–POACHED
SEKEL PEAR | WITH ROBERT PIERRE,
HEARTY GREENS AND
CANDIED WALNUTS

RED WINE–POACHED SEKEL PEAR WITH PIERRE ROBERT, HEARTY GREENS AND CANDIED WALNUTS

serves 6

The Sekel pear's petite size is ideal for poaching and stuffing with a triple cream cheese such as Pierre Robert. The pear's deep red color is a result of leaving them in their poaching liquid overnight. I then reduce the poaching liquid for the vinaigrette, which instills an intense pear flavor. Heartier, slightly bitter greens such as frisee, arugula or endive envelop the sweet and creamy distinctiveness of this salad.

POACHED PEARS
4 cups port wine
4 cups red wine
2 cups sugar
2 cinnamon sticks
6 whole cloves
1 star anise
1 whole vanilla bean, split
6 bay leaves
20 black peppercorns
12 Sekel pears, peeled and cored (if Sekel are not available, French Butter or Bosc pears can be substituted)
8 ounces Pierre Robert Cheese, rind removed
See technique on page 155

To make the poaching liquid, combine wines, sugar and spices in a nonreactive pot; bring to a simmer for 20 minutes. This removes the raw alcohol flavor and infuses the spices. Peel the pears in a straight continuous line from the stem down to the bottom. Using a melon baller, remove the seeds and core from the bottom of the pear. Add pears to poaching liquid and cover with a tea towel to keep the pears submerged. Cook at a simmer until easily pierced with a paring knife. Cooking time can range from 15 to 30 minutes depending on the ripeness of the pear. Remove the pot from the heat and let pears cool in the poaching liquid. Refrigerate submerged in the liquid overnight to create the deep red color throughout. Set the cheese out at room temperature for 1 hour to soften. Transfer cheese to a piping bag fitted with a smooth tip. Remove the pears from the poaching liquid and pat dry; reserve the liquid. Place the tip of the piping bag as far inside the pear as possible and fill with cheese.

RED WINE PEAR SYRUP
1 cup pear poaching liquid

Strain 1 cup of the pear poaching liquid into a nonreactive pot and slowly reduce to 1/3 cup; let cool. Reserve 2 tablespoons for the Red Wine Pear Vinaigrette and transfer remaining syrup to a squeeze bottle to sauce the plate.

RED WINE PEAR VINAIGRETTE
1/4 cup pear vinegar
2 tablespoons Red Wine Pear Syrup
2 tablespoons diced shallots
2 teaspoons salt
1/2 teaspoon Coleman's dry mustard
3/4 cup canola oil
1 teaspoon black pepper

Place vinegar, Red Wine Pear Syrup, shallots, salt and dry mustard in a mixing bowl and let sit for 15 minutes. Slowly add the oil in a steady stream while whisking constantly and then add pepper.

CANDIED WALNUTS
3 quarts oil
1/4 cup powdered sugar
2 teaspoons salt
1 teaspoon cayenne
1 cup walnut halves

Heat the oil to 325 ° F in a pot large enough to allow the oil to rise up during frying. Place powdered sugar, salt and cayenne in a mixing bowl. Bring a pot of water to a boil and then add the walnuts and boil for 5 minutes; drain. While the walnuts are still hot, toss with the sugar mixture. The sugar will dissolve and coat the walnuts. Add the walnuts to the oil and fry until browned and crunchy; drain on a paper towel.

FINISH AND PLATE
2 heads green endive
2 heads red endive
2 heads frisee
1 bunch watercress
Baby arugula
Salt

Cut off the base of the endives and separate into spears. Cut away any browned leaves from the frisee and discard. Wash frisee under cold running water. Cut off the base and separate into leaves; spin dry. Place the watercress and arugula in a bowl of cold water and gently swish around to loosen grit and dirt. Let sit undisturbed for 5 minutes to allow grit to settle to the bottom. Scoop out the greens from the top; drain in a colander and spin dry. Drizzle Red Wine Pear Syrup on the plate; cut a wedge from the Poached Pear and lay flat on the plate to show the cheese center. Toss frisee, endive, watercress and arugula with the Candied Walnuts, Red Wine Pear Vinaigrette and salt to taste. Place salad next to the pear.

From The List
SAVENNIERES

Powerful long-lived chenin with great density, enough to take on the extremes of the dish

TECHNIQUE

1. Peel pear from the stem down to the bottom in a straight continuous line.

2. Starting at the bottom of each pear, turn a melon baller in a circular motion to cut out the seeds and hollow the center of the pear.

3. Add pears to poaching liquid, cover with a tea towel and cook until done.

4. Let pears cool in poaching liquid overnight to create the deep ruby-red color.

5. Place cheese in a piping bag fitted with a straight tip.

6. Place the tip as far inside each pear as possible, using care not to split the pear while filling with cheese.

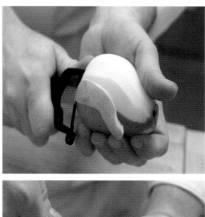

FILLING POACHED PEARS

SALAD OF GRILLED BLACK MISSION FIGS, BITTER GREENS AND BLEU de HAUT JURA CHEESE WITH A PORT REDUCTION

serves 6

Bleu de Haut Jura cheese, also known as Bleu de Gex, is an aged cow's milk blue cheese from the Jura Mountains in France. Originally this cheese maintained its blue hue from cows grazing on blooms from alpine violets in the spring. The dry, firm and salty nature of this blue cheese perfectly accents the sweetness of the black mission fig.

PORT WINE FIG VINAIGRETTE
2 tablespoons red wine vinegar
1 tablespoon Port Syrup (see page 251)
1 tablespoon Fig Jam (see page 257)
1 tablespoon diced shallot
1/4 teaspoon salt
1/8 teaspoon Coleman's dry mustard
6 tablespoons canola oil
1/8 teaspoon pepper

Place the vinegar, Port Syrup, Fig Jam, shallot, salt and mustard in a bowl and let sit for 15 minutes. Add the oil in a slow, steady stream while whisking constantly; add pepper.

SPICED PECANS
1 tablespoon softened butter
2 teaspoons brown sugar
2 teaspoons salt
1/2 teaspoon cayenne pepper
2 teaspoons fresh rosemary
1/2 cup pecans

Preheat oven to 350° F. Mix the butter, brown sugar, salt, cayenne pepper and rosemary together in a bowl. Place the pecans on a parchment-lined baking sheet and bake for 8 minutes, or until browned and fragrant. Immediately add the hot pecans to the bowl with the butter mixture; toss to incorporate and arrange in a single layer on the sheet pan to cool.

FINISH AND PLATE
1 head green endive
1 head red endive
1 head frisee
6 large figs
2 tablespoons sugar
2 tablespoons butter
6 (2-ounce) wedges Bleu de Haut Jura

Cut off the base of the endives and separate into individual leaves. With a pair of scissors, cut away any browned leaves from the frisee and discard; wash frisee under cold running water. Cut away the base, separate into leaves, and spin dry. Cut each fig in half and coat the cut side with sugar, shaking off excess. Melt butter in a skillet over medium heat; add figs, cut side down, and cook until caramelized, about 2 minutes. Remove from heat. Drizzle the plate with Port Syrup and place 2 fig halves towards the front of the plate. Set a wedge of Bleu de Haut Jura next to the fig. Toss greens in a bowl together with Spiced Pecans, a pinch of salt and Port Wine Vinaigrette to taste. Place a small mound of the salad behind the figs and cheese.

From The List
MONTLOUIS

Wine

Semidry chenin blanc with nutty and mineral qualities to embrace fig and blue cheese

SALAD OF GRILLED BLACK MISSION
FIGS, BITTER GREENS AND | BLEU DE HAUT JURA CHEESE
WITH A PORT REDUCTION

SEAFOOD BOURIDE WITH RED PEPPER PICADA

serves 6

When planning a menu, one should always consider how many bites or sips of a preparation can be consumed before the initial impact of flavors begins to diminish. This soup has plenty of garlic and is infused with aioli, but the Red Pepper Picada serves as the awakening point, keeping the palate in constant yearning. Mild-flavored white fish such as grouper, halibut or seabass works best with this dish.

BOURIDE SOUP BASE

2 cups leeks, white part only
2 tablespoons olive oil
1/2 cup julienned yellow onion
1 tablespoon chopped garlic
1 teaspoon fennel seeds
1/2 teaspoon orange zest
1/4 cup pernod
2 cups clam juice
2 cups Fish Fumet (see page 252)
1 cup water

Cut off and discard the green tops and root end of the leeks leaving only the white bases. Cut leeks in half lengthwise and roughly chop; place in a large bowl filled with cold water, gently breaking up the leeks to loosen any grit, and let sit for 5 minutes to allow grit to settle to the bottom of the bowl. Scoop the leeks off the top of the water and place in a colander to drain. Heat the oil in a pot over medium heat; add onion, leek and garlic. Cook until onion is translucent, about 5 minutes; add fennel seeds, orange zest and pernod and continue to cook until almost all the pernod has evaporated, about 5 minutes. Add clam juice, Fish Fumet and water; simmer for 20 minutes and then transfer to the container of a blender, cover and puree until smooth. Keep hot.

AIOLI

3 tablespoons pernod
6 large egg yolks
2 teaspoons minced garlic
2 tablespoons lemon juice
2 teaspoons white wine vinegar
1 teaspoon salt
1/4 teaspoon cayenne pepper
1 cup canola oil
2 tablespoons extra virgin olive oil

Chef's Note: The aioli is used for binding the bouride, so it needs to be richer than a traditional aioli; hence, the extra egg yolks. In a small pot over medium heat, ignite pernod; when flame dies out, remove from heat and cool. Place egg yolks in a large bowl; add garlic, lemon juice, vinegar, salt, cooled pernod and cayenne. Whisking constantly, add oils in a slow, steady stream to emulsify. Refrigerate until ready to use.

GROUPER

4 (3-ounce) pieces grouper or other white fish, such as halibut or seabass
Salt and pepper
3 tablespoons canola oil
2 tablespoons butter
1/2 teaspoon lemon juice

Season the fish with salt and pepper. Heat canola oil in a sauté pan. Add fish, skin side up, and cook until browned lightly, about 3 minutes. Turn fish over and cook another 3 minutes. Holding the fish in place with a spatula, drain off excess oil and add butter; return to the heat. When butter begins to foam, add lemon juice and baste the fish by spooning the foamy butter over the fish. Keep warm.

RED PEPPER PICADA
1 cup toasted sliced almonds
1 tablespoon canola oil
1/4 cup olive oil
2 cups pugliese bread, cut into 1/2-inch cubes
6 roasted red peppers (peeled and seeded)
2 cloves garlic
1 teaspoon crushed red chiles
1/2 teaspoon sherry vinegar
Salt and pepper

Preheat oven to 350° F. Toss the almonds with canola oil. Lay out on a sheet pan and bake for 8 minutes, or until golden brown. Heat the olive oil in a skillet over medium heat, add the bread cubes and fry until golden brown, about 6 minutes. Place all ingredients in the bowl of a food processor fitted with a metal blade and puree until a smooth paste, stopping once to scrape down the sides. Adjust seasoning to taste with salt and pepper

GARLIC BREAD CRUMBS
1 cup panko
1/4 cup olive oil
2 tablespoons butter
4 cloves garlic, chopped
3/4 teaspoon salt
1/4 teaspoon black pepper

Preheat oven to 350° F. Spread panko out in a thin layer on a sheet pan and toast in oven for 8 minutes, or until golden brown. Transfer to a mixing bowl. Heat oil and butter together in a skillet. When butter has melted, add the garlic and cook until garlic is soft but not browned, about 3 minutes. Pour garlic mixture over toasted panko and mix until fully incorporated. Season with salt and pepper.

FINISH AND PLATE
Salt and pepper
1 tablespoon chopped fresh parsley

Place the Aioli in a mixing bowl. Slowly pour in the hot Bouride Soup Base while whisking constantly to incorporate. *Chef's Note: This process is called tempering and is done to slowly equalize the temperature and consistency of the aioli and the soup base and prevent the egg from curdling. It is best to temper in the aioli just before serving; if the soup boils after aioli is added, it will cause the soup to separate.* Adjust seasoning to taste with salt and pepper. Pour soup into bowls, placing a piece of Grouper in the center. Top with a spoonful of Red Pepper Picada, sprinkle with Garlic Bread Crumbs and fresh parsley.

From The List
MENETOU-SALON

Good, racy, grassy note, sauvignon blanc similar to sancerre, not to be served too cold with bouride

PANCETTA-WRAPPED
SIKA VENISON LOIN | WITH PISTACHIO PUREE,
HUCKLEBERRY SAUCE AND
PUMPKIN DUMPLINGS

PANCETTA-WRAPPED SIKA VENISON LOIN WITH PISTACHIO PUREE, HUCKLEBERRY SAUCE AND PUMPKIN DUMPLINGS

serves 6

The venison from Broken Arrow Ranch is as close to wild as possible. The herds have a wide range to roam freely. Their diet is all natural and their aging process ensures a tender, flavorful meat that, when paired with the traditional accompaniment of huckleberry, stands out.

PUMPKIN DUMPLINGS
1 (2-pound) pumpkin
Canola oil
1 whole egg
1 egg yolk
1 1/3 cups flour
2 teaspoons salt
1 teaspoon sugar
1/2 teaspoon nutmeg
See technique on page 163

Preheat oven to 350° F. Cut the pumpkin in half across and scoop out the seeds. Rub with oil; place cut side down on a parchment-lined baking sheet. Bake for 45 minutes, or until soft to the touch; let cool. Scoop out pulp and discard the outer skin. Place pulp in a strainer over a bowl and let drain overnight. Pass pumpkin through a food mill and transfer puree to a 12-inch nonstick skillet and slowly cook over low heat to remove moisture. Move constantly with a heatproof spatula or wooden spoon to prevent scorching. Cook like this for about 10 minutes, or until thickened and noticeably dryer. Transfer to a mixing bowl and let cool. In another bowl, whisk together the egg and egg yolk. Make a well in the center of the pumpkin, pour in the egg and mix well. Gently fold in the flour, salt, sugar and nutmeg. Do not overwork as this will make the dumplings tough. Bring a large pot of salted water to a boil; using two spoons, form quenelles by scooping about 2 tablespoons of the batter in one spoon, pushing with the other spoon to form a football shape; repeat until smooth on all sides. Push quenelle into the water. *Chef's Note:* Test one dumpling to see if it holds together. If the dumpling falls apart, you may need to add a little more flour. The dumplings are done when they start to float. Transfer to an ice water bath when done; drain and toss with a little oil. Refrigerate until ready to use.

PISTACHIO PUREE
1 cup pistachios
2 tablespoons diced shallot
2 tablespoons Cabernet Syrup (see page 250)
1 tablespoon port wine
1 tablespoon pistachio oil
1/4 teaspoon salt
1/8 teaspoon pepper

Preheat oven to 350° F. Place the pistachios on a parchment-lined sheet pan and bake for 8 minutes, or until lightly browned and fragrant. When cool, transfer pistachios to the bowl of a food processor fitted with a metal blade; add shallot and, with the processor running, add Cabernet Syrup, port wine and pistachio oil, occasionally stopping to scrape down the sides until pistachios are a coarse paste. Season with salt and pepper.

VENISON LOIN
1 (8-inch) piece cleaned venison loin
24 slices pancetta bacon
3 tablespoons canola oil

Preheat oven to 350° F. Clean the venison loin of all sinew and then lay flat on a cutting board. To butterfly the venison loin for stuffing, cut three-fourths of the way through the loin starting along the narrow rounded side; open loin and lay flat. Form a cylinder with the Pistachio Puree roughly 1/2 inch in diameter. Place the cylinder in the center of the butterflied venison loin and wrap the meat around. Lay out the pancetta bacon, slightly overlapping, on a sheet of plastic wrap. Roll the venison in the pancetta and then roll in the plastic wrap, leaving about 4 inches of plastic wrap on each end of the venison. Twist and tie each end of the plastic wrap to form a tight cylinder. Transfer to the freezer for 30 minutes, or until firm but not frozen. This helps keep the round shape while tying. Remove the plastic wrap and tie with butcher's twine every 1 1/2 inches to secure the bacon during cooking. Heat canola oil in a 14-inch skillet, add the venison loin and brown on all sides, about 8 minutes. Transfer to oven for 4 to 5 minutes for rare and 6 to 8 minutes for medium-rare.

HUCKLEBERRY SAUCE

2 tablespoons canola oil
4 ounces venison scrap meat, cut into 1/2-inch pieces
1/4 cup water
1/4 cup diced shallots
1 clove garlic
5 sprigs thyme
3 bay leaves
8 pieces juniper berries, crushed
2 whole allspice
1 clove
1/4 cup gin
1/4 cup water
1 cup Veal Stock (see page 253)
1/4 cup Huckleberry Gastrique (see page 249)

FINISH AND PLATE

3 tablespoons butter
8 whole sage leaves
12 whole steamed chestnuts
2 tablespoons diced shallot
Salt and pepper

In a heavy 2-quart saucepan, heat the oil until almost smoking. Carefully add the venison, one piece at a time. When the meat is deeply browned on the bottom, use a pair of tongs to turn the meat over and brown the other side. Add the water and after the steam subsides, scrape the browned bits from the bottom of the pan. When the water is completely evaporated and the meat begins to sizzle and brown again, add the shallots, garlic, thyme, bay leaves and spices. When the shallots and garlic are translucent, about 2 minutes, move pan away from the heat and carefully add the gin and 1/4 cup water. *Chef's Note:* You do not want to ignite the gin, as it creates a high flame that takes awhile to burn out. Place the pot back on a low burner and slowly cook until the liquid is almost evaporated. Add the Veal Stock and simmer for 30 minutes, skimming frequently. Strain through chinois into another pot and then add Huckleberry Gastrique. Slowly reduce by one-fourth and keep warm.

Heat the butter in a 12-inch nonstick skillet until it begins to brown. Add the Pumpkin Dumplings, sage leaves, chestnuts and shallot. Season with salt and pepper. Continue to cook, tossing frequently, until the dumplings are lightly browned, about 3 minutes. Place 5 dumplings in a semicircle towards the back of each plate. Slice a 1 1/2-inch-thick slice from the Venison Loin and place in front of the dumplings. Spoon Huckleberry Sauce around plate.

From The List
NEW WORLD CABERNET FRANC
LANG AND REED WINERY

Proven varietal
and a good
name in napa
to follow
when it
comes to
loire style
cabernet franc

TECHNIQUE

1. Scoop 2 tablespoons of dumpling batter into one spoon.

2., 3. & 4. Shape batter into a small oval using the second spoon with the first, repeating until smooth on all sides.

5. Drop dumpling into boiling salted water.

6. When dumplings are done, they will float. Skim them off the surface and transfer to an ice water bath.

QUENELLE PUMPKIN DUMPLINGS

ALASKAN HALIBUT WITH POTATO RÖSTI, SAVOY SPINACH, PERNOD-POACHED OYSTERS AND SEVRUGA CAVIAR

serves 6

The anise flavor of pernod is the star of this dish. However, you never want liquor to dominate flavor. By flaming off the alcohol and emulsifying it with butter and oyster liquor, it creates a smooth well-balanced sauce that is excellent with most seafood.

ALASKAN HALIBUT
6 (5-ounce) portions Alaskan halibut
6 (8-inch) pieces butcher's twine
Salt and pepper
3 tablespoons canola oil
3 tablespoons butter
1 tablespoon lemon juice
See technique on page 167

Cut the halibut across the fillet into 1 1/2-inch-wide slices; turn the slices onto their sides; roll up, skin side in, and tie with butcher's twine. *Chef's Note: The main advantage to cutting fish across and tying it with twine is that it creates an equal thickness all the way across, allowing the fish to cook evenly.* Season halibut with salt and pepper. Heat the oil in a skillet over medium heat and arrange the halibut in the skillet and cook until the bottom has formed a brown crust, about 3 minutes; turn over and repeat with other side. Holding the halibut in place with a spatula, drain off excess oil, return to heat and add add butter. When butter starts to foam, add the lemon juice and baste the fish with the lemon butter. Remove from heat and keep warm. The fish will be slightly undercooked; however, the carryover cooking (residual heat from pan) will continue to cook the fish until plating.

POTATO RÖSTI
5 medium russet potatoes, peeled
Salt and pepper
6 tablespoons Clarified Butter (see page 246), divided

Preheat oven to 350° F. Grate potatoes on the largest side of a box grater; place grated potatoes in a kitchen towel, twist, and squeeze to remove excess water. Transfer the potatoes to a large mixing bowl and toss with salt and pepper to taste. In a 14-inch ovenproof non-stick skillet, heat 3 tablespoons Clarified Butter over medium heat. Add the potatoes and flatten them out evenly with a spatula; reduce heat and cook until crisp and evenly browned on the bottom, about 8 minutes. Occasionally check the color by lifting up one edge of the potatoes with a spatula. Turn the rösti over by flipping them with the skillet or turning them over into another skillet the same size. Drizzle the remaining Clarified Butter around the outer edge of the skillet. When second side is nicely browned, transfer to oven for 12 minutes. Remove from the oven and slide out of the skillet onto a cutting board. Cut into rounds with a 3-inch ring mold. Keep warm.

ALASKAN HALIBUT WITH POTATO RÖSTI, SAVOY SPINACH, PERNOD-POACHED OYSTERS AND SEVRUGA CAVIAR

SAVOY SPINACH
1 pound savoy spinach
2 tablespoons olive oil
2 teaspoons diced shallot
Salt and pepper

Remove and discard the stems of the spinach and place leaves in a large bowl of cold water. Gently swish around to loosen grit; let sit for 5 minutes to allow the grit to settle to the bottom. Scoop the spinach from the top and transfer to a colander to drain. Heat oil over medium heat in a large sauté pan and add the shallot; sauté until translucent, about 1 minute. Add the spinach and season with salt and pepper. Cook until spinach is wilted, immediately wrap in a towel to keep warm until plating.

OYSTERS
12 medium oysters such as Hog Island, beausoleil or malpeque, shucked and liquid reserved
2 tablespoons butter
2 tablespoons pernod
2 tablespoons lemon juice
2 tablespoons reserved oyster liquid
1/4 cup Beurre Blanc (see page 246)
Salt
Lemon juice
2 tablespoons chives
1 ounce sevruga caviar, divided

Shuck oysters over a bowl to reserve liquid; remove the oysters from their shell and strain liquid through a chinois or cheesecloth. Place butter, pernod, lemon juice and oyster liquid in a small sauté pan over high heat. Allow the pernod to ignite and when the flame dies out, add the oysters and Beurre Blanc; remove from heat. *Chef's Note: By placing an equal amount of whole butter and liquor in the saucepan over high heat, it will ignite as it comes to a boil. When the flame dies, you have an emulsion that can then be stabilized by adding stock or Beurre Blanc.* Adjust the seasoning with salt and lemon juice. Just before serving, add the chives and half the caviar, reserving the remaining caviar for garnish. Once caviar is added, do not return to heat as the eggs will cook and coagulate the sauce.

FINISH AND PLATE

Place a Potato Rösti round in the center of each plate and then cover with Savoy Spinach. Remove string and place Alaskan Halibut fillet on top of spinach. Place 2 Oysters and remaining sevruga caviar on top. Spoon sauce over and around fish.

From The List
CHENIN BLANC FROM
CHAPPELLET VINEYARDS NAPA
consistent
well-priced
example of
chenin blanc,
richer and
more friendly
then loire style,
definitely
suitable

TECHNIQUE

1. Cut the halibut across the fillet into 1 1/2-inch-wide slices.

2. Turn the slices on their sides.

3. Roll up skin side in and tie with butcher's twine.

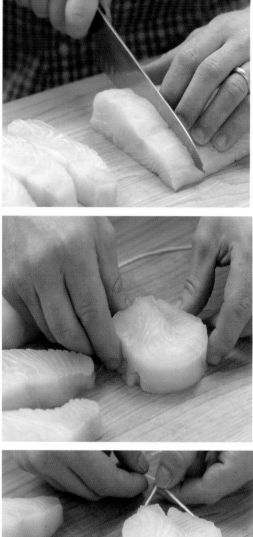

TYING
FISH
ROUNDS

ROAST DUCK BREAST WITH STAR ANISE CONSOMMÉ, PEKING DUCK WONTONS, SOY-BRAISED MUSHROOMS AND PLUM SAUCE

ROAST DUCK BREAST WITH STAR ANISE CONSOMMÉ, PEKING DUCK WONTONS, SOY-BRAISED MUSHROOMS AND PLUM SAUCE

serves 6

My first taste of Peking duck had just arrived in a box from Honolulu, its contents still warm. We were preparing an event menu featuring traditional Peking duck. The next thing I knew, all chefs in proximity, including me, were staring at a picked-clean duck carcass with little realization of what had just happened. A stern lecture followed, but it was worth getting caught up in the taste that I can still remember.

STAR ANISE DUCK CONSOMMÉ

3 1/2 quarts Asian Duck Stock (see page 252)
16 egg whites
1 cup julienned yellow onion
1/2 cup julienned celery
1/2 cup julienned carrot
1/2 cup julienned leeks
6 sprigs thyme
12 pieces parsley stem
1 star anise
8 ounces duck meat, ground
1 tablespoon sherry vinegar
1/4 cup soy sauce

Pour stock into a heavy-bottom pot. In a large bowl, whisk together egg whites, julienned vegetables, herbs, star anise and duck meat; whisk the contents of the bowl into the duck stock. Add the vinegar and place the pot over medium-low heat. During the first 10 minutes, whisk occasionally, scraping the bottom to prevent the egg white and meat from scorching. When you notice small flecks of white, this is signaling that the egg white is starting to coagulate; stop whisking and let the consommé cook over medium-low heat until all the vegetables, meat and egg whites start rising to the surface and create what is called a raft. With a small ladle, push a hole through the center of the raft to allow the liquid to percolate up through its center, this is called a chimney. From this point, let the consommé simmer for about 45 minutes, or until the liquid coming up through the center is completely clear. Remove consommé from heat. Line a chinois with a triple layer of cheesecloth and place over a large soup bain. Place the bottom point of a conical-shaped strainer over the center chimney and let it sink gently into the consommé. Ladle the consommé that has come through the conical strainer into the chinois until all liquid has been ladled through. *Chef's Note:* Do not disturb the raft, as it can break apart and release impurities that will affect the clarity of the consommé. Add the soy sauce and keep warm.

CHINESE 5 SPICE

1 1/2 sticks cinnamon
1 tablespoon fennel seeds
1 teaspoon whole cloves
4 whole star anise
1 tablespoon Szechwan peppercorns

Break up the cinnamon sticks, place all ingredients in a spice grinder and then grind to a powder. Set aside. *Chef's Note:* I prefer grinding my own whole spices. It imparts more vibrant flavor, however, pre-ground 5 spice will do.

ROAST DUCK BREAST

6 boneless Muscovy duck breasts
Salt and pepper
1 tablespoon Chinese 5 Spice
6 tablespoons canola oil

The goal when cooking duck breast is to render off as much fat under the skin as possible without overcooking the meat. Season the duck breasts with salt, pepper and Chinese 5 Spice on both sides. Divide the oil between two large heavy skillets over high heat; carefully add three duck breasts to each pan, skin side down. Allow the duck breasts to sear on high heat for 45 seconds to seal in the juices. Turn the burner to medium-low and let the duck breast slowly render its fat. During the cooking process you need to check the duck breasts frequently to make sure they are not burning around the edges; move the breasts around in the pan to ensure even cooking. When the skin is browned and crisp, about 10 minutes, drain off most of the fat. Turn the breasts over, increase heat to medium and cook until about medium, another 3 minutes; transfer to a resting rack and keep warm.

PEKING DUCK WONTONS

2 tablespoons finely chopped green onions
1/4 cup Shiitake Duxelles (see page 256)
1/4 cup peking duck meat and skin, finely chopped
1 egg white
2 tablespoons cornstarch
12 wonton wrappers

Mix together the green onions, Shiitake Duxelles and peking duck. In a bowl, whisk egg white and cornstarch together. Lay out the wonton wrappers, 4 at a time to prevent them from drying out, and brush the edges with egg white mixture. Place a tablespoon of the duck filling in the center; fold the wonton wrapper over, creating a triangle, and seal by pressing firmly around edges. Pull the two outer points of the triangle together and press to seal. *Chef's Note: You can purchase peking duck at most good Chinese restaurants with a 24-hour notice.*

SOY-BRAISED ASIAN MUSHROOMS

3 cups assorted mushrooms, cut in wedges
3 tablespoons canola oil
1 teaspoon grated ginger
1/4 cup Sweet Soy (see page 253)

Chef's Note: Any combination of shiitake, oyster, alba, Trumpet Royale, enoki, matsutake or maitake mushrooms will yield great results. These mushrooms can also be used with Asian-style salads or soups. Cut the mushrooms into wedges where possible, enoki or alba can be cooked whole. Heat oil in a large skillet over high heat and then add the mushrooms, being careful not to overcrowd the pan. Cook until the mushrooms begin to brown, about 3 minutes; add the ginger, reduce heat to medium and then add the Sweet Soy, cooking 3 minutes more, or until the mushrooms are nicely glazed.

GINGER THREADS
1 (2-inch) piece fresh ginger, peeled
2 quarts oil

Peel the ginger and slice into paper-thin sheets using a Japanese mandolin. Lay the sheets down in stacks of 3 on a cutting board and, with a sharp knife, cut the ginger into thin julienne. Heat the oil to 325° F in a pot large enough to allow the oil to rise up during cooking and sprinkle the ginger into the hot oil, breaking up any clumps so they are fried as individual threads; transfer to a paper towel–lined plate to drain.

SEARED FOIE GRAS
6 (1-ounce) pieces foie gras
Salt and pepper
Fleur de Sel

Score the foie gras on one side and season with salt and pepper. Let the foie gras sit out for 15 minutes before cooking to come to room temperature. Add the foie gras, scored side down, to a hot skillet and cook until a brown crust forms, about 10 seconds. Turn over and cook 10 seconds more; transfer to a paper towel–lined plate. Sprinkle with fleur de sel.

FINISH AND PLATE
Julienned green onion
Plum Sauce (see page 253)

Bring a pot of water to a boil and cook the Peking Duck Wontons for 2 minutes. Drain and place 2 wontons in each bowl; fill with Star Anise Duck Consommé and garnish with green onions. Spoon Plum Sauce on the plate in a zigzag pattern. Mound some of the Soy-Braised Asian Mushrooms in front of the consommé. Slice the duck breast and fan out on the mushrooms. Top with Seared Foie Gras and Ginger Threads.

From The List
SANCERRE ROUGE

Wine

Pinot noir with a good structure and high acidity, top years recommended, it will hold to the star anise, soy and plum

BUTTERNUT SQUASH RAVIOLI WITH SAGE-PECAN BROWN BUTTER

serves 6

A little mascarpone with the roasted butternut squash can go a long way in flavoring these ravioli. The hint of sweetness divides the intensity of the squash, allowing your palate to acknowledge the change of seasons. Sage and pecans foreshadow that autumnal food is upon us.

BUTTERNUT SQUASH RAVIOLI
1 butternut squash
Canola oil
1/4 cup mascarpone
Salt
Freshly grated nutmeg
Pasta Dough (see page 247)
1 egg, whisked lightly

Preheat oven to 350° F. Cut the squash in half lengthwise and scoop out the seeds. Brush with oil and lay cut sides down on a lined baking sheet. Bake for 35 minutes, or until soft to the touch at the thickest point; cool and scoop out the pulp, discarding the skin. Place the squash in a strainer or colander and let drain for 6 hours; discard liquid. Puree squash in a food processor until smooth. Transfer puree to a mixing bowl and whisk in the mascarpone; season with salt and nutmeg. Roll out the pasta using a pasta machine, then cut the sheets of pasta with a round cutter into 2 3/4-inch circles. Brush the edges of the pasta with the egg, place 2 teaspoons of the filling in the center of each pasta circle and then fold the pasta over the filling to create a half-circle ravioli, using care not to trap any air. Seal by pressing down around the edges with a fork.

SAGE-PECAN BROWN BUTTER
10 tablespoons butter
1/4 cup milk solids (see page 246)
2 teaspoons chopped garlic
2 teaspoons diced shallot
12 sage leaves
1/2 cup toasted pecans
1 teaspoon lemon juice
Salt and pepper

Chef's Note: Have all ingredients ready to go before starting the brown butter, as it moves quickly. Melt the butter in a saucepan over medium heat; when completely melted, add the milk solids and turn up heat to medium-high. Continue to cook until light flecks of brown appear and the butter exudes a nutty aroma. Add the garlic, shallot, sage leaves, pecans and lemon juice; remove from the heat and season to taste with salt and pepper.

FINISH AND PLATE
Shaved Parmesan
Balsamic Syrup (see page 250)

Bring pot of salted water to a boil; add Butternut Squash Ravioli and cook for 3 minutes. Drain and toss ravioli with the hot Sage-Pecan Brown Butter; divide ravioli between six bowls and top with shaved Parmesan. Drizzle with Balsamic Syrup.

From The List
VOUVRAY MOELLEUX

Wine

Somewhat sweet chenin blanc to embrace sweet squash but with plenty of backbone to challenge the sage pecan and brown butter

BUTTERNUT SQUASH RAVIOLI | WITH SAGE-PECAN
BROWN BUTTER

BLACK TRUFFLES, SHELLFISH & PONDERING THE SOUL OF FOOD

MENU FIVE

Amuse-Bouche

LOBSTER RILLETTE WITH CAULIFLOWER PUREE AND
CAVIAR ON A POTATO GAUFRETTE *178*

Course One

DUNGENESS CRAB TASTING *183*

CARPACCIO OF FALLOW VENISON WITH
"WALDORF" SALAD AND GIN SORBET *187*

TWICE-BAKED FINGERLING POTATO WITH
CREAMY TRUFFLE VINAIGRETTE *188*

TRIO OF DAY BOAT SCALLOP PREPARATIONS *190*

Course Two

BABY LETTUCES WITH CRISPY ROOT VEGETABLE
CHIPS AND BLACK TRUFFLE VINAIGRETTE *195*

COMPOSED MAINE LOBSTER SALAD WITH SATSUMA
MANDARINS, HEARTS OF PALM AND BASIL OIL *196*

MONTEREY BAY SPOT PRAWN AND COCONUT SOUP *201*

Course Three

PAN-ROASTED WILD STRIPED BASS WITH OLIVE OIL
FORK-MASHED POTATOES, CHORIZO AND MUSSELS *202*

GRILLED RIB-EYE STEAK WITH CRISPY POTATO CAKE AND
OYSTER MUSHROOM–CAMBAZOLA COMPOTE *205*

WALNUT-CRUSTED KUROBUTA PORK LOIN WITH PARSNIP
PUREE, CARAMELIZED APPLES AND RED WINE SYRUP *206*

CASTROVILLE ARTICHOKE WITH CARAMELIZED FENNEL AND
ITALIAN BUTTER BEAN CASSOULET *209*

Crisp winter weather means our favorite bay area crustacean, the San Francisco Dungeness crab, abounds as cooler waters indicate the time is right for shellfish. Most shellfish spawn or molt during the summer months when the waters are warm, and, as soon as ocean temperatures drop, we are quick to feature the sea's procession of Monterey Bay spot prawns, lobster and mussels. We begin this anticipated voyage with a Dungeness Crab Tasting, page 183.

CHEF'S NOTES

A key factor in the purchasing of shellfish is to buy as close to the source as possible, minimizing the time from ocean to table. Picking lobster, page 198, and boiling crab are everyday occurrences as we inevitably witness root vegetables replacing our summer pantry of peas, corn and tomatoes. For now, their fate unfolds as the key element in a salad of Baby Lettuces with Black Truffle Vinaigrette, page 195, to which they are sliced thin and fried, creating a Crispy Root Vegetable Chip.

Black truffle season is also upon us, and it heralds a perfect time for down-to-earth transitional flavor pairings, thus keeping us in constant test mode. Our "ramekin experimentation" gave us our answer to the question of pairing the unique flavor of black truffle with shellfish. By placing Beurre Blanc, page 246, in four ramekins, adding a different truffle infusion to each, and tasting, we found that black truffle was more seafood friendly. It was also the exact flavor element that completed the Trio of Day Boat Scallop Preparations, page 190. The theory of this easy exercise can be used in any kitchen to research flavor combinations and can be applied to vinaigrettes as well as sauces.

Pan-Roasted Wild Striped Sea Bass with Olive Oil Fork-Mashed Potatoes, Chorizo and Mussels, page 202, is outlined for this evening's menu. The inspiration came yesterday during a discussion about the strong influence cultural heritage has on cuisine. Its 6 p.m. the next day, and willingly our conversation resumes about the soul of food, not its science. We get into our rhythm for the evening and plate the first course with our passion for food enabled.

LOBSTER RILLETTE WITH CAULIFLOWER PUREE AND CAVIAR ON A POTATO GAUFRETTE

serves 6

LOBSTER RILLETTE

8 ounces cooked lobster claws and knuckles (see page 196)
2 tablespoons mayonnaise
2 tablespoons pernod
2 tablespoons butter
1 tablespoon chopped chives
2 teaspoons chopped chervil
1/2 teaspoon salt
Pinch cayenne pepper
1 teaspoon lemon juice

Place lobster meat and mayonnaise in the bowl of a stand mixer fitted with a paddle attachment; run on medium speed until lobster meat is shredded. Cook the pernod and butter together in a small skillet over high heat and let the alcohol in the pernod ignite. When all the alcohol is gone and the flame burns off, remove from heat and let cool for 10 minutes. This mixture should still be slightly warm when added. Turn mixer on low speed and add the pernod butter in a steady stream until incorporated. Turn off mixer and fold in herbs, salt, cayenne pepper and lemon juice. Taste and adjust seasoning if needed. Refrigerate for 2 hours to set.

CAULIFLOWER PUREE

1 head cauliflower
3/4 cup heavy cream
Salt and white pepper

Bring a large pot of salted water to a boil; cut cauliflower into florets. Blanch until soft. Drain and allow to steam in a colander to evaporate the excess moisture. In another pot, reduce the cream to a thick consistency; add cauliflower and mash with a heavy whisk over medium heat to release moisture. Transfer to the container of a blender, cover, and puree. Season with salt and white pepper. Transfer to a storage container and refrigerate for 2 hours to set.

POTATO GAUFRETTE

1 russet potato
3 quarts peanut or rice bran oil
See technique on page 180

Set up a French mandolin to the waffle-cut blade setting. Peel the potato and run it once through the blade; discard first piece and adjust the thickness if needed. Turn the potato 90 degrees in your hand and run through the blade again. The potato slice should have a criscross pattern like a tennis racket. Turn the potato back to its original angle and slice again, turning between each slice. Watch the potato slices, as the mandolin blade tends to move and requires adjusting to maintain a uniform thickness. Rinse the gaufrettes in cold water. With a ring mold, cut 1 1/2-inch circles out of the center of each gaufrette, discarding the outer piece. Heat the oil to 350° F in a pot large enough for the oil to rise up during frying. Fry in batches until golden brown and crispy, about 3 minutes; drain on paper towels.

FINISH AND PLATE

Sevruga caviar
Chervil sprigs

Put chilled Cauliflower Puree in a piping bag fitted with a star tip. Place about 2 teaspoons Lobster Rillette in the center of each Potato Gaufrette. Pipe 1 teaspoon Cauliflower Puree on top and finish with a dollop of sevruga caviar and a sprig of chervil.

Lobster Rillette
WITH CAULIFLOWER PUREE AND
CAVIAR ON A POTATO GAUFRETTE

AMUSE-BOUCHE

SERVE BEFORE

TECHNIQUE

1. Run the potato through the blade, creating a waffle cut.

2. Discard the first piece and then rotate the potato 90 degrees in your hand; run through the blade again to create the gaufrette cut.

3. Adjust the mandolin's thickness setting so there are holes between the crisscross pattern in each slice.

4. & 5. Each time you pass the blade, rotate the potato slice 90 degrees.

SLICING POTATO GAUFRETTES

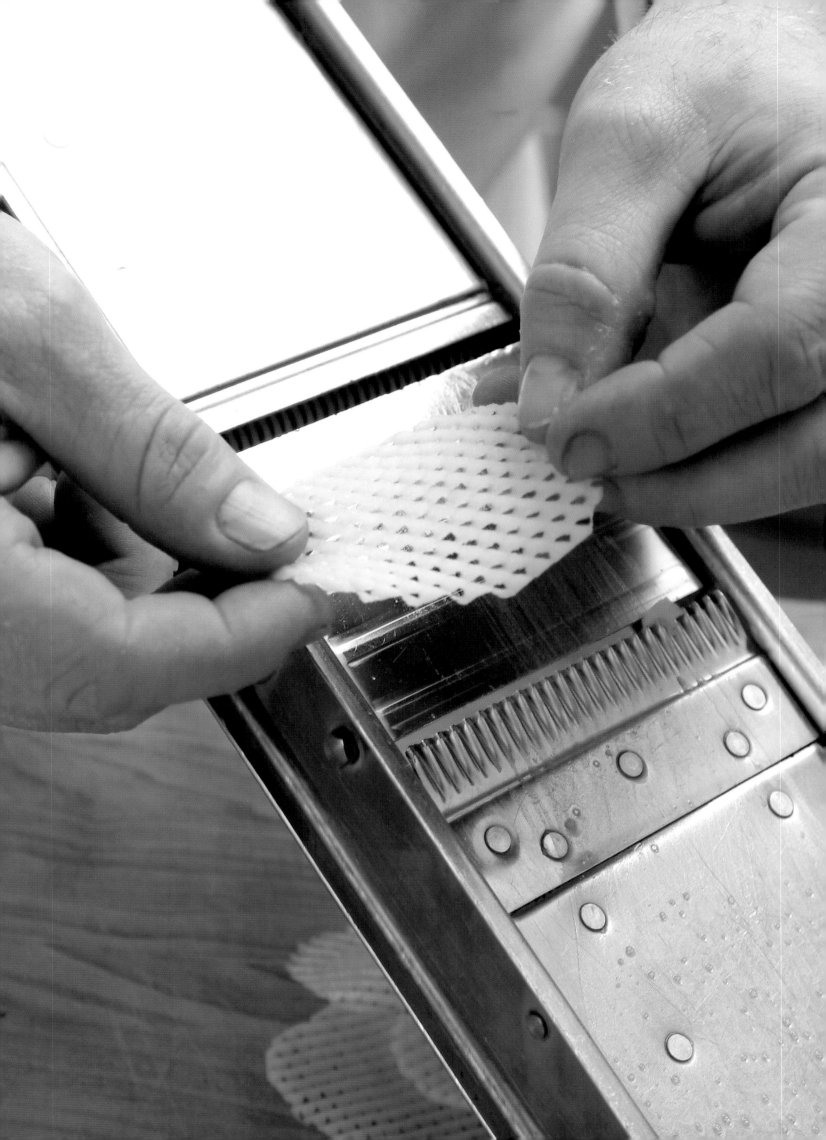

DUNGENESS CRAB TASTING

DUNGENESS CRAB TASTING

serves 6

The taste of fresh-cooked crab always creates the desire to build a dish, or three in this case, around its flavor. Picking crab can be a trying technique, and we included ours on page 29. This trio of tastes keeps the palate interested with a journey of sweet, savory and pure crab flavor.

CRAB

10 quarts water
1 cup diced (1-inch) onion
1/2 cup diced (1-inch) celery
1/2 cup diced (1-inch) carrot
1/2 cup diced (1-inch) leek
1 thumb-size piece ginger
1 lemon, cut in half
6 tablespoons salt
5 bay leaves
15 parsley sprigs
2 (2 1/2-pound) live Dungeness crabs

Place all ingredients except the crabs in a large pot and bring to a boil. Carefully drop crabs into pot and simmer for 10 minutes. Remove crab from pot and lay on its back to cool. Once cool, pick crabmeat (according to instructions on page 29). Reserve shells and "butter" for the Bisque. Reserve 12 of the larger, more intact crab legs for the salad on this dish and the remaining meat for the crab cakes.

CRAB CAKES

12 ounces Dungeness crabmeat
1 egg, lightly beaten
1 tablespoon mayonnaise
1 tablespoon + 1 teaspoon melted butter
2 tablespoons chopped chives
1 teaspoon lemon juice
Salt
Cayenne pepper
1 cup panko

Place crabmeat from above in a strainer and gently press down to remove any excess liquid. Transfer to a large bowl; add egg, mayonnaise, butter, chives and lemon juice. Gently mix together and season to taste with salt and cayenne pepper. Form into 8 small cakes by pressing into a small ring mold. Gently roll in panko and refrigerate for 1 hour.

CRAB BISQUE

Reserved Dungeness crabmeat
2 tablespoons canola oil
1 cup diced (1-inch) yellow onion
1/2 cup diced (1-inch) celery
1/2 cup diced (1-inch) leeks
1/2 cup diced (1-inch) carrot
2 cloves garlic, crushed
2 Roma tomatoes, cut in quarters
2 tablespoons tomato paste
1 cup sherry
2 cups water
4 cups heavy cream
1/2 ounce ginger, crushed
1 sprig tarragon
1/4 vanilla bean
12 parsley stems
Salt and cayenne pepper

Crush crab shells in a stand mixer with paddle attachment on slow speed for 5 minutes. Heat oil in a large pot over high heat and then add the reserved crab shells and "butter" from above; cook for 5 minutes, stirring occasionally with a wooden spoon to loosen the bits that stick to the bottom of the pot. Add the onion, celery, leeks, carrot and garlic; sauté until the vegetables start to soften, about 5 minutes. Add the tomatoes and tomato paste; cook until the tomatoes are soft, about 10 minutes more. Add the sherry and cook until reduced to almost dry; add water and simmer about 20 minutes, or until reduced by half. Add cream, ginger, tarragon, vanilla bean and parsley. Bring to a simmer for 20 minutes; strain and season with salt and cayenne pepper. Keep warm until ready to serve.

TOMATO TARRAGON NAGE
1 tablespoon butter
1 teaspoon diced shallot
1/4 cup Beurre Blanc (see page 246)
2 tablespoons Oven-Roasted Tomatoes (see page 256)
1 teaspoon chopped tarragon
Salt
Lemon juice

Melt butter in a small skillet over medium heat, add shallot and cook until translucent, about 1 minute. Add the tomatoes and cook 1 more minute. Add the Beurre Blanc and tarragon; simmer for 30 seconds. Adjust seasoning with salt and lemon juice to taste.

FINISH AND PLATE
3 tablespoons Clarified Butter (see page 246)
Creamy Mustard Vinaigrette (see page 247)

Preheat oven to 350° F. Heat Clarified Butter in a skillet over medium heat; add the Crab Cakes and cook for 2 minutes, or until panko crust is golden brown. Turn over and cook until second side is browned, about 2 more minutes; transfer to the oven and bake for 5 minutes. Place a pool of Creamy Mustard Vinaigrette at one end of the plate and top with 2 crab legs; at the other end, fill espresso cups with the hot Crab Bisque. Place a pool of Tomato Tarragon Nage in center of plate and top with a Crab Cake.

From The List
SHARP BLANC de BLANC
OR SPARKLING WINE

Wine

crisp and cleansing, lifting the appetite even higher with each variation within the dish

SHELLFISH, like clams, mussels and oysters should be eaten the day of purchase or the following day at the latest.

STORING SHELLFISH

To store clams and mussels, wrap in a damp towel and place in the coldest part of the refrigerator.

Oysters need to be stored cupped side down between two damp towels with a small amount of ice on top.

Live lobsters, crabs and prawns should be cooked immediately. To store for a short period of time prior to cooking, wrap in damp newspaper and place in the coldest part of the refrigerator.

CARPACCIO OF
FALLOW VENISON | WITH "WALDORF" SALAD
AND GIN SORBET

CARPACCIO OF FALLOW VENISON WITH "WALDORF" SALAD AND GIN SORBET

serves 6

Juniper is the flavor element in gin; venison and juniper berries have been longtime companions in the category of flavor combinations. Gin Sorbet alongside the carpaccio keeps flavors traditional yet interesting. The spicy crust and quick searing gives the venison the heightened taste element I strive for at Sierra Mar. I suggest using Broken Arrow Ranch fallow venison due to its proper aging, tenderness and full flavor.

VENISON SPICE
1 tablespoon coriander
1 teaspoon black pepper
4 juniper berries
1/4 teaspoon cumin
1 whole allspice
1 clove

Place all ingredients into a spice grinder and process to coarse grind. Store in an airtight container.

VENISON
1 (3-inch-long) piece center-cut venison loin
1 teaspoon salt
3 tablespoons canola oil

Season venison loin liberally with salt and 1/2 teaspoon of the Venison Spice. Cover with plastic wrap and let sit at room temperature for 30 minutes. In a skillet, heat oil until almost smoking; add the venison and sear each side for about 10 seconds; remove from pan, let cool and then roll in plastic wrap. Twist each end of the plastic wrap in opposite directions and tie to compress the loin into a cylinder. Place in freezer for 1 hour, or until firm but not frozen solid. Slice thinly on a meat slicer and lay out on wax paper. *Chef's Note: If you do not have a meat slicer, carefully cut the venison slices by hand to about 1/8 inch thick. Place slices between plastic wrap and gently pound flat with a meat mallet.*

GIN SORBET
2 cups water
3 tablespoons + 1 teaspoon sugar
2 juniper berries
12 whole black peppercorns, cracked
1/3 cup gin

Mix water with sugar, juniper berries and cracked black peppercorns in a pot and heat until sugar is dissolved. Strain and chill. Add gin and run in ice cream machine according to the manufacturer's instructions.

FINISH AND PLATE
1/4 cup julienned celery root
1/4 cup julienned apple
1/4 cup chive sticks
Creamy Cider Vinaigrette (see page 247)
Good-quality extra virgin olive oil
Cracked pepper
Fleur de sel

Overlap 5 paper-thin slices of the Venison in a semicircle on each plate. Put the celery root, apple and chive sticks in a bowl and toss with Creamy Cider Vinaigrette. Place salad behind the venison and place one scoop of Gin Sorbet in the center of the plate in front of each salad. Drizzle the Venison with oil; season with cracked pepper and fleur de sel.

From The List
HERBACEOUS WHITE
ALBARINO OR SAUVIGNON

Wine

Light white will take on the sorbet while staying faithful to the carpaccio

TWICE-BAKED FINGERLING POTATO WITH CREAMY TRUFFLE VINAIGRETTE

serves 6

I'm lucky my wife is a great cook. (We actually met over one of my recipes, but that's another story.) I always have a wonderful-tasting dish to look forward to on the drive home. She proclaims she didn't invent the twice-baked potato; however, she did remind me just how exquisite the potato can be.

FINGERLING POTATOES
6 fingerling potatoes
2 tablespoons butter, melted
Salt and pepper

Preheat oven to 350° F. Rub fingerling potatoes with melted butter; season generously with salt and pepper. Arrange on a sheet pan and bake for approximately 30 minutes, or until easily pierced with a pairing knife. With a paring knife, cut an oval shape out of the top of potatoes; carefully hollow out the inside of the potato with a small melon baller.

POTATO FILLING
1 pound Yukon gold potatoes, peeled
2 quarts water
1 tablespoon salt
6 tablespoons cold butter, cut in cubes
1/3 cup heated cream
2 tablespoons truffle butter (see Purveyor's List, page 258)
Salt and white pepper
2 tablespoons chopped chives

Cut peeled potatoes into quarters; place in a medium-size pot, cover with water and add salt; bring to a boil, then reduce heat to a simmer and cook approximately 20 minutes, or until potatoes are easily pierced with a paring knife. Strain through a colander and allow potatoes to steam dry for 2 minutes. Run the potatoes through a food mill with the cold butter; fold in the heated cream, truffle butter, salt, white pepper, and chives. Transfer to a piping bag with star tip and keep warm.

FINISH AND PLATE
Creamy Truffle Vinaigrette (see page 247)
12 chive spears
6 sprigs chervil
Small white truffle

Preheat oven to 350° F. Pipe the Potato Filling into fingerling potatoes; bake until filling is lightly browned, about 12 minutes. Serve potato on a pool of Creamy Truffle Vinaigrette. Garnish with chive spears and chervil; shave fresh white truffle tableside if desired.

From The List

OLD AND NEW WORLD
RHONE WHITES

Wine

Roussanne or a blend of Roussanne Marsanne and Viognier

TWICE-BAKED
FINGERLING POTATO | WITH CREAMY
TRUFFLE VINAIGRETTE

TRIO OF DAY BOAT SCALLOP PREPARATIONS

serves 6

The most important element for this recipe is to find dry-pack day boat or diver scallops. (Dry pack simply means that the scallops are not injected with a preservative.) This results in a pure, sweet scallop flavor, and when seared, the scallops caramelize nicely. The beauty of these preparations is that each will stand alone as a first course, or work elegantly together in a trio. Prepare the Potato Puree, Beurre Blanc, Crispy Pancetta and Truffle Vinaigrette ahead of time.

DAY BOAT SCALLOPS
18 medium day boat scallops
6 (5-inch) strips pancetta bacon, thinly sliced (smoked bacon can be substituted)
1/2 pound savoy spinach
1 tablespoon butter
1 tablespoon diced shallot
Salt and pepper
1/4 cup canola oil

Wrap 6 scallops in the pancetta bacon and tie with butcher's twine. Season all the scallops with salt and pepper, keeping in mind that the pancetta is mildly salty. Heat the canola oil divided between two 12-inch nonstick or cast-iron skillets. Add the bacon-wrapped scallops to one skillet and 6 of the plain scallops to the other skillet. *Chef's Note: I cook only 6 scallops at a time to avoid overcrowding. Too many scallops at one time will cool down the pan quickly and allow some of the juices to escape from the scallops, thus preventing a brown crust from forming and resulting in a steamed scallop rather than a seared one.* Cook all scallops undisturbed until a brown crust forms, about 1 to 2 minutes, turn over and cook until medium-rare, about 2 minutes more. Transfer to a platter and keep warm. Repeat for remaining 6 scallops. For the pancetta-wrapped scallops, after searing top and bottom, turn on their sides and slowly roll in the pan to crisp the bacon. Cut and remove the butcher's twine and transfer to a platter. Keep warm.

SPINACH
1/2 pound savoy spinach
1 tablespoon butter
1 tablespoon diced shallot
Salt and pepper

Prepare the spinach by removing the stems and placing spinach leaves in a large bowl of cold water. Swish the spinach around to loosen grit. Let spinach set undisturbed for 5 minutes to allow the grit to settle to the bottom of the bowl. Gently scoop out spinach and transfer to a colander to drain. Heat butter in a 12-inch skillet over medium heat, add the shallot and cook until translucent, about 1 minute. Add the spinach and season with salt and pepper; cook until spinach is wilted and then transfer to a terry-cloth towel. Fold towel over spinach and keep warm.

GRAIN-MUSTARD BEURRE BLANC
1 teaspoon whole grain mustard
3 tablespoons Beurre Blanc (see page 246)
Salt
Lemon juice

In a small sauté pan, whisk together the mustard and the Beurre Blanc. Heat briefly and adjust the seasoning with salt and lemon juice as needed. *Chef's Note: This sauce can come to a boil briefly without breaking; should it begin to break, just whisk in a little more Beurre Blanc.*

CHAMPAGNE-CAVIAR BUTTER
1/4 cup Beurre Blanc (see page 246)
2 teaspoons champagne or sparkling wine
2 teaspoons chopped chives
1 teaspoon sevruga caviar
Salt
Lemon juice

FINISH AND PLATE
Pancetta Crisps (see page 255)
Black Truffle Vinaigrette (see page 247)
Potato Puree (see page 256)
1 small black truffle, cut into batonettes
1 ounce sevruga caviar

Place the Beurre Blanc and champagne together in a small sauté pan over medium heat; at the first sign of boiling, remove from heat, add the chives and caviar at the last second. Taste and adjust seasoning with salt and lemon juice if needed. After caviar is in the sauce, do not reheat, as caviar will cook and cause the sauce to coagulate. *Chef's Note:* I prefer sevruga caviar for this sauce because of its stronger flavor; however, American sturgeon, hackle-back, or wild or farm-raised osetra are good substitutions.

At one end of the plate, place a pancetta-wrapped Day Boat Scallop, sauce with 2 teaspoons of the Grain-Mustard Beurre Blanc and garnish with a Crispy Pancetta Bacon strip. Place one seared scallop in the middle of the plate and sauce with Black Truffle Vinaigrette. Garnish with a quenelle of Potato Puree and truffle batonettes, if desired. Place a small mound of spinach at the other end of the plate and top with another seared scallop. Sauce with the Champagne-Caviar Butter and garnish with sevruga caviar.

From The List
WHITE BURGUNDY OR
MEURSAULT PREMIER CRU

Wine

Needs richness
cream minerals
and acidity
such as
Matrot
Darnat
Bouchard

BABY LETTUCES WITH CRISPY ROOT VEGETABLE CHIPS AND CREAMY TRUFFLE VINAIGRETTE

BABY LETTUCES WITH CRISPY ROOT VEGETABLE CHIPS AND BLACK TRUFFLE VINAIGRETTE

serves 6

Thanks to Michael Gagliardi, we can satisfy our truffle craving anytime of the year with his black truffle puree and black truffle oil (see Purveyors, page 258). White truffle oil has a synthetic taste that is too overpowering for this vinaigrette. Black truffle has a more subtle flavor; therefore, our Truffle Vinaigrette can be enjoyed not only during the December–March black truffle season, but year-round.

CRISPY VEGETABLE CHIPS
3 quarts rice bran or peanut oil
Flour
Salt and pepper
1 carrot
1 parsnip
1 large red beet
1 shallot

Heat the oil to 350° F in a pot large enough to allow the oil to rise during frying. Season flour with salt and pepper. Peel and discard the outer layer of each vegetable. With a vegetable peeler, peel the entire length of the carrot into a bowl and toss with seasoned flour; repeat until the carrot is too small to peel. Shake off excess flour and fry in small batches until crispy, about 3 minutes; transfer to a paper towel–lined plate to drain. Repeat this process with the parsnip, and beet. For the shallot, slice into thin rings on a Japanese mandolin, toss in flour, separate into individual rings, and fry.

FINISH AND PLATE
6 heads baby lettuce, such as baby lolla rosa, red oak leaf or Bibb
Salt and pepper
Black Truffle Vinaigrette (see page 247)

Clean baby lettuces by pulling off and discarding the outer leaves. Cut off the remaining leaves one by one with a pair of kitchen shears. Place all the lettuces together in a large tub of cold water and gently swish to loosen grit. Let the lettuces sit undisturbed for 5 minutes to allow the grit to settle to the bottom. Gently scoop the lettuce out of the water, drain in a colander and spin dry in a salad spinner. Transfer lettuce to a small bowl and season lightly with salt and pepper. Drizzle the Black Truffle Vinaigrette around the outside of the bowl and gently toss the salad. Plate the salad by layering dressed baby lettuces with the Crispy Vegetable Chips.

From The List

Wine

GRECO Di TUFO FROM CAMPANIA ITALY
Light, but present earthiness slight nutty note still well structured

COMPOSED MAINE LOBSTER SALAD WITH SATSUMA MANDARINS, HEARTS OF PALM AND BASIL OIL

serves 6

Shellfish are at their best during the cooler weather, and the fruit of that season—citrus—is the ideal union of flavor fashioned by nature. The reduction of mandarin juice used to emulsify and flavor the vinaigrette is an example of fortifying, giving more depth and sauce-like consistency to the vinaigrette. The lobster should be served chilled.

POACHED LOBSTER

10 quarts water
2 cups white wine
2 cups diced onion
1 cup diced (1-inch) celery
1 cup diced (1-inch) carrot
1 cup diced (1-inch) leek
2 whole lemons
20 parsley stems
6 bay leaves
1/2 cup salt
6 (1 1/4-pound) live Maine lobsters or Pacific spiny lobsters
See technique on page 198

Place all ingredients except lobsters in a large stockpot and simmer for 30 minutes. Bring to a full boil; plunge lobsters in and cook for 8 minutes; remove and place in an ice bath. When cool, remove the lobster meat from its shell (see page 198, but leave lobster tail whole); reserve the claws and knuckles for the Lobster Rillette on page 178.

MANDARIN VINAIGRETTE

1 1/2 cups mandarin orange or tangerine juice
2 tablespoons champagne vinegar
1 tablespoon diced shallots
1/2 teaspoon salt
1/4 teaspoon dry mustard
6 tablespoons canola oil
1/8 teaspoon freshly ground black pepper

Place mandarin orange or tangerine juice in a nonreactive pot and slowly reduce to 1/4 cup; let cool. Add mandarin orange reduction to vinegar, shallots, salt and dry mustard in a mixing bowl and let sit 15 minutes. Add the oil in a slow, steady stream while whisking constantly to emulsify. Finish with the black pepper. *Chef's Note: Any variety of mandarin orange can be used for this vinaigrette.*

FINISH AND PLATE

6 lobster tails, sliced (from above)
48 Satsuma mandarin segments
1 pound hearts of palm, sliced on the bias
3 heads endive
1 head frisee
Sprigs of chervil
Salt and pepper
Basil Oil (see page 248)

Slice the lobster tails into 5 even slices and fan out in a semi-circle on each plate. Place a few of the mandarin segments on top of the lobster. *Chef's Note: For the mandarin segments, peel the outer skin of 4 mandarins and separate the segments into a heatproof bowl. Pour simmering water over to cover and let sit 2 minutes; drain. The white pith on the segments will easily rub off with a towel.* Separate the endive leaves and wash and cut the frisee. Toss sliced hearts of palm, endive, frisee, chervil and remaining mandarin segments with salt, pepper and the Mandarin Vinaigrette to taste. Place a small salad behind the lobster and then sauce the plate with the remaining vinaigrette and Basil Oil.

From The List
SPATLESE MOSEL RIESLING

Wine

Sweet for the lobster, high acidity for mandarins, floral and aromatic for basil oil

COMPOSED MAINE
LOBSTER SALAD

WITH SATSUMA MANDARINS,
HEARTS OF PALM AND BASIL OIL

TECHNIQUE

1. Remove claws. Grasp the lobster in both hands, twist and pull off the tail.

2. Cut through the thin shell on bottom of lobster tail with kitchen shears.

3. Pull out lobster tail meat.

4. Cut tail in half.

5. Lift out digestive tract.

6. Cut 1/4 inch into each side of the claw, twisting the knife side to side to loosen the shell.

7. Grasp and pull off bottom part of the claw shell.

8. Twist and pull smaller pincer of claw—this should remove the cartilage in the center.

PICKING LOBSTER

MONTEREY BAY SPOT PRAWN AND COCONUT SOUP

MONTEREY BAY SPOT PRAWN AND COCONUT SOUP

serves 6

The classic Hawaiian dish of coconut fried shrimp is the flavor combination at the heart of this soup. It takes on a refined elegance when lemongrass, galangal, coconut milk and jasmine rice join in. Thai basil and mint give the broth its aromatic, perfume-like qualities. Most fresh or high-quality frozen whole prawns can be substituted for live spot prawns.

PRAWN AND COCONUT SOUP

18 large spot prawns or other head-on shrimp
3 tablespoons canola oil
1 cup (1-inch) diced onion
1/2 cup (1-inch) diced carrot
1/2 cup (1-inch) diced leek
1 clove garlic
15 stalks lemongrass
1 thumb-size piece galangal
2 tomatoes, cut into quarters
1 tablespoon tomato paste
1 tablespoon tamarind paste
2 quarts water
1/4 cup jasmine rice
2 cans (14 ounces each) coconut milk
1 kaffir lime leaf
Salt
Siracha

If the prawns are still alive, submerge in ice water to make dormant. Separate the prawn head and tail by twisting and pulling. Reserve the heads for the soup stock. Peel the tails and reserve the meat for the finish and reserve the shells for the soup stock; add the shells from the tails to the heads. Heat oil in a heavy pot, add prawn heads and shells, crushing with a heavy wooden spoon while cooking for 5 minutes, or until the shells are pulverized and turning pink. Add onion, carrot, leek, garlic, lemongrass and galangal. Cook until the onion is trans-lucent, about 5 minutes. Add tomatoes, tomato paste and tamarind. Cook until the tomatoes begin to break down, about 10 minutes. Add the water and rice and simmer 45 minutes. *Chef's Note:* The jasmine rice is used in this soup as a thickener and its exotic floral flavor. Add the coconut milk and lime leaf and simmer 15 minutes more. Strain through a fine sieve into another pot, pressing all the solids with the back of a ladle to extract all the liquid. Season with salt and siracha. Keep warm.

FINISH AND PLATE

18 shiitake mushrooms
18 shrimp tails
18 mint leaves
24 Thai basil leaves
1/2 cup chopped (1/2-inch) green onion

Remove the mushroom stems and save for Mushroom Jus on page 251. Cut the caps into quarters. Return the soup base to medium heat. Add the shiitake mushrooms and simmer until softened, about 3 minutes. Add the peeled prawn tails and simmer for 2 minutes more, or until tails are cooked through. Tear the mint and Thai basil leaves into the soup and top with green onion.

From The List
PINOT GRIS FROM OREGON

"Alsatian" spices and aromatics with a touch of sweetness

PAN-ROASTED WILD STRIPED BASS WITH OLIVE OIL FORK-MASHED POTATOES, CHORIZO AND MUSSELS

serves 6

When you are surrounded by a particular heritage, conversing about cuisine is always a favorite topic. With names like Zoellin, Cardoza and daCruz, my friends and I have discussed the soul of classic Portuguese fare. Paying homage to my friends' favorite sausage and clams memories, I substitute mussels with our house-made chorizo sausage for this dish.

OLIVE OIL FORK-MASHED POTATOES
1 pound fingerling potatoes
Cold water
4 teaspoons salt
6 tablespoons extra virgin olive oil
Salt

In a large pot, cover the fingerling potatoes with cold water; add salt and bring to a simmer. Cook until potatoes are pierced easily with a paring knife, about 25 minutes. Pour potatoes into a colander and let steam for 1 minute; transfer to a large bowl. Add the olive oil in a slow, steady stream while mashing the potatoes with a fork. The texture will still be somewhat coarse, with chunks of potato. Adjust the seasoning with salt to taste. Keep warm until plating.

GREMOLATA
3 tablespoons Italian parsley
2 teaspoons garlic
2 teaspoons lemon zest

Pick and chop the Italian parsley leaves. Mince the garlic and zest the lemon with a microplane. Mix all ingredients together in a bowl. *Chef's Note: Gremolata is traditionally used as an accompaniment to osso bucco.*

FINISH AND PLATE
6 (5-ounce) portions wild striped bass
Salt and pepper
4 tablespoons canola oil, divided
2 tablespoons butter
1 teaspoon lemon juice
6 ounces chorizo sausage, broken into pieces
2 tablespoons garlic
Beurre Blanc Reduction (see page 246)
1 pound mussels, scrubbed
1/3 cup Oven-Roasted Tomatoes (see page 256)
1/4 cup butter
Lemon juice
Salt
Black pepper

Season the seabass with salt and pepper. Heat 3 tablespoons oil in a large skillet over medium heat and add fish skin side down; press down on the fish with a spatula for 10 seconds to prevent the skin from curling. Cook until the first side is browned and the skin is crisp, about 3 minutes. Turn over and brown the other side; holding the fish in place with a spatula, drain off the oil, return to the heat and add 2 tablespoons butter; when foamy, add 1 teaspoon lemon juice and 1 teaspoon Gremolata. Baste the fish with the butter, remove from heat and keep warm. Heat remaining oil in a 12-inch skillet and add the sausage; cook over high heat until browned, about 3 minutes. Add the garlic and cook until it is translucent but not browned. Add Beurre Blanc Reduction, mussels and Oven-Roasted Tomatoes; cover and cook until mussels are open, about 2 minutes. Discard any that are not open. Transfer mussels from the skillet to a warm bowl. Reduce the cooking liquid by one-fourth. Turn off the heat and whisk in butter one piece at a time until incorporated. Finish with remaining Gremolata, salt, pepper and lemon juice to taste. Return mussels to the pan and toss with the broth. Place Olive Oil Fork-Mashed Potatoes in the center of a bowl, spoon sausage, mussels and broth around and place fish on top of the potatoes.

From The List
BANDOL OR COTE
de PROVENCE ROSE

Wine

Move forward, do not let the color bother you

PAN-ROASTED WILD STRIPED BASS | WITH OLIVE OIL FORK-MASHED POTATOES, CHORIZO AND MUSSELS

GRILLED RIB-EYE STEAK | WITH CRISPY POTATO CAKE AND OYSTER MUSHROOM—CAMBAZOLA COMPOTE

GRILLED RIB-EYE STEAK WITH CRISPY POTATO CAKE AND OYSTER MUSHROOM–CAMBAZOLA COMPOTE

serves 6

Cambazola is a blue Brie cheese with a mild flavor and when melted, it retains a creamy texture. Locally cultivated Big Sur oyster mushrooms have a hint of shellfish flavor, giving a subtle taste dimension to the compote without overpowering the steak. You can substitute other blue cheese such as St. Agur or Gorgonzola in place of Cambazola.

RIB-EYE STEAK
6 (4 1/2-ounce) rib-eye steaks
Salt and pepper

Season the steaks with salt and pepper about 4 hours prior to grilling; cover with plastic wrap and refrigerate. Let covered steaks sit at room temperature 30 minutes before grilling. *Chef's Note: Meats at room temperature cook more evenly.* Place steaks on a hot broiler and cook for 2 minutes; turn 180 degrees to create a crisscross mark, cooking another 2 minutes. This helps to develop a more even brown crust, and the high heat of the broiler seals in the juices. Turn steaks over and repeat for second side until medium-rare. Let steaks rest for 3 minutes before plating.

OYSTER MUSHROOM–CAMBAZOLA COMPOTE
5 cups oyster mushrooms
6 ounces Cambazola cheese
3 tablespoons canola oil
2 cups julienned red onion
1/2 teaspoon salt
1/4 teaspoon pepper
2 tablespoons chopped chives

Cut off the mushroom stems and reserve for Mushroom Jus (see page 251). Remove the rind from the Cambazola. Heat the oil in a large skillet over high heat. Add the onion and cook for 2 minutes, or until lightly browned. Add the mushrooms and cook for another 5 to 6 minutes. Stir the onions and mushrooms frequently in the skillet to avoid burning; add the salt, pepper and cheese. Remove from heat; the residual heat from the mushrooms and onions will slowly melt the cheese. *Chef's Note: This gentle melting keeps the cheese from separating and becoming oily.* Just before serving, fold in the chives.

CRISPY POTATO CAKES
3 quarts rice bran or peanut oil
1 large russet potato
Salt and pepper
3 tablespoons canola oil

Heat the oil to 350° F in a pot large enough for the oil to rise up during frying. Using the medium teeth of a Japanese mandolin, julienne the potatoes lengthwise. Toss potato in a bowl with salt and pepper. Heat the canola oil in a 14-inch nonstick skillet and form the julienned potatoes into 3-inch rounds; cook until lightly browned on the bottom, about 2 minutes. Turn over and cook until just holding together. At this point, transfer to the hot frying oil and fry until golden brown and crispy, about 3 minutes. Transfer to a paper towel–lined plate.

FINISH AND PLATE
Sautéed Swiss Chard (see page 256)
Cabernet Syrup (see page 250)

Place Swiss Chard in the center of each plate, top with a Crispy Potato Cake, Rib-Eye Steak and Oyster Mushroom–Cambazola Compote. Drizzle Cabernet Syrup around plate.

From The List

CABERNET SAUVIGNON
FROM NAPA OR SONOMA

Obvious for rib-eye yet its ripe fruit and tannins will take on the blue cheese very well

WALNUT-CRUSTED KUROBUTA PORK LOIN WITH PARSNIP PUREE, CARAMELIZED APPLES AND RED WINE SYRUP

serves 6

With the resurgence of pure, unadulterated heritage meats, or meats from non-crossbred animals, comes Kurobuta pork. Snake River Farms imported this pure all-natural Berkshire pork breeding stock, making Kurobuta pork available in the United States. The marbling, one of this pork's main features, creates a rich, flavorful, succulent texture. If Kurobuta is not available to you, brined conventional pork can be substituted and directions are listed below.

WALNUT CRUST
1 (8-ounce) loaf Brioche (see page 246)
6 tablespoons butter, softened
2 cups walnuts
1 tablespoon walnut oil
2 teaspoons salt
1/2 teaspoon black pepper

Puree the bread, butter and walnuts in a food processor fitted with a metal blade, stopping occasionally to scrape down the sides. When mixture forms a smooth paste, add the oil, salt and pepper. Transfer to a sheet of plastic wrap; roll into a cylinder that is about the same size and shape as the pork loin to be crusted, roughly 1 1/2-x-3 1/2 inches. Refrigerate crust until firm, about 4 hours. Unroll crust from plastic and cut into 1/4-inch-thick slices.

KUROBUTA PORK LOINS
6 (5-ounce) portions Kurobuta pork loin, at least 1 inch thick, or conventional pork (brine as instructed below)
Salt and pepper
3 tablespoons canola oil

Preheat oven to 350° F. If using Kurobuta pork, season liberally with salt and pepper 4 hours before cooking. Heat canola oil in a 14-inch skillet over high heat; add the pork and cook until a brown crust forms, about 4 minutes per side; top with a 1/4-inch-thick slice of Walnut Crust. Transfer to the oven for 3 to 4 minutes, or until cooked to medium and the crust is browned anb bubbly. *Chef's Note:* The pork will continue to cook while browning the walnut crust.

If using conventional pork, submerge in Brine (see page 257); dry thoroughly and season lightly with salt and pepper. Proceed as above but use a lower heat. *Chef's Note:* If brining, the sugar content of the brine will cause the pork to burn easily. To brown the pork loins evenly, move them around frequently and make sure to reduce the heat slightly.

RED ONION MARMALADE
1 1/2 cups julienned red onion (about 2 medium onions)
1 cup red wine
1/4 cup + 1 tablespoon sugar
1 bay leaf
1 tablespoon red wine vinegar

Place all ingredients in a saucepan and cook slowly over low heat until thickened to the consistency of syrup, about 30 minutes.

WALNUT-CRUSTED
KUROBUTA PORK LOIN WITH PARSNIP PUREE,
CARAMELIZED APPLES
AND RED WINE SYRUP

CARAMELIZED APPLES
3 tablespoons Clarified Butter (see page 246)
2 apples peeled, cored and cut into wedges
2 tablespoons Apple Cider Gastrique (see page 249)

PARSNIP PUREE
3 cups parsnips, peeled and coarsley chopped
4 cups cold water
2 teaspoons salt
2 tablespoons butter
Salt

FINISH AND PLATE
Beet greens (cook like Sautéed Swiss Chard on page 256)
Red Wine Syrup (see page 251)

Heat Clarified Butter in a 12-inch nonstick skillet; add the apple wedges, arranging in a single layer. Brown wedges, turning over one at a time. When the second side is lightly browned; add the Apple Cider Gastrique and toss. Continue cooking until apples are cooked through and glazed with the gastrique, about 2 to 3 minutes.

Chef's Note: Select young, small, tender parsnips, avoiding larger starchy parsnips with a woody center. Cover parsnip with cold water; add 2 teaspoons salt; bring to a simmer. Cook until tender and easily pierced with a paring knife, about 15 minutes. Drain parsnips into a colander and let steam for 1 minute. Transfer to a food processor fitted with a metal blade; with machine running, add the butter and puree until smooth. Season with salt. Keep warm.

Place beet greens toward the front of each plate and top with a Kurobuta Pork Loin. Place a few wedges of Caramelized Apples on top of pork and then Red Onion Marmalade. Place 2 quenelles of Parsnip Puree behind the pork and sauce with Red Wine Syrup.

From The List
WASHINGTON STATE SYRAH

Between new- and old-world style, fruity enough for apples yet rustic enough for pork

CASTROVILLE ARTICHOKE WITH CARAMELIZED FENNEL AND ITALIAN BUTTER BEAN CASSOULET

serves 6

Italian butter beans are fresh shelling beans and can be found at most regional farmers markets. Fresh beans don't require presoaking, but preparing them is tricky due to their shorter cooking time. Taste the beans for doneness all through the cooking process and salt at the end. Carryover cooking, or residual heat that continues to cook beans after they are removed from heat, can be minimized by placing the pot into ice water for quick cooling.

CARAMELIZED FENNEL
3 heads fennel
3 tablespoons olive oil
Salt and pepper

Preheat oven to 350° F. Cut off the tops of the fennel; peel off the tough outer layer. Cut each bulb into quarters. Lay each wedge on its side and cut out as much of the core as possible while leaving enough to just hold wedge together. Heat the oil in a skillet over medium heat and arrange the fennel wedges in the skillet on their sides; season with salt and pepper and cook over medium heat until caramelized, about 3 minutes. Turn over and cook another 3 minutes; transfer to to the oven for 2 minutes more.

ITALIAN BUTTER BEANS
5 pounds fresh Italian butter shelling beans
8 sage leaves
4 cloves garlic, lightly crushed
6 cups water
2 tablespoons extra virgin olive oil
1 tablespoon salt

Chef's Note: If Italian butter beans are not available, fresh cannelini or cranberry beans can be substituted. If substituting dried beans, soak overnight and extend cooking time by 10 minutes. Shell and then wash the beans under running water. Make a sachet with the sage and garlic by tying up in a cheesecloth. Place beans, water, sachet and oil in a nonreactive pot. Slowly bring to a simmer and skim foam as beans cook. Check beans frequently for doneness starting a few minutes after reaching a simmer. When beans are almost done, about 20 minutes, add the salt and remove from heat. Place pot into an ice bath if needed. Cool and store in their liquid. *Chef's Note:* Pay particular attention during the last 5 minutes of cooking. If over-cooked, beans will split open.

FINISH AND PLATE
2 tablespoons sherry vinegar
1/4 cup olive oil
1/4 cup Roasted Tomatoes (see page 256)
24 kalamata olives, pitted
2 tablespoons Basil Puree (see page 255)
6 artichokes cooked en Barigoule (see page 56)
Garlic Breadcrumbs (see page 257)

Place cooked Italian Butter Beans and their liquid in a medium pot with sherry vinegar and oil; simmer for 5 minutes. Add Roasted Tomatoes and cook another 2 minutes. Add olives and Basil Puree and remove from heat. To plate, place 3 wedges of Caramelized Fennel in the bottom of a bowl, add 1 hot artichoke cooked en Barigoule, and fill each artichoke with Italian Butter Bean mixture, allowing to spill over and fill the bowl. Top with Garlic Breadcrumbs.

From The List
ITALIAN GAVI DI GAVI
FROM LA SCOLCA

Wine

Artichoke challenges any wine; this example will take on the variables of flavor

SLOW BRAISING OF FLAVORS & BIG SUR CHANTERELLES, A RUSTIC SPIRIT OF TASTE

Amuse-Bouche

MOREL MUSHROOM WITH RAMP CUSTARD
AND ASPARAGUS SOUP   214

Course One

BIG SUR CHANTERELLE MUSHROOM RISOTTO   217

DAY BOAT SCALLOPS WITH SEARED FOIE GRAS,
BLOOD ORANGE AND CANDIED FENNEL   218

BRAISED NIMAN RANCH BEEF SHORT RIB WITH
TOASTED BARLEY "RISOTTO" AND
GLAZED ROOT VEGETABLES   220

THAI SPICE–CRUSTED LOBSTER WITH MANGO-VANILLA
BUTTER AND GREEN PAPAYA SALAD   223

Course Two

MÂCHE SALAD WITH WILD MUSHROOM
AND GOAT CHEESE CROSTINI   227

GUINEA HEN CONSOMMÉ WITH
MOREL MUSHROOMS   228

BUTTERNUT SQUASH AND PEAR SOUP WITH
CHESTNUT CREAM   232

Course Three

ROAST RACK OF JAMISON FARMS LAMB WITH
BRAISED LAMB SHANK RISOTTO AND
PORCINI MUSHROOM JUS   235

MOREL MUSHROOM STROGANOFF   237

PAN-ROASTED RIB-EYE CAP WITH GRUYERE
POTATO GRATIN, AND CHORON SABAYON   241

PORCINI MUSHROOM–DUSTED MONKFISH
WITH FRENCH LENTIL RAGOUT AND
BALSAMIC BROWN BUTTER   245

MOREL MUSHROOM
STROGANOFF   SEE PAGE 237

This final menu emphasizes the hearty flavor of wild mushrooms and slow-braising techniques that warm away the chill of winter. The taste of slow-braised beef short ribs is the essence of flavor enhancing while creating a texture that is tender and moist. Winter's tropical mango and green papayas samba toward blood oranges and candied fennel, teasing our thoughts with a summer vacation somewhere in the South Pacific. We add contrast to seafood by infusing the season's sweet acidic citrus, giving a lighter but true to place option until spring is once again upon us.

CHEF'S NOTES

One of the keys to cooking meaty fungi is high heat, see our pan-roasting technique on page 257. By browning them much like a steak, the end result is a duo of texture and taste that perfects the Big Sur Chanterelle Mushroom Risotto, page 217, and the Morel Mushroom Stroganoff, page 237. From the kitchen we also share our Risotto Base, page 253, that is actually done in two parts—saving a tremendous amount of time but not at the sacrifice of quality. Mushroom jus is a mushroom stock that is used as a base to build on and remains a key component to our vegetarian dishes. We have expanded its use in certain cases in place of veal or chicken stock because of its pure intense flavor, see page 252 for recipe.

Each day in the kitchen we welcome change, presence and the intuitiveness required to participate. It's not about just reading a recipe, as much as it's about experiencing it. Alejandro is pan-roasting chanterelles and their earthy smell is intoxicating the entire restaurant. We each stop what we are doing to sample their goodness. Our spirit of taste pleased, we continue on, satisfied and thankful.

MOREL MUSHROOM WITH RAMP CUSTARD AND ASPARAGUS SOUP

serves 6

MOREL MUSHROOMS
6 medium morel mushrooms
1/4 cup ramps, blanched and chopped
6 tablespoons milk
6 tablespoons heavy cream
1/2 teaspoon cornstarch
2 eggs
1 teaspoon salt
1/4 teaspoon cayenne pepper

Preheat oven to 350° F. Select 6 perfect and unbroken morel mushrooms. Place morel mushrooms in a large bowl of warm salted water and swish around to loosen any grit and dirt; let sit undisturbed for 5 minutes to allow grit to settle to the bottom. Scoop mushrooms off the top and transfer to a colander to drain. Repeat if mushrooms are particularly dirty. For the custard, clean and blanch the ramps in rapidly boiling salted water until tender, about 1 minute., refresh in ice water, squeeze out excess water and roughly chop. Place milk, cream and ramps in a small pot and simmer for 5 minutes. Transfer to the container of a blender, add the cornstarch, cover, and run on high until smooth. Place the eggs in a mixing bowl and temper in the hot cream mixture by adding in a slow steady stream and whisking constantly to incorporate. Season with salt and cayenne pepper. Place the morel mushrooms stem side up in individual ramekins or small muffin tins to stand upright. Using a funnel or squeeze bottle, fill the mushrooms with the custard. Arrange the ramekins in a roasting pan and place in oven. Pour in enough water to come halfway up the ramekins. Cover roasting pan with aluminum foil and bake 20 minutes or until set.

ASPARAGUS SOUP
2 tablespoons butter
1/2 cup diced (1/2 inch) leeks
1 cup Vegetable Stock (see page 253)
1/4 cup heavy cream
1 teaspoon salt
1/4 teaspoon white pepper
1 cup asparagus spears

Melt butter in a small pot. Add the leeks and saute until softened. Add the Vegetable Stock and simmer for 20 minutes; add the cream and return to a simmer for 2 minutes. Bring a pot of salted water to a rolling boil, add the asapargus and cook until soft, about 3 minutes, refresh in ice water. Transfer the soup base to the container of a blender, add the asapargus and cover. Blend on high until smooth and frothy. Season with salt and pepper.

FINISH AND PLATE

Spoon the soup into 6 small bowls. Cut the Morel Mushrooms in half on the bias and place in the middle of the soup.

Morel Mushroom
WITH RAMP CUSTARD AND
ASPARAGUS SOUP

AMUSE-BOUCHE

SERVE BEFORE

BIG SUR CHANTERELLE MUSHROOM RISOTTO

BIG SUR CHANTERELLE MUSHROOM RISOTTO

serves 6

Late in the year, Big Sur chanterelle mushrooms just foraged from the Los Padres Wilderness are brought right to our kitchen door and I'm always tempted to have every item on the menu feature a chanterelle preparation. Here we capture the spirit of our local fungi in a creamy mushroom risotto.

1 batch Risotto Base (see page 253)
1 3/4 cups hot Mushroom Jus (see page 251)
2 cups Pan-Roasted Chanterelles (see page 257)
2 tablespoons butter
3 tablespoons Parmesan
1 1/2 teaspoons lemon juice
1 1/2 teaspoons salt
1/4 teaspoon pepper
2 tablespoons truffle butter
1 tablespoon chives

Add the Risotto Base in a small pot and then add enough hot Mushroom Jus to barely cover the rice. Over medium heat, bring to a simmer, stirring frequently with a wooden spoon. Continue adding more jus as it is absorbed to keep the rice covered. When most of the jus has been absorbed, add the Pan-Roasted Chanterelles; stir to mix and continue to cook for 1 minute more. At this point, the rice should be suspended in a creamy liquid and the grains of the rice should be cooked through but firm. Remove from heat and fold in the remaining ingredients; adjust seasoning. Serve immediately. *Chef's Note:* Check the consistency by eating a few grains of rice. If the rice is too hard, add a little more Mushroom Jus.

From The List
CARIGAGNE VARIETAL
BY ITSELF OR BLENDED

Wine

Corbieres shows earth, white pepper dusty tannins and mature fruit

DAY BOAT SCALLOPS WITH SEARED FOIE GRAS, BLOOD ORANGE AND CANDIED FENNEL

serves 6

Blood oranges and the light bitter notes of their flavor make them more than an ideal component to this dish. Their slight bitter-acid elements mingle defined boundaries between the sweet scallop and rich foie gras flavors. Saba comes from cooked Trebbiano grapes, which are used primarily to make balsamic vinegar. I always look forward to featuring this elegant appetizer.

DAY BOAT SCALLOPS
3 tablespoons canola oil
12 medium day boat scallops
Salt and pepper

Heat oil in a 12-inch skillet over medium heat; season scallops with salt and pepper. Arrange 6 scallops in the skillet and cook about 1 to 2 minutes, or until a light brown crust forms. Turn scallops over and cook another 1 to 2 minutes, or until medium rare; keep warm. Repeat procedure with remaining scallops.

CANDIED FENNEL
1 bulb fennel
1 cup water
1/2 cup sugar
1 tablespoon lemon juice
2 tablespoons pernod

Remove stalk-like tops and tough outer layer from the fennel bulb. Starting at the top, cut into paper-thin slices across on a Japanese mandolin. Bring water, sugar, lemon juice and pernod to a boil; add fennel. Immediately remove from heat and let cool.

BLOOD ORANGE VANILLA EMULSION
1 cup blood orange juice
1 vanilla bean, split in half
1/4 cup olive oil

Put blood orange juice and vanilla bean in a nonreactive saucepan. Reduce slowly over low heat until liquid has a syrup consistency, about 20 minutes. Transfer syrup to a small mixing bowl and slowly add the oil, whisking constantly to emulsify. Strain through a fine sieve and transfer to a squeeze bottle.

FINISH AND PLATE
2 blood oranges
Saba (see Purveyors page 258)
Basil Oil (see page 248)
Fleur de sel
6 Seared Foie Gras (see page 171)

Peel the blood oranges, removing all the pith; using a small sharp knife, cut along either side of the membrane to release the segments of orange. Drizzle the Saba, Basil Oil and Blood Orange Vanilla Emulsion on each plate. Stack 2 scallops in the center of the plate; surround with blood orange segments. Top scallops with Seared Foie Gras, a pinch of fleur de sel and a nest of Candied Fennel.

From The List
LATE HARVEST RIESLING FROM ALSACE

Wine

Enough structure to take on the oranges and embrace the sweetness in the foie gras and candied fennel

DAY BOAT SCALLOPS | WITH SEARED FOIE GRAS, BLOOD ORANGE AND CANDIED FENNEL

BRAISED NIMAN RANCH BEEF SHORT RIB WITH TOASTED BARLEY "RISOTTO" AND GLAZED ROOT VEGETABLES

serves 6

Even in fine dining kitchens we crave rustic, slow-cooked comfort food as the year comes to an end. Our favorite is braised short ribs with toasted barley cooked in the style of risotto and glazed root vegetables to complete the rustic adventure. And we wouldn't be Sierra Mar if we didn't surprise your palate with a tangy Horseradish Gremolata just to keep things interesting.

BRAISED SHORT RIBS

2 pounds (2-inch cut) beef short ribs
Salt and freshly ground black pepper
1/4 cup canola oil
1 1/2 cups diced (1-inch) onion
3/4 cups diced (1-inch) carrot
1/2 cup diced (1-inch) celery
2 cups red wine
2 cups Madeira wine
2 cups Chicken Stock (see page 252)
2 cups Veal Stock (see page 253)
8 sprigs thyme

Preheat oven to 225° F. Thoroughly season short ribs on all sides with salt and pepper; refrigerate and allow to sit 6 hours or overnight. Heat the oil in a heavy skillet over high heat and brown the ribs on all sides, about 2 minutes on each side. Brown ribs in several batches, if needed, to avoid overcrowding the pan. Transfer ribs to a roasting pan. In the same skillet, brown the onion, carrot and celery, about 5 minutes; add to the roasting pan with the ribs. Place red wine and Madeira wine in a separate pot and bring to a boil for 5 minutes to remove the raw alcohol flavor. Pour wine, Chicken Stock and Veal Stock over the ribs. The liquid should come about three-fourths of the way up the sides of the ribs. Add the thyme and cover roasting pan with aluminum foil. Braise in oven for 6 hours on the middle rack. When done, meat will practically fall off the bone; let cool to room temperature. Strain off most of the braising liquid through a chinois into a 4-quart nonreactive pot, leaving enough liquid to keep ribs moist. Bring strained liquid to a simmer, skimming frequently until reduced by half, about 1 hour. Keep warm.

TOASTED BARLEY "RISOTTO"

1 cup pearl barley
2 tablespoons canola oil
1/4 cup diced yellow onion
1 1/2 cups Chicken Stock (see page 252) or hot water
3/4 cup Mushroom Jus (see page 251)
1 cup pan-roasted chanterelle mushrooms
1 1/2 teaspoons salt
1/4 teaspoon black pepper
1 1/2 teaspoons lemon juice
2 tablespoons butter
1 tablespoon truffle butter

Preheat oven to 350° F. Place barley in a single layer on a sheet pan and toast in oven for 15 minutes. The barley should be lightly browned and have a nutty aroma when done. Heat the oil in a small pan over medium heat; add onion and sauté until translucent, about 2 minutes. Add the barley and stir to coat with oil; add hot Chicken Stock or water to the barley to just cover the grains and then reduce heat to a simmer. Continue adding the stock to keep the grains covered throughout the cooking process. When all the stock is incorporated, add the Mushroom Jus and continue to cook until the barley is still slightly chewy and has a creamy texture. Add the mushrooms, cook 1 minute more and then add salt, pepper, lemon juice, butter and the truffle butter. Adjust seasoning if needed. Serve immediately.

HORSERADISH GREMOLATA

3 tablespoons chopped Italian parsley
1 teaspoon grated lemon peel
2 teaspoons grated fresh horseradish

Pick the leaves from the Italian parsley, wash and dry. Add lemon peel and horseradish to the parsley and chop together. *Chef's Note:* Prepared horseradish can be used, but reduce amount to 1 teaspoon.

GLAZED ROOT VEGETABLES
12 baby round carrots
12 baby turnips
12 medium shallots
4 1/2 cups Chicken Stock (see page 252)
3 tablespoons butter
1 tablespoon sugar
3/4 teaspoon salt
1/4 teaspoon pepper

Trim off the tops of the carrots and turnips. Peel the carrots, turnips and shallots. In each of three small pots, add 1 1/2 cups Chicken Stock, 1 tablespoon butter, 1 teaspoon sugar, 1/4 teaspoon salt and a pinch of pepper. Add the carrots to one pot, turnips to another and shallots to the third. The liquid should come about halfway up the vegetables. Bring each pot to a boil over medium heat and slowly reduce the liquid. (The goal is to have all the liquid reduced to a glaze with each root vegetable just cooked through, turning the vegetables occasionally.) When the liquid is reduced to a syruplike consistency, move each vegetable around to coat and caramelize or "glaze" and check each vegetable for doneness, add more stock to any that are still undercooked. Keep warm until plating.

FINISH AND PLATE

Mound some of the Toasted Barley "Risotto" in the center of each plate. Top with one Braised Short Rib and then drizzle the rib sauce around the barley. Place Glazed Root Vegetables, alternating varieties, around the outside. Sprinkle the rib with Horseradish Gremolata.

From The List
ZINFANDEL FROM
SONOMA DRY CREEK AREA

Spice, pepper
zest, sweet
fruit and
sharp earthy
finish to
match this
dish

THAI SPICE–CRUSTED LOBSTER WITH MANGO-VANILLA BUTTER AND GREEN PAPAYA SALAD

THAI SPICE–CRUSTED LOBSTER WITH MANGO-VANILLA BUTTER AND GREEN PAPAYA SALAD

serves 6

The philosophy behind *China Moon Cookbook,* by Barbara Tropp, initially motivated me to start making my own spicy, acidic and aromatic seasonings using whole spices and fresh exotic ingredients. Looking beyond premade and working from scratch has played a key role in the outcome of my food for as long as I can remember. Sometimes giving in to convenience isn't worth giving up on flavor.

MANGO-VANILLA BUTTER
1 cup white wine
2 tablespoons mirin
1 tablespoon lime juice
1/4 cup diced shallot
1/2 vanilla bean, split in half
3/4 cup peeled and diced Manila mango
1/2 cup butter
1 teaspoon salt

Place the wine, mirin, lime juice, shallot, vanilla bean and mango in a 2-quart nonreactive pot; simmer gently until almost dry. Mash the mango with a whisk while reducing; add the butter, one piece at a time, whisking constantly to incorporate. Strain through a fine sieve, pressing down on the solids with the bottom of a ladle, extracting as much mango pulp as possible. Season to taste with salt and more lime juice if necessary.

LOBSTER
Salt
4 gallons water
3 (1 1/4-pound) live Maine lobsters
See technique on page 198

Bring lightly salted water to a boil; turn off the heat and add the lobsters, letting them poach for 90 seconds. Transfer lobsters to an ice water bath; remove claws and return claws to the hot water for an additional 4 minutes before returning to the ice water. Using a twisting motion, separate the head from the tail; reserve the head and shells for lobster bisque or stock. Using a pair of poultry shears, cut through the thin shell on the bottom of the tail and remove the meat. Trim off the ragged pieces at the front of the tail and reserve for Lobster Rillette (see page 178). Cut the tail meat in half lengthwise and remove the digestive tract. Hold each claw up on its side and cut 1/4 inch down into the shell just below the smaller pincer part of the claw; turn claw to its other side and cut 1/4 inch down the other side. Grasp the small pincer part of the claw and turn slightly as you pull to remove it from the shell. The cartilage inside the claw should come out with this small shell. Remove the rest of the shell and reserve for the stock or bisque. Use a knife and a small fork to remove the elbow meat; reserve for Lobster Rillette.

THAI SPICE RUB
14 stalks lemongrass
6 kaffir lime leaves
2 tablespoons coriander seeds
3 tablespoons diced shallot
2 teaspoons grated galangal
2 Thai chiles, deseeded
2/3 cup canola oil

Cut off and discard the bottom 1/2 inch and the tough top 5 inches of each lemongrass stalk; peel off and discard the fibrous outer layers, about 4 layers. Thinly slice the tender center and place in the container of a blender, add the kaffir lime leaves, coriander, shallot, galangal and Thai chiles. Run the blender on medium and add the oil in a steady stream. When all the oil is incorporated, turn the blender to high and puree until smooth.

GREEN PAPAYA SALAD DRESSING
2 tablespoons garlic
2 tablespoons palm sugar
1/4 cup fish sauce
1/3 cup lime juice
1 tablespoon siracha

With mortar and pestle, grind garlic and palm sugar into a fine paste. Slowly add the fish sauce, lime juice and siracha. Refrigerate until ready to use.

GREEN PAPAYA SALAD
1/2 green papaya
1 tablespoon julienned mint
1 tablespoon julienned cilantro
1 tablespoon julienned basil
1/4 cup peanuts, roasted and chopped

Peel the green papaya and then cut in half lengthwise and remove the seeds. Julienne into long strands using a Japanese mandolin fitted with medium-size teeth. Toss the julienned green papaya in a bowl with julienned herbs and peanuts. Dress with Green Papaya Salad Dressing right before serving.

FINISH AND PLATE
6 tablespoons butter
Mint Oil (see page 249)

Preheat oven to 350° F. Rub lobster tails and claws with Thai Spice Rub. Melt 3 tablespoons of butter in each of two 12-inch ovenproof skillets over medium heat. When the butter begins to foam, add the lobster tails to one skillet, red side down, and the claws to the other; cook 10 seconds. Turn tails and claws over and then transfer to the oven for 30 to 45 seconds. Place a pool of Mango-Vanilla Butter in the center of each plate; drizzle Mint Oil around. Arrange a half tail on top of the sauce, dress the Green Papaya Salad and place a small amount on top of the tail, followed by 1 claw. Top claw with another small mound of Green Papaya Salad.

From The List
SAUTERNES

Wine

Botrytis, sweetness, acidity, complexity— this dish calls for it

MÂCHE SALAD | WITH WILD MUSHROOM AND
GOAT CHEESE CROSTINI

MÂCHE SALAD WITH WILD MUSHROOM AND GOAT CHEESE CROSTINI

serves 6

The taste of wild mushrooms paired with goat cheese and sherry vinegar circulate a flavor trio full of action. This recipe can also work as an appetizer or be served as a crostini hors d'oeuvre. You can use domestic mushrooms such as portabella or crimini if wild mushrooms are not available.

CROSTINI
1 Brioche loaf (see page 246)
3 tablespoons butter
Salt and pepper

Slice the Brioche into thin slices. In a nonstick skillet, heat 1 1/2 tablespoons butter over medium heat; add the Brioche slices and lightly season with salt and pepper. Cook until golden brown, about 2 minutes. Turn over and add remaining butter and then cook until second side is browned; keep warm.

HERBED GOAT CHEESE
1/2 cup soft ripened goat cheese, such as Laura Chenel or Redwood Hill Farms
2 tablespoons chopped chives
1 teaspoon chopped tarragon
1 teaspoon black truffle oil

Mix all ingredients together and set aside until ready to use.

FINISH AND PLATE
Pan-Roasted Wild Mushrooms (see page 257)
Sherry Vinaigrette (see page 248)
Crispy Shallots (see page 254)
1 pound mâche
Picked chervil and parsley
Salt and freshly ground pepper
Balsamic Syrup (see page 250)

Chef's Note: Any wild mushroom can be used for this dish. My favorites are chanterelles, porcinis or morels. Spread a little Herbed Goat Cheese on each Crostini. Lightly dress the roasted mushrooms with the Sherry Vinaigrette and arrange on top of crostini; top with Crispy Shallots. Lightly season the mâche, chervil and parsley with salt and fresh ground pepper; toss with Sherry Vinaigrette to taste. Place a small mâche salad next to the crostini on the plate; dot the plate with Balsamic Syrup.

From The List
WHITE BORDEAUX
SAUVIGNON-SEMILLION BLEND

Wine

Complexity
of two
varietals
will embrace
the goat
cheese and
remain delicate
enough for
the mâche

GUINEA HEN CONSOMMÉ WITH MOREL MUSHROOMS

serves 6

Consommé is not difficult; it just requires attention to detail and is truly worth any and all effort. For me, consommé is the truest distillation of a meat's flavor, as it is impossible to disguise any flaw. Guinea Hen Mousse is used to fill the morel which allows an additional taste element to surface. Dried morels reconstituted can be substituted for fresh.

GUINEA HEN
1 (2 1/2-pound) guinea hen
See technique on page 90

Place guinea hen breast side up, wings closest to you on a cutting board. Cut off and reserve the wings. With your finger, find the cartilage running down the center of the breast. With a boning knife, make a cut just to the right of the cartilage and cut all the way from the front to the back, getting as close to the cartilage as possible. When you reach the end closest to you, which is the wishbone, follow it down and to the right until you come to the wing joint. Pull the wing down to expose the joint so it is easier to cut through the gap. Cut through the skin above the thigh, exposing the thigh joint, and pull the thigh down and away from the bird to expose or dislocate the joint. Cut through the joint and cut down the breastplate all the way to the wing to remove the meat from the carcass, lay half of bird on cutting board and then cut through the skin connecting the breast with the thigh. Remove the tender from the inside of the breast and reserve for Guinea Hen Mousse. Separate the leg and thigh by cutting between the bones at the joint; reserve the legs for the Guinea Hen Potpie. Place the thigh skin side down and make an incision on either side of the thigh bone, slip your knife point under the bone and remove it, reserving the thigh meat for the roulade and the bone for stock. After breaking down the other side, chop the bones into 2-inch pieces with a heavy cleaver for the Guinea Hen Jus (see page 251).

GUINEA HEN MOUSSE
6 ounces guinea hen meat (see page 88)
1 whole egg
1 egg white
3/4 cup cream
1 tablespoon salt
2 tablespoons pepper
1 tablespoon black truffle puree
2 tablespoons chives

Put the bowl of a food processor in the freezer for 30 minutes. Place guinea hen meat in processor bowl and run until the meat is minced, about 30 seconds. Add the egg and egg white; continue running until egg is incorporated. Stop processor. *Chef's Note:* It is important to only run the processor while ingredients are being added. If the mousse is overprocessed, it will be tough and chewy. With processor running again, add half of the cream in a steady stream. Stop processor and scrape down the sides with a rubber spatula. With machine running again, add the remaining cream in a steady stream. Push mousse through a tamis sieve, season with salt and pepper, followed by the truffle puree and chives. *Chef's Note:* To test seasoning, drop an almond-size piece into simmering water, poach about 3 minutes. Taste and adjust seasoning if needed.

GUINEA HEN ROULADE
2 guinea hen thighs, deboned and pounded
Salt and pepper
2 tablespoons canola oil
2 tablespoons butter
5 sprigs thyme
See technique page 93

Preheat oven to 350° F. Season thighs with salt and pepper; place 3 tablespoons Guinea Hen Mousse in the center of each thigh and roll up to enclose. Tie each with three pieces of butcher's twine; refrigerate. Heat oil in a 12-inch ovenproof skillet over medium heat; place roulades in skillet and brown on all sides, about 8 minutes total. Hold the roulades in place with a spatula and drain off the oil; return to heat and then add the butter. When the butter becomes foamy, add the thyme. Baste with the thyme butter and transfer to the oven for 9 minutes; keep warm.

MOREL MUSHROOMS
6 pieces large morel mushrooms
Warm water
Salt
2 quarts lightly salted Chicken Stock (see page 252)

Choose 6 large, unbroken morel mushrooms and place in warm water with a little salt. To loosen any dirt, gently swish the mushrooms in the water; let sit for 5 minutes and then scoop the mushrooms out of the water and lay out on paper towels to drain. Place the remaining Guinea Hen Mousse in a piping bag fitted with a small smooth tip. Hold the mushroom in one hand and put the tip of the piping bag as far inside the mushroom as possible and then gently fill completely with the mousse, pulling the piping bag out slowly as the top of the mushroom begins to fill. Be careful not to overfill and break the mushroom. Bring stock to a simmer; add the mushrooms and poach about 5 minutes, or until mousse is set. Remove morels from liquid and drain on paper towels; keep warm.

GUINEA HEN CONSOMMÉ
12 cups Guinea Hen Stock (see page 252)
1 tablespoon sherry vinegar
1 cup julienned onion
1/2 cup julienned carrot
1/2 cup julienned celery
1/2 cup julienned leek
12 pieces parsley stems
6 sprigs thyme
1/4 cup dried black trumpet mushrooms
2 1/2 cups egg whites
8 ounces ground guinea hen meat or chicken
See technique on page 230

Place stock and vinegar in an 8-quart heavy-bottom stockpot. In a large bowl, whisk together the vegetables, herbs, dried mushrooms, egg whites and meat. Add to the stocks, mixing vigorously to incorporate. Place over low heat, whisking occasionally in the early stages of cooking, scraping the bottom to prevent the egg white and meat from scorching. When you see the first signs of the egg white coagulating and rising to the surface, stop whisking; allow the egg white, vegetables and meat to rise and form a "raft" on the surface. Once the raft forms, using a ladle, cut a hole in the center of the raft (this is called a chimney) to encourage the liquid below to percolate through the center and clarify itself. Let the consommé simmer this way for about 45 minutes or until the liquid coming through the chimney is clear. Line a chinois with a triple layer of cheesecloth and set over a bain-marie. With care, place the bottom point of a china cap strainer in the center chimney of the consommé and let it sink to the bottom of the pot. Ladle the clear liquid that accumulates in the center of the china cap through the cheesecloth; season to taste with salt; keep hot.

FINISH AND PLATE
Stuffed morel mushrooms, sliced
1 black truffle, optional

Slice the Guinea Hen Roulades into 6 slices. Cut the truffle into batonettes. Place 1 slice of galantine in each bowl, fill with hot Guinea Hen Consommé and float Morel Mushroom rounds and truffle on top.

From The List
JURA REGION OF FRANCE
PALE AND AROMATIC RED BLEND

Very distinctive
aromatic, light
earthy fruit
worth the
effort to find

TECHNIQUE

1. Place vegetables, meat and herbs in a mixing bowl and add the egg whites.

2. Whisk vigorously to incorporate.

3. Whisk the egg white and vegetable mixture into the stock seasoned with a little vinegar to aid clarification.

4. Place over low heat and whisk occasionally, scraping the bottom to prevent scorching until you see the first sign of coagulating and rising to the surface; stop whisking.

5. Allow the egg white and vegetable to rise and form a raft on the surface.

6. Using a ladle, cut a hole in the center of the raft (this is called a chimney) and let the consommé simmer this way for about 45 minutes.

7. Line a chinois with a triple layer of cheesecloth and place over a bain marie.

8. Place the bottom point of a conical strainer in the center chimney and let it sink to the bottom of the pot.

9. Ladle out the consommé that collects in the conical strainer and pour through the cheesecloth-lined chinois.

GUINEA HEN CONSOMME

BUTTERNUT SQUASH AND PEAR SOUP WITH CHESTNUT CREAM

serves 6

Every chef has his or her favorite, and during winter months, this soup is one of mine. I am not alone in this thought, as this is the most requested Sierra Mar recipe to date. A hint of pear divides the linear richness of butternut squash with a balance of sweet and slightly acidic undertones, adding another flavor dimension to this recipe.

SQUASH FOR VESSEL
3 medium acorn squash
1/4 cup canola oil

Preheat oven to 350° F. Cut off the bottom ends of each squash just enough to create a flat surface for the squash bowl to sit flat. Cut each squash in half across and remove seeds. Brush inside flesh of squash with oil; place cut side up on a Silpat-lined sheet pan. Bake for 35 minutes, or until done; set aside and keep warm.

BUTTERNUT SQUASH SOUP
1 large butternut squash (about 2 pounds)
1 tablespoon canola oil
2 tablespoons butter
1/2 cup julienned shallot
2 ripe d'anjou pears, peeled, cored and chopped
6 cups water
Salt and pepper
Fresh nutmeg

Preheat oven to 350° F. Cut butternut squash in half lengthwise and remove seeds. Brush with oil and place cut side down on a baking sheet; bake until soft to the touch, about 35 minutes. Remove from the oven and let cool; scoop out flesh with a spoon and discard peel. Melt butter in a pot over medium heat; add shallot and sauté until translucent, about 3 minutes. Add squash pulp, pears and water; bring to a boil and then reduce heat. Simmer for 30 minutes and then transfer to the container of a blender, cover and run on high until smooth. Season with salt, pepper and fresh nutmeg; keep warm.

CHESTNUT CREAM
1/4 cup heavy cream
1/4 cup chopped (1-inch) steamed chestnuts
1/2 cup crème fraîche
Salt
Pinch of white pepper
Pinch of nutmeg

Place the heavy cream and chestnuts in a small saucepan and simmer over medium heat for 5 minutes. Transfer to the container of a blender, cover and puree until smooth, adding a little more cream if needed. Place cooled cream mixture and crème fraîche in a stand mixer with the whisk attachment and whip to soft peaks; add salt, white pepper and nutmeg to taste.

FINISH AND PLATE

Fill the Squash Vessels with hot soup. Top with a dollop of Chestnut Cream and serve.

From The List
VIOGNIER, CLEAN BUT RICH

Strong aromatics invite the soup and sweetness

ROAST RACK OF
JAMISON FARMS LAMB | WITH BRAISED LAMB SHANK RISOTTO
AND PORCINI MUSHROOM JUS

ROAST RACK OF JAMISON FARMS LAMB WITH BRAISED LAMB SHANK RISOTTO AND PORCINI MUSHROOM JUS

serves 6

Here is a perfect example of a rustic slow-braising technique. Porcini mushrooms blend well within a much slower cooking time and their liquor-like flavor doesn't overrule the dish. The lamb shanks in this hearty winter time dish could also be served whole over a bean ragout. Jamison Farms is a small family farm in Pennsylvania that produces the best lamb I have ever tasted.

BRAISED LAMB SHANKS

2 lamb shanks
2 tablespoons salt
1 750 ML bottle red wine
2 tablespoons canola oil
1 cup large-dice yellow onion
1/2 cup large-dice carrot
1/2 cup large-dice celery
3 whole cloves garlic
1 sprig rosemary
2 teaspoons whole black peppercorns
2 cups Veal Stock (see page 253)

Preheat oven to 225° F. Season the lamb shanks with salt and refrigerate for 6 hours or overnight; this allows the salt to penetrate all the way through the meat. Bring the wine to a boil in a 2-quart saucepan for 5 minutes to remove the raw alcohol flavor; set aside to cool. Remove the lamb shanks from the refrigerator and wipe off the salt with a towel. Heat canola oil in a 14-inch skillet over medium heat and then add the lamb shanks; brown on all sides, roughly 5 minutes per side. Place shanks in a roasting pan just large enough to hold them without touching each other. In the same skillet, add the onion, carrot, celery and garlic; sauté until browned, about 5 to 8 minutes. Add the browned vegetables, rosemary, red wine, black peppercorns and Veal Stock to the roasting pan with the lamb shanks. Cover pan with aluminum foil and braise in oven for 5 to 6 hours, or until the meat easily pulls away from the bone. When cool enough to touch, remove the lamb shanks from the braising liquid and pick all the meat from the bones, discarding any bones and tough sinew. Strain the braising liquid through a fine sieve into a metal container; skim off and discard any fat. The reserved braising liquid will be used for the Lamb Porcini Mushroom Sauce.

ROAST RACK OF LAMB

2 Jamison Farms lamb racks
Salt and pepper, to taste
3 tablespoons canola oil
2 tablespoons butter
1 sprig rosemary

Preheat oven to 350° F. Four hours before cooking, generously season the lamb rack with salt and pepper; refrigerate. One hour before cooking, remove from the refrigerator and let sit at room temperature, covered with plastic wrap. Heat the oil over high heat in a 14-inch skillet; add the lamb rack, bone side up. Cook until a brown crust forms on the bottom, about 5 minutes. Turn the lamb and brown each side in the same manner, about 8 to 10 minutes total, ending with the rack bone side down. Drain off oil and then add butter. When the butter is foamy, add rosemary and baste the lamb rack. Transfer to the oven for 12 minutes for medium-rare or an internal temperature of 140° F. Remove from the oven and let rest for 5 minutes before serving.

LAMB PORCINI MUSHROOM SAUCE
1/2 cup boiling water
1/3 cup dried porcini mushrooms
2 tablespoons canola oil
2 tablespoons finely diced shallot
2 tablespoons finely chopped garlic
1/2 cup dry sherry wine
1 1/2 cups Veal Stock (see page 253)
1 cup lamb shank braising liquid (from previous page)
1 sprig rosemary
1/2 cup Pan-Roasted Porcini Mushrooms,
optional (see page 257)

Pour boiling water over dried porcini mushrooms and let steep for 15 minutes; strain porcinis through a fine sieve, reserving the liquid. Heat canola oil in a 2-quart saucepan over medium heat and add the shallot, garlic, and reconstituted mushrooms; sauté until shallots are translucent, about 2 minutes. Add the reserved mushroom liquid and sherry; simmer until almost dry, about 15 minutes. Add the Veal Stock and lamb shank braising liquid; simmer for 30 minutes, skimming frequently, and then add the rosemary, simmering 1 minute more. Strain sauce through a fine sieve and add the Pan-Roasted Porcini Mushrooms and simmer for 5 minutes more; keep warm.

LAMB SHANK RISOTTO
Risotto Base (see page 253)
3/4 cup Mushroom Jus (see page 251)
2 tablespoons butter
3 tablespoons Parmesan
1 1/2 teaspoons salt
1/4 teaspoon pepper
1 1/2 teaspoons lemon juice
1 tablespoon chopped chives

Place the Risotto Base in a small pot and then add enough hot Mushroom Jus to barely cover the rice. Over medium heat, bring to a simmer, stirring frequently with a wooden spoon. Continue adding more jus as it is absorbed to keep the rice covered. Once all the Mushroom Jus is absorbed, the rice should be cooked through but still firm. Add Braised Lamb Shanks and cook 1 minute more, remove from the heat and add the butter, Parmesan, salt, pepper, lemon juice and chives. Adjust seasoning to taste; serve immediately.

FINISH AND PLATE
Italian parsley

Place a mound of Lamb Shank Risotto in the center of each plate. Slice the Roast Rack of Lamb into 6 portions and place 1 chop on each plate in front of the risotto. Spoon the Lamb Porcini Mushroom around and garnish with parsley.

From The List
PASO ROBLES WEST SIDE
RHONE BLEND OR SYRAH

Big full body wines make sure the high alcohol content is in balance with the other components

MOREL MUSHROOM STROGANOFF

serves 6

Fresh wild morels usually follow the snow melt. We obtain most of our blond morels that are used in this stroganoff from the Pacific Northwest. Vegetarians appreciate the meaty richness and firm texture of the earthy morel sauce tossed with a fresh-made batch of fettuccini. When shopping for morels, they should be firm, dry, and have a fresh earthy scent.

STROGANOFF SAUCE
2 cups Mushroom Jus (see page 251)
2 cups Pan-Roasted Morel Mushrooms (see page 257)
6 tablespoons crème fraîche
2 tablespoons truffle butter
2 tablespoons diced chives
1 1/2 teaspoons lemon juice
1/2 teaspoon salt
1/4 teaspoon pepper

Clean the morel mushrooms (see page 238). Simmer the Mushroom Jus and Pan-Roasted Mushrooms together for 5 minutes to infuse the flavors. Whisk in the crème fraîche and continue cooking for 1 minute; remove from heat and add the truffle butter, chives, lemon juice, salt and pepper. Taste and adjust seasonings. Keep warm.

FINISH AND PLATE
1/2 pound asparagus tips
12 ramps
Pasta, cut to fettuccine (see page 247)
Salt
Shaved Parmesan cheese

Blanch the asparagus in rapidly boiling salted water until tender and then refresh in ice water; cut into 1-inch-long pieces on a bias. Clean the ramps by cutting off the root base and three-fourths of the green top. Peel off the outer translucent layer and blanch for 30 seconds in rapidly boiling salted water, refresh and then cut into 1-inch-long pieces. Cook fettuccine in salted boiling water until al dente, about 2 minutes; drain in a colander. Add the ramps and asparagus to the Stroganoff Sauce and cook for 1 minute to warm through; toss with the pasta and top with shaved Parmesan cheese. Serve immediately.

From The List
AMARONE OR VALPOLICELLA CLASSICO

Concentrated
rustic yet
fruity, rich
and earthy
look to top
Veneto producers

TECHNIQUE

1. Cut off the stem from the base of the morel mushroom and reserve for Mushroom Jus or Mushroom Nage.

2. Cut mushroom into 1/2-inch-thick rings.

3. Or cut in half lengthwise.

4. Place mushrooms in a bowl of lightly salted warm water and swish around to loosen grit.

5. Let sit for 5 minutes to allow the grit to settle to the bottom. Gently scoop mushrooms off the top and transfer to a paper towel–lined plate to drain.

CLEANING MOREL MUSHROOMS

PAN-ROASTED
RIB-EYE CAP . WITH GRUYÈRE POTATO GRATIN,
AND CHORON SABAYON

PAN-ROASTED RIB-EYE CAP WITH GRUYÈRE POTATO GRATIN, AND CHORON SABAYON

serves 6

The cap meat of the rib-eye is the most flavorful, juicy and tender cut of beef. To get a rib-eye cap, you have to purchase the entire rib-eye and then have your butcher separate the cap and clean it of all sinew and fat. You can substitute whole rib-eye or hanger steak here.

GRUYÈRE POTATO GRATIN

2 tablespoons butter
2 teaspoons chopped garlic
1 teaspoon diced shallot
1 1/4 cups heavy cream
2 teaspoons salt
1 teaspoon pepper
3 medium russet potatoes (about 2 pounds)
1/2 thinly julienned onion
1 tablespoon chopped thyme
1/4 cup grated gruyère cheese (about 4 ounces)

Preheat oven to 350° F. In a saucepan, melt butter over medium heat. Add garlic and shallot and sauté until translucent, about 2 minutes. Add the cream and bring to a simmer for 5 minutes. Season with salt and pepper; strain through a fine sieve and set aside. Peel the potatoes and slice into thin rounds with a Japanese mandolin. In a 4-x-6-inch baking dish, arrange two layers of potato slices, scatter with a third of the onion, thyme and gruyère cheese. Cover with a little of the seasoned cream; repeat this three times, ending with a layer of potatoes. Cover with the rest of the cream. Press down on the potatoes to evenly distribute the cream. Cover with aluminum foil and bake for 40 minutes. Remove the foil and bake another 10 minutes, or until browned on top and easily pierced with a paring knife. Keep warm.

CHORON REDUCTION

1/2 cup white wine vinegar
6 sprigs tarragon
2 tablespoons chopped shallot
2 tablespoons Oven-Roasted Tomatoes (see page 256)
1/2 teaspoon black pepper

Place all ingredients in a nonreactive pot and bring to a simmer; slowly reduce by half. Remove from heat, strain and let cool before adding to egg yolks for Choron Sabayon.

CHORON SABAYON

4 egg yolks
1 teaspoon salt
1/4 teaspoon pepper
1/4 cup heavy cream, whipped to medium peaks

Bring a medium pot of water to a simmer; place a bowl of ice aside for cooling the sabayon. In a large bowl, mix egg yolks, 1/4 cup Choron Reduction, salt and pepper; whisk vigorously until frothy. Place bowl over the pot of simmering water and whisk vigorously until thick and pale yellow in color, about 5 minutes. Place same bowl over ice and whisk sabayon base until cool. Gently fold in whipped cream; adjust seasoning with salt and pepper if needed. This can be made up to 3 hours ahead and refrigerated.

PAN-ROASTED RIB-EYE CAP

6 (5-ounce) rib-eye steaks
Salt and pepper
6 tablespoons canola oil
6 tablespoons butter
10 sprigs thyme
Fleur de sel

Preheat oven to 350° F. Season the steaks with salt and pepper 4 hours ahead, allowing the salt to penetrate all the way through. About 1 hour before cooking, remove the steaks from the refrigerator and let come to room temperature. Heat 3 tablespoons oil over high heat in each of two heavy skillets. *Chef's Note:* The steaks need high heat to sear properly—this aids in the carmelization of the meat and seals in the juices. If the skillet is overloaded with meat, it will cool too much, resulting in the juices being lost, preventing carmelization. Therefore, it is best to use two skillets to pan-roast 6 steaks. When the skillets are very hot but not smoking, carefully add 3 steaks to each pan. When the rib-eye has a nice brown crust, about 4 minutes, turn over and sear other side. When second side has browned, hold the steaks in place with a spatula and drain off all the cooking oil; return to heat and add 2 tablespoons of butter to each pan. When the butter melts and begins to foam, add the thyme sprigs right on top of the butter. Baste the rib-eye repeatedly with the thyme butter; finish in oven until desired doneness, about 5 minutes for medium-rare. Allow to rest for 5 minutes before cutting. Season with fleur de sel before serving.

BONE MARROW

3 beef marrow bones
Salt and pepper
Flour to dredge
3 tablespoons canola oil

To extract the bone marrow, press on the marrow with your thumb from the end with the smallest opening. If the marrow does not come out, set the marrow bone in warm tap water for a minute to loosen up. Cut the marrow in 1/2-inch-thick discs. Season with salt and pepper and then dredge in flour. Add oil to a 12-inch skillet over high heat. Add the marrow pieces and cook about 15 seconds per side, or until browned and crispy; transfer to a paper towel–lined plate to drain. Serve immediately.

FINISH AND PLATE

Red Wine Sauce (see page 251)
Pan-Roasted Chanterelles (see page 257)

Cut Gruyère Potato Gratin into 6 circles with a 2-inch round cutter. Place gratin and a mound of Swiss Chard on each plate. Slice the Pan-Roasted Rib-Eye Cap and place on top. Spoon a dollop of Choron Sabayon on top. Sauce the plate with Red Wine Sauce. Place 2 pieces of Bone Marrow and scatter Pan-Roasted Chanterelles around the plate.

From The List
BORDEAUX HAUT MEDOC

Wine

classic style
at a good
value ratio

Craig and Patrick in the Monterey studio.

This book would have never made it to the printer if it wasn't for the dedication of local photographer, Patrick Tregenza.

tregenza.net

Patrick Tregenza's work has appeared in *Graphis*, *The Wall Street Journal*, *USA Today*, *The Wine Spectator* and *Food Arts*.

The food and technique photos were shot at his studio in historic downtown Monterey, California on my days off from the restaurant.

Patrick's ability to capture the soul of food through a lens can only be described as pure talent.

I am grateful for Patrick and his amazing contribution to this project.

PORCINI MUSHROOM-
DUSTED MONKFISH

WITH FRENCH LENTIL
RAGOUT AND BALSAMIC
BROWN BUTTER

PORCINI MUSHROOM–DUSTED MONKFISH WITH FRENCH LENTIL RAGOUT AND BALSAMIC BROWN BUTTER

serves 6

Monkfish is a hearty rich fish with a lobster-like texture and subtle shellfish flavor. It is the tail portion of angler fish and perfectly suited for heartier meat-like preparations. Achieving a brown crust on a monkfish can be difficult—the problem is solved by simply dusting the fish with dry porcini powder. Grinding your own porcini powder is convenient and a must, as most premade porcini powders lack flavor.

MONKFISH
1/4 cup dry porcini mushrooms
6 (5-ounce) pieces monkfish
Salt and pepper
3 tablespoons canola oil
2 tablespoons butter
1 tablespoon lemon juice
6 sprigs thyme

Preheat oven to 350° F. Grind porcinis to a powder in a spice grinder to make about 2 tablespoons powder. Season monkfish with salt and pepper and dust with porcini powder. Heat the oil in a 14-inch skillet over high heat and add the monkfish; brown all over, about 2 minutes per side. Hold the fish in place with a spatula and drain off oil; return to heat and add the butter. When the butter is foamy and beginning to brown, add lemon juice and thyme sprigs. Baste the monkfish with the brown butter. Monkfish requires a slightly longer cooking time due to its dense texture; therefore, after basting, transfer to the oven until cooked through, about 5 minutes. Remove from oven and keep warm.

FRENCH LENTILS
1 1/4 cups green lentils
3 cups water
1/2 yellow onion
1 (6-inch) piece celery stalk
1 (3-inch) piece carrot, cut in half
1 bay leaf
1 teaspoon salt

Place lentils in a fine strainer and rinse under cold running water. Place all ingredients together, except the salt, in a 2-quart pot and bring to a simmer for about 15 to 20 minutes. The lentils will continue to cook a little from the residual heat, so remove from the stove when the lentils are tender but still firm; add the salt and transfer to a baking pan and cool in the cooking liquid. When cool, remove the bay leaf and vegetables and then strain off cooking liquid.

LENTIL RAGOUT
1 1/4 cups cubed pancetta (about 1/2 pound)
2 tablespoons butter
1/2 cup leeks, cut into 1/2-inch rounds
3 cups cooked Green Lentils (see above)
1 cup Chicken Stock (see page 252)
2 tablespoons Fines Herbes (see page 255)

Fry the pancetta in a nonstick pan until browned and crispy; transfer to a paper towel–line plate. Melt butter in saucepan over medium heat; add leek and saute until translucent, about 2 minutes. Add 3 cups cooked French lentils, pancetta cubes and Chicken Stock; continue cooking for another 2 minutes, or until the stock has reduced and glazes the lentils. Stir in Fines Herbes right before serving.

BALSAMIC BROWN BUTTER
2 tablespoons balsamic vinegar
2 tablespoons Balsamic Syrup (see page 250)
2 teaspoons diced shallot
8 tablespoons butter
1/2 teaspoon garlic
1/2 teaspoon thyme

Place vinegar, Balsamic Syrup and shallot in a mixing bowl. Heat butter over medium heat until foamy and beginning to brown; add garlic and thyme to the brown butter and immediately add the brown butter mixture to the vinegar and syrup in a slow, steady stream while whisking constantly to emulsify.

FINISH AND PLATE

Mound Lentil Ragout in the center of each plate and top with a piece of Monkfish. Spoon the Balsamic Brown Butter around and serve.

From The List
BURGUNDY BEAUNE OR
SAVIGNY Les BEAUNE OR A BLAGNY

Wine

Consider the challenge of balsamic, a well-built burgundy would respect and complete all components

BASIC RECIPES

CLARIFIED BUTTER AND MILK SOLIDS

2 pounds unsalted butter

Melt the butter over low heat until foam rises to the surface and milk solids drop to the bottom of the pot. With a ladle, skim off the foam as it rises to the surface. Ladle off all the butter fat into another container, this is the clarified butter, and leave the water and milk solids, which are reserved for adding to Brown Butter Sauces.

FROMAGE BLANC BATTER

2/3 cup flour
1/2 cup cornstarch
2 tablespoons baking powder
1 egg
1/3 cup fromage blanc
Water

Chef's Note: Fromage blanc is a fresh cow's milk farmer's cheese. Mix flour, cornstarch and baking powder together in bowl. In another bowl, whisk egg into fromage blanc. Whisk the egg and cheese mixture into the flour mixture, adding just enough water to create a batter consistency.

BEURRE BLANC
YIELDS 1 1/4 CUPS

1/3 cup clam juice
1/3 cup Fish Fumet (see page 252)
2 tablespoons julienned shallot
1 tablespoon lemon juice
2/3 cup dry white wine
1 bay leaf
1 cup unsalted butter, softened and
    divided
Salt

Place the clam juice, fumet, shallot, lemon juice, wine and bay leaf in a medium pot.

Bring to a boil, reduce heat and simmer slowly until reduced by half, or until about 2/3 cup of liquid remains. Strain through a chinois into another small pot. Soften butter by leaving it at room temperature for 3 hours or placing it in the microwave for 20 seconds. Put 1/4 cup softened butter in the container of a blender. Bring the wine reduction back to a boil and pour over the butter in the blender, cover and run the blender on high a few seconds until the butter has emulsified with the reduction. Working quickly and with the blender running on high, add the remaining softened butter, 1/4 cup at a time, with the blender running on high until the emulsion slightly thickens. Adjust seasoning with salt and lemon juice to taste. Transfer to a clean warmed thermos or metal bain and keep warm.

BEURRE BLANC REDUCTION
YIELDS 2 CUPS

2/3 cup clam juice
2/3 cup Fish Fumet (see page 252)
3 tablespoons julienned shallot
1 tablespoon lemon juice
1 1/2 cups dry white wine
2 bay leaves

Place all ingredients in a medium pot. Bring to a boil, reduce heat and simmer slowly until reduced by one-third, or to approximately 2 cups of liquid; strain and reserve for the chorizo mussel sauce.

BRIOCHE
YIELDS 6 (4-X-9-INCH) LOAVES

2 tablespoons yeast
1 1/4 cups flour
1 1/3 cups milk
13 eggs
7 1/2 cups flour
1/3 cup sugar
6 teaspoons salt
1 pound 6 ounces butter, softened or
    2 1/2 cups whipped

Preheat oven to 350° F. Mix yeast and 1 1/4 cups flour. Warm milk to 105° F and add to yeast mixture. Before adding, be sure milk is warm, not hot to the touch. Whisk milk in for 1 minute to develop gluten. Let sit 20 minutes. Mixture should have a light, bubbly texture when ready. In the meantime, mix dry ingredients in a separate bowl. Once yeast mixture is ready, whisk in the eggs and beat until incorporated. Place mixture into a stand mixer fitted with a dough hook. On low speed, slowly start adding the dry ingredients. Once incorporated, switch speed to medium and let run 10 minutes or until dough stretches to thin membrane when pulled. At this stage, add one-third of the softened butter and mix until incorporated. Transfer dough to bowl and cover with plastic wrap sprayed with nonstick spray. Refrigerate overnight. Turn out dough on floured surface and cut twelve equal portions. Cup each portion with the palm of your hand and roll with a circular motion until dough forms a smooth ball. Place two balls of dough into each 4-x-9-inch loaf pan. Let rise until doubled, about 2 hours. Bake for 16 to 20 minutes, or until firm with nicely golden brown crust. *Chef's Note:* This recipe yields six loaves. Once baked, Brioche can be frozen for up to one month. To defrost, leave out at room temperature for about 45 minutes to 1 hour. Having it on hand will be convenient when cooking from this book as it is used in many of the recipes.

PASTA DOUGH

1 pound flour (about 5 cups)
4 large eggs
2 teaspoons cold water

Mound the flour in the center of a work table; make a well in the center. Crack eggs into a small bowl and whisk together with the water. Pour egg mixture into the well and, with the tips of your fingers, rotate the eggs in a circular motion, gathering a little flour with each swirl. Continue until it begins to form into a ball. Knead until smooth and elastic, about 5 minutes. Wrap in plastic and let rest in the refrigerator for 2 hours. Run the dough through a pasta machine into sheets. Cut according to recipe.

PÂTÉ BRISEE
YIELDS 10 POTPIES

3 cups flour
1 tablespoon baking powder
2 teaspoons salt
1 teaspoon sugar
1/2 pound unsalted cold butter, diced
3/4 cup milk

Mix flour, baking powder, salt and sugar in the bowl of a stand mixer. Add the butter and run at low speed for 5 minutes, or until the pieces of butter are pea-sized. Add the milk and mix for a few seconds more. Turn out the dough on a floured surface. Knead lightly, gathering dough into a ball. Wrap with plastic and refrigerate for 1 hour. On a marble slab or flat cold surface, roll out dough to 1/8-inch thickness and cut out rounds according to recipe. Once cut, this dough freezes well.

BLACK TRUFFLE VINAIGRETTE
YIELDS 1/2 CUP

2 tablespoons white wine vinegar
1 tablespoon diced shallots
1/2 teaspoon salt
1 tablespoon black truffle puree
6 tablespoons canola oil
1 teaspoon black truffle oil
1/4 teaspoon freshly ground black pepper

Place vinegar, shallots and salt in a small bowl; let sit 15 minutes. Add the black truffle puree and slowly add the canola oil in a steady stream while whisking constantly. Add the black truffle oil and freshly ground black pepper.

CHAMPAGNE VINAIGRETTE
YIELDS 1/2 CUP

2 tablespoons champagne vinegar
1 tablespoon diced shallot
1 teaspoon salt
1/2 teaspoon Dijon mustard
6 tablespoons canola oil
1/2 teaspoon freshly ground pepper

Place vinegar, shallot, salt and mustard in a mixing bowl and let sit for 15 minutes. Slowly add the oil, whisking constantly. Add the freshly ground pepper.

CHIANTI WINE VINAIGRETTE
YIELDS 1/2 CUP

2 tablespoons chianti vinegar
1 teaspoon water
2 teaspoons shallots
1/4 teaspoon salt
6 tablespoons extra virgin olive oil
1/8 teaspoon freshly ground pepper

Place the vinegar, water, shallots and salt in a bowl; let sit for 15 minutes. Add the olive oil in a slow steady stream while whisking constantly; add freshly ground pepper.

CREAMY CIDER VINAIGRETTE
YIELDS 3/4 CUP

2 tablespoons apple cider vinegar
1 tablespoon Apple Cider Gastrique
   (see page 249)
2 teaspoons diced shallot
1/4 teaspoon salt
1/4 teaspoon dry mustard
1 tablespoon mayonnaise
3 tablespoons crème fraîche
1/4 cup canola oil
1/4 teaspoon black pepper

Place vinegar, gastrique, shallot, salt and mustard in a bowl and let steep 15 minutes; whisk in mayonnaise and crème fraîche. Add the oil in a slow steady stream while whisking constantly to emulsify. Season with pepper.

CREAMY MUSTARD VINAIGRETTE
YIELDS 3/4 CUP

2 tablespoons white wine vinegar
1 tablespoon diced shallot
1 teaspoon salt
2 tablespoons mayonnaise
1 1/2 tablespoons crème fraîche
2 teaspoons grain mustard
1/4 cup canola oil
1/2 teaspoon freshly ground pepper

Place the vinegar, shallot and salt in a small bowl; let steep for 15 minutes. Add the mayonnaise, crème fraîche and mustard. Add the oil in a slow steady stream while whisking constantly to emulsify. Season with pepper.

CREAMY TRUFFLE VINAIGRETTE
YIELDS 3/4 CUP

2 tablespoons white wine vinegar
1 tablespoon diced shallots
1 teaspoon salt
2 tablespoons mayonnaise
1 1/2 tablespoons crème fraîche
2 teaspoons black truffle puree
1/4 cup canola oil
1/2 teaspoon freshly ground pepper
1 teaspoon black truffle oil

Place the vinegar, shallot and salt in a small bowl; let steep for 15 minutes. Add the mayonnaise, crème fraîche and truffle puree. Add oil in a slow, steady stream, whisking constantly to emulsify, and then add freshly ground pepper and truffle oil.

DILL-SHALLOT VINAIGRETTE
YIELDS 1/2 CUP

2 tablespoons unseasoned rice vinegar
1 teaspoon salt
1 tablespoon diced shallot
1/3 cup canola oil
1/4 teaspoon black pepper
2 teaspoons chopped fresh dill

Place vinegar, salt and shallot in a mixing bowl and set aside for 15 minutes. Slowly add the oil in a steady stream while whisking constantly. Add the pepper. A few minutes before serving, add chopped dill. *Chef's Note: The vinegar will discolor the dill if added too soon.*

MISO VINAIGRETTE
YIELDS 3/4 CUP

3 tablespoons miso paste, red or white
2 tablespoons pickled ginger vinegar
2 tablespoons seasoned rice vinegar
10 tablespoons canola oil

Chef's Note: Pickled ginger vinegar is simply the liquid in a jar of pickled ginger. If you do not have pickled ginger vinegar, you may substitute 2 tablespoons seasoned rice vinegar. Place the miso in a large bowl, add vinegars and whisk until smooth. Add oil in a slow, steady stream while whisking constantly to emulsify.

PUMPKIN SEED VINAIGRETTE
YIELDS 1 CUP

2 tablespoons pumpkin seeds, shelled
1 teaspoon canola oil
1/4 cup apple cider vinegar
4 teaspoons diced shallot
1 teaspoon salt
1/2 teaspoon Coleman's dry mustard
10 tablespoons canola oil
2 tablespoons pumpkin seed oil
1/2 teaspoon freshly ground black pepper

Preheat oven to 350° F. Toss the pumpkin seeds with half the canola oil; place on a baking sheet and toast in the oven for 6 minutes, or until brown and fragrant. Place vinegar and toasted pumpkin seeds in a blender and puree until smooth. Strain through a chinois, pressing down with the bottom of a ladle to extract all the liquid. The yield

un batidor whisk

should be 4 tablespoons; if not, apple cider vinegar can be added to reach measurement. Place the strained cider vinegar-pumpkin seeds puree in a bowl with the shallots, salt and dry mustard; let steep for 15 minutes. Add the oils in a steady stream while whisking constantly to emulsify. Add freshly ground pepper.

SHERRY VINAIGRETTE
YIELDS 1/2 CUP

1/4 cup dry sherry
1/4 cup Chicken Stock (see page 252)
2 teaspoons diced shallot
1 sprig thyme
2 tablespoons sherry vinegar
1 tablespoon diced shallot
1/2 teaspoon salt
6 tablespoons canola oil
1/4 teaspoon freshly ground black pepper

Place first four ingredients in a nonreactive pot and slowly reduce to 2 tablespoons; strain into a mixing bowl. Add vinegar, 1 tablespoon shallot and salt to the same bowl and let sit for 15 minutes. Add oil in a slow steady stream while whisking constantly to emulsify. Add freshly ground pepper.

WILD MUSHROOM VINAIGRETTE
YIELDS 3 CUPS

1 cup Guinea Hen Jus (see page 251)
2 tablespoons sherry vinegar
1/2 teaspoon grain mustard
1/2 teaspoon salt
2 teaspoons black truffle puree
1 tablespoon diced shallot
1/3 cup canola oil
1 cup Pan-Roasted Mushrooms (see page 257)
1/2 teaspoon freshly ground black pepper

Slowly reduce Guinea Hen Jus to 2 tablespoons. *Chef's Note: You may substitute chicken stock.* Transfer the reduced jus to a bowl and add vinegar, mustard, salt, truffle puree and shallot. Mix well and let sit for 15 minutes; add the oil in a slow, steady stream whisking constantly to emulsify. Roughly chop the Pan-Roasted Mushrooms and add to the mixture with freshly ground black pepper.

BASIL OIL
YIELDS 1/3 CUP

1 1/2 cups packed fresh basil leaves
1/2 cup canola or rice bran oil

Chef's Note: For green oils (basil, mint and parsley), the amount of oil can vary slightly according to the size of blender container used. Just remember you need enough oil to barely cover the herbs and be above the top of the blender's blades to ensure a smooth puree. Pick the basil leave and discard the stems. Bring a large pot of water to a boil. Add the basil leaves and submerge into the water with a skimmer. Blanch for 15 seconds and then refresh under cold running water. Ring out the excess water, roughly chop the basil and transfer to the container of a blender. Add oil, cover, and blend on high for 4 minutes. Pour into a cheesecloth-lined sieve over a bain-marie. Drain for 2 hours; store in a squeeze bottle and refrigerate until ready to use.

BEET OIL
YIELDS 1/2 CUP

About 3 large beets
1/4 cup canola oil

Run beets through a juice extractor to yield 1 cup of beet juice. In a 1-quart saucepan, slowly reduce juice to 1/4 cup over low heat and then transfer to the container of a blender. Add the oil, cover, and run on high for 30 seconds; store in a squeeze bottle with a fine tip. *Chef's Note: The mottled broken look is the goal for presentation; therefore, it is important not to emulsify the oil and beet juice completely.*

MINT OIL
YIELDS 1/3 CUP

1 1/2 cups mint leaves, packed
    (roughly 2 bunches)
1/2 cup canola oil

Pick the mint leaves, discarding stems. Bring a large pot of water to a boil. Add the mint leaves and submerge them into the water with a skimmer. Blanch for 15 seconds and then refresh under cold running water. Ring out the excess water and transfer to the container of a blender. Add oil, cover, and blend on high for 4 minutes. Pour into a cheesecloth-lined sieve over a bain-marie and let drain for 2 hours. Store in a squeeze bottle.

PARSLEY OIL
YIELDS 1/3 CUP

1 1/2 cups packed parsley leaves
    (about 2 bunches)
1/2 cup canola oil

Pick the parsley leaves, discarding the stems. Bring a large pot of water to a boil. Add parsley leaves and submerge into the water with a skimmer. Cook for 15 seconds and then refresh under cold running water. Ring out the excess water and transfer to the container of a blender. Add oil, cover, and blend on high for 3 minutes. Pour into a cheesecloth-lined sieve over a bain-marie and let drain for 2 hours. Store in a squeeze bottle.

APPLE CIDER GASTRIQUE
YIELDS 1/4 CUP

2 tablespoons water
1/4 cup sugar
1/4 cup apple cider vinegar
1 bay leaf
1/2 cinnamon stick
1 clove
1 small piece star anise
1 teaspoon whole black pepper
1/2 vanilla bean, split in half

In a 1-quart saucepan over medium heat, mix water and sugar together. Have a pastry brush and some water nearby, as during cooking, the sugar may crystallize on the sides of the pot and you'll need to brush down the sides of the pot with a wet pastry brush. This helps to prevent the sugar from re-crystallizing when the gastrique is cool. As sugar syrup cooks, it will begin to brown around the edges first; gently swirl pan to prevent burning in spots. Do not mix the sugar syrup with a utensil once it begins to thicken. Continue cooking until sugar syrup turns a golden brown, remove from heat and carefully add the vinegar. Return to the heat and add spices; cook until mixture is smooth, about 2 minutes. Strain through a fine sieve while still warm.

FENNEL GASTRIQUE
YIELDS 1/4 CUP

2 tablespoons water
1/4 cup sugar
2 tablespoons white wine vinegar
2 teaspoons fennel seed

In a 1-quart saucepan over medium heat, mix water and sugar together. Have a pastry brush and some water nearby, as during cooking, the sugar may crystallize on the sides of the pot and you'll need to brush the sides of the pot with a wet pastry brush. This helps to prevent the sugar from re-crystallizing when the gastrique is cool. As sugar syrup cooks, it will begin to brown around the edges first; gently swirl pan to prevent burning in spots. Do not mix the sugar syrup with a utensil once it begins to thicken. Continue cooking until sugar syrup turns a golden brown, remove from heat and carefully add the vinegar. Return to the heat and add the fennel seed; cook until mixture is smooth, about 2 minutes. Strain through a fine sieve while still warm.

HUCKLEBERRY GASTRIQUE
YIELDS 1/2 CUP

2 tablespoons water
1/4 cup sugar
1/4 cup red wine vinegar
1/4 cup huckleberries

In a 1-quart saucepan over medium heat, mix water and sugar together. Have a pastry brush and some water nearby, as during cooking, the sugar may crystallize on the sides of the pot and you'll need to brush the sides of the pot with a wet pastry brush. This helps to prevent the sugar from re-crystallizing when the gastrique is cool. As sugar syrup cooks, it will begin to brown around the edges first; gently swirl pan to prevent burning in spots. Do not mix the sugar syrup with a utensil once it begins to thicken. Continue cooking until sugar syrup turns a golden brown, remove from heat and carefully add the vinegar. Return to the heat and add the huckleberries; cook until mixture is smooth, about 2 minutes.

PEAR GASTRIQUE
YIELDS 1/4 CUP

2 tablespoons water
1/4 cup sugar
1/4 cup pear vinegar
1 bay leaf
1/2 cinnamon stick
1 clove
1 small piece star anise
1 teaspoon whole black pepper
1/2 vanilla bean, split in half

In a 1-quart saucepan over medium heat, mix water and sugar together. Have a pastry brush and some water nearby, as during cooking, the sugar may crystallize on the sides of the pot and you'll need to brush the sides of the pot with a wet pastry brush. This helps to prevent the sugar from re-crystallizing when the gastrique is cool. As sugar syrup cooks, it will begin to brown around the edges first; gently swirl pan to prevent burning in spots. Do not mix the sugar syrup with a utensil once it begins to thicken. Continue cooking until sugar syrup turns a golden brown, remove from heat and carefully add the vinegar. Return to the heat and add the spices; cook until mixture is smooth, about 2 minutes. Strain through a fine sieve while still warm.

RED WINE GASTRIQUE
YIELDS 1/4 CUP

2 tablespoons water
1/4 cup sugar
1/4 cup red wine vinegar

In a 1-quart saucepan over medium heat, mix water and sugar together. Have a pastry brush and some water nearby, as during cooking, the sugar may crystallize on the sides of the pot and you'll need to brush the sides of the pot with a wet pastry brush. This helps to prevent the sugar from re-crystallizing when the gastrique is cool. As sugar syrup cooks, it will begin to brown around the edges first; gently swirl pan to prevent burning in spots. Do not mix the sugar syrup with a utensil once it begins to thicken. Continue cooking until sugar syrup turns a golden brown, remove from heat and carefully add the vinegar. Return to the heat and cook until mixture is smooth, about 2 minutes.

SHERRY-LAVENDER GASTRIQUE
YIELDS 1/4 CUP

2 tablespoons water
1/4 cup sugar
1/4 cup sherry vinegar
1 teaspoon whole black peppercorns
5 sprigs lavender

In a 1-quart saucepan over medium heat, mix water and sugar together. Have a pastry brush and some water nearby, as during cooking, the sugar may crystallize on the sides of the pot and you'll need to brush the sides of the pot with a wet pastry brush. This helps to prevent the sugar from re-crystallizing when the gastrique is cool. As sugar syrup cooks, it will begin to brown around the edges first; gently swirl pan to prevent burning in spots. Do not mix the sugar syrup with a utensil once it begins to thicken. Continue cooking until sugar syrup turns a golden brown, remove from heat and carefully add the vinegar. Return to the heat and add the whole black peppercorns and lavender; cook until mixture is smooth, about 2 minutes. Strain through a fine sieve while still warm.

BALSAMIC REDUCTION
YIELDS 1/2 CUP

1 cup Lamb Stock (see page 252)
1 cup balsamic vinegar
2 tablespoons sugar
1 clove garlic, chopped
1 medium shallot, chopped
1 sprig thyme
2 bay leaves
1 sprig rosemary
1 tablespoon butter

Place all ingredients except the butter into a nonreactive saucepan; bring to a simmer and reduce to 1/2 cup, about 40 minutes. Strain through a chinois; return to heat and whisk in the butter. Set aside and keep warm.

BALSAMIC SYRUP
YIELDS 1/3 CUP

2 cups balsamic vinegar

Place balsamic vinegar into a small nonreactive pot and slowly reduce on the lowest heat possible to a light syrup-like consistency; store in a squeeze bottle until ready to use.

CABERNET SYRUP
YIELDS 1/2 CUP

3 cups Cabernet Savignon
1 1/2 cups Veal Stock (see page 253)
1/4 cup sugar
3 bay leaves
4 parsley stems
5 sprigs thyme
1/4 cup julienned shallots
3 cloves garlic, crushed
10 black peppercorns

Place all the ingredients in a nonreactive saucepan. Bring to a simmer, skimming frequently. Slowly reduce to a syrupy consistency, about 1 1/2 hours. Strain through a fine sieve; keep warm.

JALAPEÑO SYRUP
YIELDS 1/4 CUP

1/4 cup sugar
6 tablespoons water, divided
1 jalapeño, sliced into rings

Mix sugar and 2 tablespoons water in a small heavy-bottom pot. Over medium heat, cook sugar mixture until a golden brown caramel. Add remaining water. Cook 2 minutes more, or until the syrup is smooth. Remove from heat. Add jalapeño slices and let steep for 5 minutes and then strain. *Chef's Note:* This syrup is not overly spicy, but for less heat, remove the seeds from the jalapeño.

PORT SYRUP
YIELDS 1/3 CUP

2 cups port wine
1/4 cup sugar
1/4 vanilla bean, split
1/4 cinnamon stick
1 point star anise
1 teaspoon whole black peppercorns
1 bay leaf

Place all ingredients together in a small nonreactive pot. Bring to a simmer and slowly reduce to a syrup consistency over low heat; stir frequently. While still warm, strain through a fine sieve.

RED WINE SYRUP
YIELDS 1 CUP

3 tablespoons canola oil
1 cup diced (1-inch) onion
1/2 cup diced (1-inch) celeriac
1/2 cup diced (1-inch) carrot
1 cup diced (1-inch) apple
1/2 cup diced (1-inch) leek
4 cups red wine
2 cups port
1/2 cup prunes
2 cups Chicken Stock (see page 252)

Heat oil in a nonreactive heavy pot over high heat until almost smoking; add onion, celeriac, carrot, apple and leek. Allow the vegetables to begin caramelizing before moving. Continue to cook over high heat until caramelized, about 10 minutes. Add the red wine, port, and prunes. Turn heat to low and reduce by three-fourths, skimming frequently. Strain through a chinois into a smaller pot, pressing down with the back of a ladle to extract all the liquid. Return to low heat; add Chicken Stock and reduce to a syrup consistency, about 20 minutes. Keep warm.

RED WINE SAUCE
YIELDS 3 CUPS

3 tablespoons canola oil
4 ounces lean beef scrap, cut in 1/2 inch cubes
1/3 cup roughly chopped shallots
1 cup sliced white mushrooms
5 sprigs thyme
3 cups red wine
4 cups Veal Stock (see page 253)

In a heavy bottom pot, heat the oil until almost smoking. Add the beef pieces one at a time and let cook undisturbed until

deeply browned on the bottom; turn over one at a time. When the second side has browned, add the shallot and mushrooms. The shallots and mushrooms will begin to sweat and deglaze the pan. Stir with a wooden spoon, scraping up the browned bits on the bottom of the pan. When the mushrooms are soft and the shallot translucent, about 4 minutes, add the red wine and bring to a simmer; slowly reduce until almost dry. Add the Veal Stock and simmer slowly, skimming frequently until reduced by one-fourth. Strain through a fine sieve and season with salt and pepper to taste.

GUINEA HEN JUS
YIELDS 2 CUPS

Bones from 1 guinea hen (see page 88)
1/3 cup canola oil
1/2 cup large-dice onion
1/4 cup large-dice carrot
1/4 cup large-dice leek
1/4 cup large-dice celery
1 clove garlic, crushed
3 cups Chicken Stock (see page 252)
2 cups Veal Stock (see page 253)
3 cups water
5 black peppercorns
1 sprig thyme

With a heavy cleaver, chop the bones into 2-inch pieces. Heat the oil in a heavy-bottom 4-quart saucepan over high heat

until almost smoking. Add guinea hen bones one piece at a time. Allow bones to brown deeply and then turn over and brown other side. When second side is brown, add 1/4 cup water and scrape bottom of pan with a wooden spoon to deglaze. Keep cooking until bones caramelize again and then add the onion, carrot, leek, celery and garlic. When the vegetables begin to sweat, the liquid will deglaze the pan again. Continue to cook until the vegetables begin to brown, about 5 minutes. Add the Chicken Stock, Veal Stock and remaining water. Bring to a simmer, skimming frequently until reduced by half, about 1 1/2 hours. Strain through a chinois or fine sieve into a smaller pot, pressing down on the solids with the bottom of a ladle to extract all the liquid. Add the peppercorns and thyme. Continue to reduce slowly by one-fourth, skimming frequently. Strain again through a fine sieve. Reserve 1 cup of the jus for Wild Mush-room Vinaigrette (see page 248).

MUSHROOM JUS
YIELDS 4 CUPS

1/4 cup dry porcini
1 cup hot water
3 tablespoons canola oil
2 cups julienned yellow onions
2 cloves garlic, chopped
6 cups sliced assorted mushrooms
1/4 cup tomato paste
1 cup sherry wine
6 cups water
10 sprigs thyme
1 tablespoon soy sauce

Soak the dry porcini in hot water until hydrated. Heat the oil in a heavy-bottom pot over high heat. Add the onions and reduce heat to medium. When the onions begin to brown lightly, begin stirring frequently with a wooden spoon, scraping the bottom to loosen up any browned bits and redistribute into the onions. Occasionally add a few tablespoons of water and scrape the bottom to completely deglaze. Once the onions are golden brown, about 20 minutes, add the garlic and mushrooms. Cook until the mushrooms have given up all their liquid and begin to caramelize, about 10 minutes. Add the tomato paste and cook about 5 minutes more, or until it begins to caramelize on the bottom of the pan. Immediately add the sherry wine and porcinis with their liquid, being careful not to include the sediment at the bottom. Scrape the bottom of the pan with a wooden spoon and deglaze again, allowing the sherry and porcini liquid to reduce until almost dry. Add the water and thyme and bring to a simmer for 45 minutes. Strain liquid through a fine chinois and add soy sauce.

ROUX

7 tablespoons Clarified Butter (see page 246)
1 cup all-purpose flour

In a heavy-bottom pot, mix the butter and flour until smooth. Cook over low heat for 15 minutes, stirring frequently with a wooden spoon or heatproof spatula to avoid scorching. Remove from the heat and let cool to room temperature before using. Transfer to an airtight container and store in the refrigerator for up to 1 month. Remove from the refrigerator and bring to room temperature before using.

CHICKEN STOCK
YIELDS 4 QUARTS

5 pounds chicken bones
6 quarts water
1 1/2 cups roughly chopped yellow onions
3/4 cup roughly chopped carrots
3/4 cup roughly chopped celery
3 bay leaves
4 sprigs thyme
10 parsley stems

Cover chicken bones with cold water and over medium heat, bring to a simmer. Strain through a colander, discarding liquid. Rinse the bones with cold water and place back in pot. Add 6 quarts water and place over medium heat. Slowly bring to a boil, skimming any fat or impurities that rise to the surface. Reduce heat and simmer for 1 1/2 hours, adding more water if needed to keep bones covered. Add the vegetables and herbs and let simmer for 1 hour more, skimming frequently. Put the stock through a fine strainer and chill.

ASIAN DUCK STOCK
YIELDS 4 QUARTS

Bones from 3 ducks or from cooked peking duck, chopped in 2-inch pieces
4 quarts Chicken Stock (see this page)
2 quarts water
2 pieces star anise
1 thumb-size piece ginger
6 scallions, white part only

Preheat oven to 350° F. Rinse and pat dry the duck bones; arrange in a single layer in a roasting pan and roast in oven for 45 minutes, or until browned. Drain off any rendered fat. Place duck bones in a stockpot and cover with Chicken Stock and water. Heat the roasting pan over medium heat and add 1 cup of water to deglaze, scraping the bottom with a wooden spoon to loosen any browned bits; add the deglazing liquid to the stockpot and bring to a simmer, skimming frequently. Simmer for 2 hours, adding more water if needed to cover the bones. Add the star anise, ginger and scallions; simmer for 30 minutes more. Strain and chill.

FISH FUMET
YIELDS 3 QUARTS

2 pounds white fish bones
4 quarts water
1/2 cup white wine
1 cup roughly chopped onion
1/2 cup roughly chopped celery
1/2 cup chopped leek
3 bay leaves

10 parsley stems
1 sprig tarragon

Chef's Note: The best bones to use are from white-fleshed fish like sole or halibut. Rinse the fish bones under cold water. Chop the bones into smaller pieces, if necessary, and cover with 4 quarts water and the wine. Over medium heat, bring to a simmer, skimming frequently. Add the vegetables and herbs and continue to simmer for 40 minutes. Ladle the stock through a chinois or fine strainer.

GUINEA HEN STOCK
YIELDS 3 QUARTS

Bones from 3 guinea hens
4 quarts Chicken Stock (see this page)
2 quarts water

Preheat oven to 350° F. Rinse and pat dry the bones; arrange in a single layer roasting pan and roast in the oven for 35 minutes, or until browned. Transfer the bones to a stockpot and cover with chicken stock and water. Heat the roasting pan over medium heat and add 1 cup of the liquid, scraping the bottom with a wooden spoon to loosen any browned bits. Add to stockpot. Bring to a simmer for 2 1/2 hours, skimming frequently and adding more water if needed to keep bones covered. Strain through a chinois and cool.

LAMB STOCK
YIELDS 4 CUPS (CAN FREEZE EXCESS)

2 pounds of lamb bones and scraps
Cold water to cover
1/2 cup tomato paste
1 cup diced onion
1/2 cup diced celery
1/2 cup diced carrot
2 cloves garlic
12 sprigs rosemary

Preheat oven to 425° F. Arrange bones and scraps in a single layer in a roasting pan and roast in the oven for 45 minutes, or until a rich brown color. Transfer bones to a large pot and cover with cold water. Heat the roasting pan over medium heat and add 2 cups water to deglaze, scraping the bottom with a wooden spoon to loosen any browned bits. Add the deglazing liquid to the pot and bring to a simmer over medium heat, skimming frequently. Simmer this way for 2 hours. Place the tomato paste in a mixing bowl and add some of the hot stock and whisk together until a smooth pourable consistency. Add to lamb stock and simmer another 2 hours, adding more water if needed to keep bones covered. Add vegetables, simmer 1 hour more; add rosemary and strain.

VEAL STOCK
YIELDS 8 CUPS

4 pounds meaty veal bones, cut in 2-inch pieces
10 quarts water
1 cup tomato paste
2 cups diced (1-inch) onion
1 cup diced (1-inch) carrot
1 cup diced (1-inch) leeks
5 sprigs thyme
10 parsley stems

Place raw veal bones in a large pot. Cover with cold water and slowly bring to a boil over medium heat, skimming fat and impurities that rise to the surface. When the water reaches a boil, immediately drain through a colander; discard the liquid. Rinse the veal bones under cold water and return to the clean pot. Cover with 10 quarts water. *Chef's Note: Keep the pot offset on the burner to cause the fat and impurities to gather on one side, making it easier to skim.* Return to medium heat, skimming frequently and bring to a bare simmer for 2 hours. Place the tomato paste in a mixing bowl and whisk hot broth into the paste until thinned to a pourable consistency. Add the paste mixture back to the stock and simmer 3 hours more, continuing to skim. Add more water if needed to keep bones covered. Add the vegetables and herbs and simmer 1 hour more. Strain the liquid into another pot. Reserve the bones for a second veal stock. Return the pot of strained stock to a low simmer and slowly reduce by one-fourth.

VEGETABLE STOCK
YIELDS 2 1/2 CUPS

1 cup roughly chopped yellow onion
1/2 cup roughly diced carrot
1/4 cup roughly diced celery
1/2 cup roughly chopped leek
5 parsley stems
1 sprig tarragon
5 sprigs chervil
1 bay leaf
2 1/2 cups water
2 tablespoons white wine
5 black peppercorns

Place all ingredients in a 1-quart canning jar; cover with re-sealable lid. Submerge jar in a water bath, covering top of jar by 1 inch. Bring to a boil and simmer for 45 minutes. Remove jar from the water and allow jar of stock to cool with lid still on. To use, open jar and strain.

FIG-SHIITAKE SAUCE
YIELDS 2 CUPS

3 tablespoons canola oil
12 medium shiitake mushroom caps, cut into quarters
12 fresh black mission figs, cut in half
2 cups Guinea Hen Jus (see page 251)
1/4 cup Fig Jam (see page 257)
Salt and pepper

Heat the oil in a skillet over medium heat. Add the mushrooms and sauté for 2 minutes, or until soft. Add the figs and cook for 1 minute more. Add the Guinea Hen Jus and simmer over medium heat until reduced by one-third. Add the Fig Jam and season with salt and pepper.

PLUM SAUCE
YIELDS 2 CUPS

1/2 pound Santa Rosa plums, pitted
1/4 cup honey
2 teaspoons red wine vinegar
2 teaspoons pickled ginger

Roughly chop plums and place in a 2-quart nonreactive saucepan. Add honey, vinegar and pickled ginger and then bring to a boil over medium heat. Reduce to a simmer and continue cooking for about 25 minutes over low heat, or until the plums have completely cooked. Transfer to the container of a blender, cover, and puree until smooth. Let cool, transfer to a squeeze bottle and refrigerate until ready to use. *Chef's Note: The plum sauce may also be preserved in canning jars by using the hot water bath method.*

SWEET SOY
YIELDS 1 1/2 CUPS

1 (1-inch) square ginger, crushed
1 stalk lemongrass, crushed and roughly chopped
1 cup soy sauce
1 cup brown sugar

Place ginger, lemongrass, soy sauce and brown sugar in a nonreactive saucepan over medium heat. Bring to a simmer for 5 minutes. Set aside, allowing the lemongrass and ginger to steep in the liquid for 5 minutes; strain and chill.

GRIBICHE
YIELDS 2/3 CUP

2 eggs
2 teaspoons dijon mustard
2 tablespoons diced shallot
1 1/2 tablespoons chopped capers
2 cornichons, diced
1 tablespoon diced Fennel ala Greque
4 teaspoons red wine vinegar
4 tablespoons canola oil
2 tablespoons extra virgin olive oil
Salt and pepper
2 tablespoons fines herbes

Drop whole eggs into boiling water and cook for 3 1/2 minutes; transfer to an ice water bath. Peel and place soft-boiled eggs in a mixing bowl with mustard, shallot, capers, cornichons, fennel and vinegar. Add the oil in a steady stream, while mashing with a fork. You do not want to completely emulsify the oil and create a mayonnaise-like sauce but rather a thick relish-like consistency. Season to taste with salt and pepper. Mix in the fines herbes just before serving.

RISOTTO BASE
YIELDS 6 SERVINGS

2 cups Vegetable Stock (see this page), Chicken Stock (see page 252) or water
3 tablespoons olive oil
1/4 cup yellow onion
1 cup carnaroli risotto rice

Chef's Note: Carnaroli rice is one of three major varieties of risotto rice; arborio rice is the most popular and will work just fine here. I like carnaroli because it creates a creamier textured risotto. Place stock or water in a saucepan and bring to a simmer. In a 2-quart saucepan, heat the oil over medium heat and add the onion; cook until translucent, about 2 minutes. Add rice to the onions and stir to coat with oil; add just enough boiling stock to barely cover the rice mixture. Keep heat at a simmer, stirring occasionally, adding more liquid as needed to keep the rice covered. After the last liquid is added, simmer for 1 minute more. At this point, there should still be a creamy liquid surrounding the rice. Turn out precooked risotto into a shallow pan; mix occasionally with a spatula while cooling to keep all the rice evenly cooked. When completely cool, store in a tightly sealed container until ready to use.

BASIL PESTO
YIELDS 1 CUP

1 1/4 cups packed basil (about 2 bunches)
2 tablespoons olive oil
1/4 cup canola oil
1/4 cup pine nuts
2 cloves garlic
3 tablespoons Parmesan cheese
1 teaspoon salt
1/8 teaspoon pepper

Bring a large pot of water to a boil. Pick the basil leaves and discard the stems. Blanch basil in boiling water for 20 seconds and then pour through a strainer and refresh under cold running water. Ring out the excess water from the basil. Place the oils, pine nuts and garlic in the container of a blender, cover, and puree until it becomes a smooth paste. Add the blanched basil, blending again until smooth, adding more olive oil if needed. Be careful not to over-process or the basil will lose its bright green color. Stir in Parmesan cheese and season to taste with salt and pepper.

CILANTRO PESTO
YIELDS 1/2 CUP

3/4 cup roughly chopped cilantro, stems included
1 small clove garlic, chopped
6 tablespoons canola oil
1/2 teaspoon salt

Thoroughly wash the cilantro under cold running water before chopping. Puree garlic and oil in a blender; with blender running, add the cilantro and puree until smooth. Add salt and transfer to a squeeze bottle.

GARLIC CONFIT

24 cloves garlic
2 cups olive oil

Cut the root tips off the garlic cloves. Place oil and garlic cloves together in a small pot and heat slowly over medium heat. At the first sign of bubbles around the garlic, reduce heat to low. When the cloves are soft but not browned, about 10 minutes, remove from heat. Store oil and garlic together in the refrigerator covered. These will last several weeks. The oil can be used for salad dressings.

CRISPY LEEKS

2 large leeks
3 quarts rice bran oil or other neutral oil for frying

Remove and discard outer layer of each leek; cut off and discard green tops. Cut the white part of the leeks in half lengthwise and pull off the outer 5 or 6 layers. Press layers flat on cutting board and julienne.

Because the centers are difficult to julienne evenly, reserve them for stock. Wash the julienned leeks in a large bowl of cold water, swishing to loosen any dirt. Let sit, undisturbed, to allow the dirt to settle to the bottom of the bowl. Carefully scoop leeks off the top, drain in a colander and place in a pot of cold water. Bring water to a boil over high heat. Once boiling, strain leeks and refresh under cold running water. Place the oil in a pot large enough to allow the oil level to rise up while frying. Heat the oil to 300° F and sprinkle leeks into the oil, separating the strands with your fingers. Fry until golden brown and crispy; transfer to a paper towel to drain. *Chef's Note:* We have been using the neutral rice bran oil for several years for many reasons. Rice bran oil has a very light and delicate flavor, and food cooked with it absorbs up to 20 percent less oil. Rice bran oil also has a high smoking point, which makes it great for deep-frying, pan-searing or roasting. It is also hypoallergenic and has the highest cholesterol reduction capacity of any other oil.

CRISPY SHALLOTS
YIELDS 1 CUP

2 quarts rice bran oil or other neutral oil for frying
3 medium shallots
Flour
Salt and pepper

Chef's Note: If rice bran oil is not available, peanut or canola oil will work just fine. Place oil in a pot large enough to allow the oil to rise up when frying; heat to 300° F. Peel the shallots and with a Japanese mandolin, slice into thin rings. Season the flour with salt and pepper and then toss the shallots with the flour. Using your finger tips, break the shallots into individual rings; shake off excess flour. Fry in small batches until golden brown; transfer to a paper towel–lined plate and season lightly with salt.

CRISPY SHIITAKES
YIELDS 1 CUP

2 cups julienned shiitake mushrooms
3 tablespoons canola oil
Salt

Preheat oven to 350° F. In the kitchen, we refer to Crispy Shiitakes as vegetarian bacon bits because of their crunchy sweet and smoky flavors. Remove the stem from the mushrooms (reserve for Mushroom Jus page 251) and thinly slice the caps. Heat oil in a large skillet over medium heat. Add the mushrooms and sauté until softened and beginning to brown, about 3 minutes. Season liberally with salt. Transfer to a parchment-lined baking sheet and arrange in a single layer. Bake for 8 minutes, or until crispy. Transfer to a paper towel–lined plate. Store in single layers in an airtight container at room temperature.

PANCETTA CRISPS

Pancetta bacon, cut in 1-inch-long pieces

Preheat oven to 350° F. Lay out 1-inch-long pieces of pancetta bacon on a sheet pan between two sheets of parchment paper. Cover with another sheet pan and bake for 20 minutes or until browned and crispy. Drain on a paper towel–lined plate.

BASIL PUREE
YIELDS 1/2 CUP

3/4 cup packed basil leaves
1 small clove garlic
6 tablespoons oil

Pick the basil leaves, discarding the stems. Bring a pot of water to a boil and blanch basil leaves for 15 seconds. Pour through a strainer and refresh under cold running water; squeeze out excess water from the basil. Place the oil and garlic in the container of a blender, cover, and puree until smooth. Add the basil and puree until smooth.

PARSNIP PUREE
YIELDS 1 1/4 CUPS

3 cups peeled and cubed (1-inch)
    parsnips
4 cups cold water
2 teaspoons salt
2 tablespoons butter
Salt

Chef's Note: Select young, small, tender parsnips, avoiding larger starchy parsnips with a woody center. Place parsnip cubes

into cold water with salt; bring to a boil over high heat and then reduce heat to a simmer. Cook until tender and easily pierced with a paring knife, about 15 minutes. Drain parsnips and let steam for 1 minute. Transfer to a food processor fitted with a metal blade; while running, add the butter and puree until smooth. Season with salt.

FENNEL ALA GRECQUE

2 fennel bulbs
2 1/2 cups white vinegar
1 cup white wine
8 cloves garlic, sliced
1/2 cup julienned onion
1 lemon, cut in quarters
1 tablespoon fennel seed
6 bay leaves
1 tablespoon pepper
2 tablespoons coriander
2 1/2 cups olive oil

Cut off the tops and peel off tough outer layer of the fennel bulbs; cut into quarters. Remove as much of the core as possible, being careful to leave the wedge intact. Place all ingredients, except fennel

wedges, together in a nonreactive pot and bring to a simmer for 15 minutes. Add the fennel wedges; return to a simmer for 20 minutes, or until the fennel can be easily pierced with a paring knife. Cool and store in an airtight container in the refrigerator until ready to use.

FINES HERBES
YIELDS 1/4 CUP

1 tablespoon chopped tarragon
1 tablespoon chopped Italian parsley
1 tablespoon chopped chervil
1 tablespoon minced chives

Pick and finely chop the tarragon, parsley and chervil leaves. Mince the chives and mix together.

HERB SALAD
YIELDS 12 SMALL SALADS

1 head baby frisee
1 bunch chervil
1/2 bunch tarragon
1 bunch chives
Lemon juice
Olive oil
Salt and pepper

Wash and dry the frisee and herbs. With a pair of kitchen sheers, cut the light-colored center leaves of the frisee into a bowl, reserving the outer green leaves for a bitter greens salad mix. Pick the small fronds from the chervil, pick individual leaves from the tarragon and then cut the chives into 1-inch-long batonettes. Gently mix together. *Chef's Note:* You can also use micro greens, beet sprouts, fennel fronds, Italian parsley leaves and very small basil leaves. Because of their strong flavor and firm texture, avoid herbs like rosemary, sage and thyme. Take the amount of herb salad you need and toss in a bowl with a drop of lemon juice, a few drops oil, salt and pepper. Handle herbs gently; be careful not to overdress. Reserve remaining herbs for garnish and place them under a damp paper towel to keep from wilting.

OVEN-ROASTED TOMATOES

1 (28-ounce) can good-quality diced
   tomatoes, with juice
2 teaspoons olive oil

Preheat oven to 225° F. *Chef's Note:* Look for good-quality diced tomatoes with no sugar added. We use fresh roasted tomatoes in season; however, good-quality canned tomatoes are packed in peak season. Strain the tomatoes in a colander and thoroughly rinse the tomatoes under cold running water until the water runs clear; let them drain for about 10 minutes. Toss in a bowl with the oil and then spread in a single layer on a Silpat-lined sheet pan. Bake in a convection oven for 15 minutes, and then move the tomatoes around with a spatula—especially the ones on the outside edges, as they cook faster. Repeat this step until tomatoes are dehydrated but still moist, approximately 1 1/2 to 2 hours. Tomatoes will keep for several weeks in the refrigerator and are a key element in the flavor of Saffron Seafood Broth on page 80 and the tomato tarragon sauce on the Dungeness Crab Tasting on page 183. They can also be used to sweeten most sauces or broths.

ROASTED TOMATOES

12 Roma or Early Girl–variety tomatoes
3 cloves garlic
1/4 cup olive oil
Salt and pepper
1 teaspoon dry basil
1 teaspoon dry oregano
1 teaspoon dry thyme

Preheat oven to 225° F. Blanch and peel tomatoes (see Blanching, page 119). Cut tomatoes in half and remove the seeds. Crush the garlic cloves with the side of a knife and place in a mixing bowl with the oil; let sit for 15 minutes. Add salt, pepper and dry herbs. *Chef's Note:* When using dry herbs, we want to infuse the herb flavor into the tomatoes while roasting. Because we roast our tomatoes for 2 1/2 hours, we find the flavors of dried herbs still remain as prevalent at the end of roasting as in the beginning. Delicate herbs when fresh, such as basil, lose their strength over longer cooking times. A dry-herbs flavor, as a general rule, retains more of its essence over longer cooking periods. Toss the tomatoes in the olive oil mixture and arrange on a baking sheet lined with Silpat or parchment paper sprayed with nonstick spray. Roast tomatoes, in the oven, turning the sheet pan every 20 minutes to help tomatoes cook evenly. Roasting time should be about 2 1/2 hours. After tomatoes have cooled, if not using right away, cover with olive oil and refrigerate in an airtight container for up to 2 weeks.

POTATO PUREE
YIELDS 3 CUPS

2 large russet potatoes (about 1 1/2
   pounds)
2 large Yukon gold potatoes (about 3/4
   pound)
Cold water to cover
2 tablespoons salt
1/4 cup hot heavy cream
4 ounces cold butter, cut in cubes
1/8 teaspoon white pepper
Salt, to taste

Peel potatoes and cut the russet potatoes into quarters; cut the Yukon golds in half and then cut each half into quarters. *Chef's Note: The Yukon gold potatoes are slightly denser and take longer to cook; therefore, they must be cut into slightly smaller pieces so all potatoes are done at the same time.* Put potatoes into a medium pot and cover with cold water, add salt and bring to a boil. Immediately reduce heat to a simmer, cook until potatoes pierce easily with a paring knife, about 10 minutes. Drain potatoes into a colander and let steam for 1 minute to release moisture. Heat cream. Run the potatoes and butter together through a potato ricer and gently fold in the cream. As starch content of potatoes vary, the amount of cream needed can vary. If potatoes are a little overcooked, you may not need to add all the cream. Add white pepper and adjust the salt to taste.

QUATRE ÉPICES
YIELDS 1 TEASPOON

1/2 teaspoon freshly ground white pepper
1/4 teaspoon freshly ground nutmeg
1/8 teaspoon freshly ground cloves
1/8 teaspoon powdered ginger

Mix together and set aside until use.

SAUTÉED SWISS CHARD
YIELDS 6 SERVINGS

1 bunch red Swiss chard
2 tablespoons canola oil
1/2 teaspoon chopped garlic
2 tablespoons water
Salt and pepper

Clean the chard by grasping the stem between the index and middle finger where the leaves end and pull the leafy part through your fingers, tearing the leaf from the stem. In this recipe, use only the leaves. Wash chard by placing the leaves in a large bowl filled with cold water and swishing them around to loosen the dirt. Let the chard sit undisturbed for 5 minutes to allow all the dirt and grit to settle to the bottom of the bowl. Gently remove the leaves from the top of the water and drain in a colander. If the greens are particularly dirty, repeat cleaning process twice. Place canola oil and garlic in a large skillet over medium heat, when the garlic starts to sizzle, add the chard leaves and season immediately with the salt and pepper. With tongs, turn chard to cook evenly; continue cooking until wilted, about 2 minutes. Wrap in a terrycloth towel to prevent chard from bleeding color on the plate; keep warm.

SHIITAKE DUXELLES
YIELDS 1 CUP

5 cups shiitake mushroom caps, about
   1/2 pound
Sweet Soy (see page 253)

Remove the stems from shiitake mushrooms and reserve for Mushroom Jus (see page 251). Place mushroom caps and Sweet Soy in a 2-quart saucepan over medium heat. Simmer until the shiitakes are done, about 5 minutes. Strain the shiitakes and reserve the Sweet Soy. Place shiitakes in food processor fitted with a metal blade and pulse until finely minced. Set aside.

GARLIC BREAD CRUMBS
YIELDS 1 CUP

1 cup toasted panko
1/4 cup olive oil
2 tablespoons butter
4 cloves garlic, chopped
3/4 teaspoon salt
1/4 teaspoon black pepper

Preheat oven to 350° F. Arrange panko in a single layer on a lined baking sheet. Bake for 8 minutes, or until golden brown; transfer to a mixing bowl. Heat oil and butter together in a pan. When butter is melted, add the garlic and sauté until garlic is cooked but not browned, about 3 minutes. Pour garlic mixture over toasted panko and mix until fully incorporated. Season with salt and pepper.

PAN-ROASTED MUSHROOMS
YIELDS 3 CUPS

4 cups wild or domestic mushrooms, cleaned (about 1/2-pound)
2 tablespoons canola oil
1 tablespoon unsalted butter
2 tablespoons diced shallot
1 teaspoon chopped garlic
1/2 teaspoon thyme, picked and chopped
1/2 teaspoon salt
1/8 teaspoon black pepper
1 teaspoon lemon juice

Chef's Notes: Look for dry, firm mushrooms with a fresh clean earthy aroma, not a moldy musty smell. A chanterelle mushroom can hold a lot of water that will evaporate during the cooking process. With this cooking method you can still get good results with wet mushrooms; however you will have to use a lot more to get the same yield. To clean mushrooms, I prefer not using water if possible. Some varieties like morel and black trumpet need water to get all the grit out of the crevasses. With chanterelles I use a stiff mushroom brush to brush the dirt loose and then scrape the dirtier areas with the paring knife. With very soiled chanterelles, never submerge the mushrooms in water; just brush while holding them under a steady stream of cold water and lay out on

a sheet pan lined with dry dishtowels. Cut the mushrooms into wedges. Heat the oil in a heavy 14-inch skillet over high heat. When the oil is hot, pull the pan away from the flame to prevent flare ups, which will ruin the flavor, and carefully add the mushrooms; return to the heat. Do not overcrowd the pan. The mushrooms will give up their excess moisture and the high heat will prevent absorption of too much oil. Once all the excess liquid has evaporate, the mushrooms will begin to caramelize. Use a wooden spoon or tongs to move the mushrooms around and turn them over. The amount of time in this step will vary according to the amount of moisture in the mushrooms. There is no need to move the mushrooms until after most of the liquid has evaporated and you begin to hear sizzling. Once the mushrooms are browned all over, hold the mushrooms in place with a spatula, tilt the skillet and drain off any excess oil. Return to medium heat and add the butter. When melted and foamy, add the shallot, garlic and thyme right on top of the butter and cook for 1 minute, tossing frequently, or until the shallot is translucent; season with salt and pepper, pour onto a sheet pan to cool. I add the lemon juice only when using morel mushrooms. This technique works for all wild cultivated mushrooms, omitting garlic for morels.

FIG JAM
YIELDS 3 CUPS

1 pound granulated white sugar
2 teaspoons powdered pure apple pectin
1 pound Black Mission figs, cut into quarters
2 teaspoons butter (optional)

Preheat oven to 225° F. The butter helps prevent foaming. If not using it, it will be necessary to skim the foam that rises to the surface of the jam during cooking. In a metal bowl, mix together the sugar and apple pectin; set in a warm place for 1 hour or in preheated oven for 15 minutes. *Chef's Note:* If the sugar is warm, it will dissolve quickly when added to the fruit. In a heavy nonreactive pot, warm the figs over low heat, turning frequently with a heatproof spatula. When the figs are warm, about 5 minutes, turn heat to high and add the sugar-pectin mixture; mix well. The sugar will dissolve quickly. Add the butter if using; bring the mixture to a hard boil, stirring and scraping the bottom of the pot frequently to prevent scorching. When the jam reaches a boil, add the butter, if using, and cook at a rolling boil for 4 minutes, stirring occasionally. Use caution when stirring, the boiling jam will splatter. Remove from heat and transfer to resealable canning jars, cover and cool. Water bath process according to jar manufacturer's instructions for preserving for winter.

BRINE

2 quarts water
1 1/2 cups salt
2/3 cup brown sugar
1/4 cup maple syrup
5 bay leaves
5 sprigs thyme
5 sprigs sage
2 sprigs rosemary
2 tablespoons whole peppercorns

Mix ingredients together in a large stockpot and then bring to a boil. Remove from heat and then chill. Submerge pork in brine for 2 hours if portioned, or 4 hours if whole loins.

PURVERYOR'S

The Abalone Farm
www.abalonefarm.com
805.995.2495
Contact: Brad
Abalone

Broken Arrow Ranch
www.brokenarrowranch.com
800.962.4263
Contact: Perrin
Venison

The Cheese Shop
www.cheeseshopcarmel.com
831.625.2272
800.828.9463
*Emmi cave aged gruyere, buffalo
mozzarella*

Cheeseworks West
800.477.5262
Cheese, olives

Chefs Warehouse
www.chefswarehouse.com
*Truffle butter, truffle oil, truffle puree,
apple pectin*

Earthbound Farms
www.earthboundfarms.com
Organic lettuces and produce

Fresh and Wild
800.222.5578
*Yuzu juice, kombu seaweed, wild
mushrooms*

Greenleaf Produce
www.greenleafsf.com
415.647.2991
*Produce, sparrow lane vinegar, nut oils,
rice bran oil*

Hamakoa Farm
www.hawaiian-heart-of-palm.com
808.962.6013
Contact: Steve
Hearts of palm

Honolulu Fish Co.
www.honolulufish.com
808.833.1123
Contact: Tory
Ahi & Hawaiian fish

Jamison Farm
www.jamisonfarm.com
800.237.5262
Contact: John Jamison
Lamb

Kanaloa Seafood
www.kanaloa.com
805.966.5159
Contact: Don
Seafood

Lafayette Caviar
www.caviarlafayayette.com
415.401.8665
Contact: Jerry
Caviar

Manicaretti
www.manicaretti.com
800.799.9830
*Carnoroli rice, saba, balsamic vinegar, salt
packed capers, extra-virgin olive oil,
chestnuts*

Mightly Leaf
www.mightlyleaf.com
Organic teas

MGM Foods
650.440.0984
Contact: Michael
Wild mushrooms, truffle puree

Mikuni Wild Harvest
www.mikuniwildharvest.com
866.993.9927
Contact: Jacob
*Wild mushrooms, salmon roe, ramps,
seabeans and fresh truffles*

Mount Hope
928.634.8251
Szechwan peppercorns and spices

Newport Meat
www.newportmeat.com
949.474.4040
Beef, lamb and pork

Niman Ranch
www.nimanranch.com
510.808.0330
Pork, beef, bacon

Oils of Paicines
www.oilofpacines.com
831.422.1915
Contact: Shelley
Extra-virgin olive oil

Pacific Farms
www.freshwasabi.com
800.927.2248
Fresh wasabi

Polarica
www.polaricausa.com
800.426.3872
Peking duck, game birds and duck fat

Sea Harvest
831.646.0547
Contact: Dimas
Local seafood

Snake River Farms
www.snakeriverfarms.com
Kobe beef, Kurobuta pork

Sonoma Saveurs
www.sonomasaveurs.com
707.938.1229
Foie gras

Whole Foods
www.wholefoods.com
Emmi cave-aged gruyère

INDEX

Gastrique: Sherry-Lavender, 124, 250; in Tomato Tart Tatin, 126; Pear, 139, 250; Apple Cider, 141, 208, 249; Red Wine, 146, 250; Fennel, 148, 249; Huckleberry, 162, 249
Gazpacho, Golden Tomato Thai, 116
Gelatin, 62
Gin Sorbet, 187
Ginger Threads, 171
Glacé, rabbit, 48
Glaze, Ceylon Tea, 74
Glazed Root Vegetables, 221
Goat cheese, 32, 227
Golden Tomato Thai Gazpacho, 116
Grain Mustard Balsamic Vinaigrette, 113
Grain Mustard Beurre Blanc, 190
Grain Mustard-Tarragon Vinaigrette, 48
Graves Sauvignon/Semillion Blend, 32
Greco di Tufo (from Campania, Italy), 195
Green papaya, 116, 224
Green Papaya Salad Dressing, 224
Gremolata, 202, 220
Grenache, 87, 125
Grenadine syrup, 38, 140
Gribiche, 71, 253
Grilled Monterey Bay Sardines with Caramelized Fennel Tart Tatin, Salsa Verde and Tapenade, 148
Grilled Rib-Eye Steak with Crispy Potato Cake and Oyster Mushroom-Cambazola Compote, 205
Grilled Rib-Eye with Gruyère Potato Gratin, and Choron Sabayon, 241–42
Grilled Squab Breast with Squab Liver Mousse Crostini, Endive and Cassis Sauce, 145–47
Grouper, in Seafood Bouride, 158
Gruner Veltliner (Austria), 43
Gruyère cheese, 30, 241
Gruyère Potato Gratin, 241
Guinea Hen: preparations, 88, 90–91, 228; Mousse, 88, 229; Jus, 88, 92, 248, 251, 253; serving, 92; Roulade, 93; roasted with Blue Cheese Polenta, 123; Consommé with Morel Mushrooms, 228–29; Galantine, 228; Stock, 229, 252;

Haichiya persimmons, 140
Halibut: in Saffron Seafood Soup, 81; in Seafood Bouride, 158; Alaskan, with Potato Rösti, 164; preparing, in rounds, 167
Ham, 55
Ham broth, 55
Haricots verts, 43
Havens Classic Merlot, 53
Hawaiian pink snapper, 55
Hearts of palm, 196
Heirloom Tomato and Bread Salad, 113

Heirloom Tomato Consommé, 100
Heirloom Tomato Nigiri with Matsutake Roll and Ponzu, 110–12
Heirloom Tomato Nigiri, 110
Heirloom Tomatoes in Tomato Jam, 136
Herb Salad: with Ahi Tuna, 71; with Cured Salmon, 74; with Veal Sweetbreads, 107; with BLT Tomato Jam, 136; with Monterey Bay Sardines, 149; basic recipe, 255
Herbacious White Albarino, 187
Herbed Goat Cheese, 227
Herbed Plugra Butter, 26
Herbes de Provence, 55
Hoisin Sauce, 68
Hoisin-Braised Bacon, 74
Hoisin-Grilled Quail with Shitake Mushroom Potsticker, Peanuts and Plum Sauce, 68–69
Horseradish: Crème Fraîche, 78; Gremolata, 220
Huckleberry Gastrique, 162, 249
Huckleberry Sauce, 162

Italian Butter Beans, 209
Italian Gavi di Gavi (from La Scola), 209
Italian sprouting broccoli, 40, 49
Italian White Wine, 102

Jalapeño Syrup, 62, 250
Jam: Tomato, 136; Currant, 145; Fig, 156, 253, 257
Jamison Farm Lamb, 235
Jasmine rice, 201
Jelly, Apple-Rosemary, 140
Juniper Berries, 145
Jus: Rabbit, 48, 49; Guinea Hen, 88, 92, 248, 251, 253
Jus, Mushroom: in Mushroom Nage, 95; in Big Sur Chanterelle Mushroom Risotto, 217; in Toasted Barley "Risotto," 220; in Lamb Shank Risotto, 236; in Stroganoff Sauce, 237; basic recipe, 251

Kalamata olives, 209
Keller Estates Chardonnay, 40
Kombu seaweed, 112
Kurobuta pork, 206

Lamb, Roast Rack of, 124–25, 235–36
Lamb Loin and Tenderloin, 86–87
Lamb Porcini Mushroom Sauce, 236
Lamb Shank Risotto, 236
Lamb Stock, 250
Late Harvest Riesling (from Alsace), 218
Lavender flowers, 124
Lavender-Tomato Tart Tatin, 124, 126
Layers of Heirloom Tomato and Buffalo Mozzarella, 102

Leeks, Crispy, 95, 254
Leeks: in Saffron Seafood Soup, 80; in Seafood Bouride, 158; in Asparagus Soup, 214; in Lentil Ragout, 245
Lemon Boy Heirloom Tomato, 116
Lemongrass stalks, 116, 201, 224
Lemon-Mint Couscous, 83
Lentils, French, 245
Lentil Ragout, 245
Lettuces, baby heads, 41, 78, 195
Lighter Style, Zinfadel, 123
Lobster: Rillette, 178; storing, 185, Poached Maine or Pacific spiny, 196; preparing, 198–99; Thai Spice-Crusted, 223–24
Lobster Rillette with Cauliflower Puree and Caviar on a Potato Gaufrette, 178
Lobster tails, 196
Loire Vouvray Moelleux, 38

Mâche Salad with Wild Mushroom and Goat Cheese Crostini, 227
Mandarin Vinaigrette, 196
Mango-Vanilla Butter, 223
Market Vegetables, 49
Marmalade: Quince, 139; Persimmon, 140; Red Onion, 206
Marvel Stripe Tomato Filled with Basil Pesto and Squash Blossom Risotto, 119–20
Mascarpone, 56, 172
Matsutake Mushrooms, 110
Menetou-Salon, 159
Meursault Premier Cru, 192
Meyer Lemon Sabayon, 28
Millefeuille, 86
Mint, 44, 83
Mint leaves, 116, 201
Mint Oil, 87, 116, 224, 249
Mirin Soy-Glazed Matsutake Mushrooms, 110
Miso Vinaigrette, 115, 248
Moelleux, 141
Monkfish, 245
Monterey Bay Sardines, 148–49
Monterey Bay Spot Prawn and Coconut Soup, 201
Montlouis, 156
More Rose, 57
Morel Mushroom(s): with veal tenderloin, 53, oven–roasted, 95; with Ramp Custard and Asparagus Soup, 214; with Guinea Hen Consommé, 228–29; Stroganoff, 237; cleaning, 238
Morgan Estate Chardonnay, 40
Moulin Touchais, 147
Mousse: Foie Gras, 139; Squab Liver, 146
Mozzarella, buffalo, 102
Muscadet, 130, 149
Muscovy duck breasts, 170